Michael Spitz

Studio Newwork

Irving & Co

Ishan Khosla

Studio AAD

Kenichi Tanaka

Aron Jancso

Studiothomson

Kellenberger-White

Sulki & Min

Tankboys

Studio KXX

Studio Frith

Signal | Noise

Neil Kellerhouse

Josh King

The Luxury of Protest

Richard The

Dimo Trifonov

Umbrella

Thomas.Matthews

Marcus McCabe

Adeline Mollard

Jonty Valentine

Régis Tosetti

Micha Weidmann Studio

La Boca

Oliver Munday

Craig Ward

Tsto

Yvette Yang

Jonas Valtysson

Nick Bell Design

Cardon Webb

Ohyescoolgreat

Nod Young

Yang Liu Design

Johan Prag

Daniel Peter

Julien Vallée

Peter Orntoft

Quinta Feira

Second Story

Sawdust

Sagmeister & Walsh

Rudd Studio

Zim & Zou

Frode Skaren

Zoveck

# New Graphic Design

**The 100 Best
Contemporary
Graphic
Designers**

**Charlotte &
Peter Fiell**

**Foreword by
Steven Heller**

GOODMAN
FIELL

Published in 2013 by Goodman Fiell
An imprint of the Carlton Publishing Group
20 Mortimer Street
London W1T 3JW

www.carltonbooks.co.uk

A CIP catalogue record for this book is
available from the British Library.

ISBN 978-1-84796-044-3

Text © 2013 Charlotte & Peter Fiell
Design © 2013 Goodman Fiell
Project Editor: Isabel Wilkinson
Creative Director: Clare Baggaley
Book design and Layout: Peter Dawson and
Louise Evans, www.gradedesign.com
Production: Maria Petalidou

Printed in China

# CONTENTS

Foreword by Steven Heller 4
Introduction by Charlotte & Peter Fiell 6

## A-Z of designers

# FOREWORD

**What Does New Mean?**
**By Steven Heller**

"What's *new* about graphic design?" is a hard question to answer. Graphic design is in flux, so other important questions are first in the queue. For instance, should graphic design still be called "graphic"? Or has the practice, now integrated with motion and sound, digital and other media, morphed into something else demanding a new rubric? Yet this is an old argument that has been pondered since graphic designers emerged from the ooze of commercial art. So let's turn to what "new" means.

Newness is relative. New graphic design could be something where the inspirations are so rarefied or arcane that you and I are surprised, even shocked by the result. Or it can be something so vintage that when revived, because it has been lost for so many decades, it is *new* by virtue of being *old*. Or what about something that emotionally "feels" fresh – you know it's true, but can't explain why? In fact, you will see all these manifestations while making your way through this book of 100 contemporary graphic designers (who incidentally range in age from their 20s to 60s and beyond, so they are not all exactly *new* in a chronological sense). You will see, however, a range of methods and approaches that convey what is arguably the newest development of all in graphic design – the ability to communicate a personal voice; not just a distinctive style, but a style that evokes indescribable emotion, more than pure function.

Back in time, until not too distant history, such attributes as individual "voice" or "personality" were downplayed or forbidden as obstacles in promoting a client's message. Paul Rand, whose advertising work had its share of emotional attributes, was once told to remove his signature from an ad he had designed. Annoyed by the request, he refused because that simple signature validated him as an individual, not a pair of hands. "Service with a smile" was the common way commercial art was always practised. It didn't hurt to have a stylistic accent, but there should be no other distraction that could interfere with the real purpose of old graphic design – selling the message.

Today, the taboos against displaying *persona* – and even self-indulgence at times – are things of the past. So, what's *new* about graphic design is its expressive excess – not in the negative sense, either.

Whether it was intentional or happenstance, the majority of the work you are about to experience – most of it client-driven, but not all – has expressive resonance. This needn't be overt, but it is present in nuanced ways. The way in which Alva, the Portuguese studio, makes its typography so kinetic in the newspaper *Proximo Futuro* can only be an act of expressive willpower (newspapers don't like their readers to have kinetically produced eye flutters). This is not your typical periodical – it is *new* graphic design. Marian Bantjes' exquisitely ornate, complicatedly layered typographic compositions are nothing if not expressive explorations. What's more, the works shown here are not her best-known icons – it is her new graphic design. Jonathan Barnbrook has been expressing himself through type and image for years yet, never content to rest on laurels, he continues to test the limits of old type and new technologies – the work here does not repeat the successes of the past, it is new graphic design. These designers and many others before you are, after many years, still pushing boundaries, reinvigorating their talents, which contributes to the overall sense of excitement in graphic design.

Yet the designers whose work I have never seen before are my reason to leaf through this book. This is the quintessence of "new" – new to me, at any rate. Despite our interconnected online, handheld, pad-driven contemporary universe, even the most avid graphic design fan cannot engage with all the work that is out there. Jonathan Budenz is a revelation for me. His nuanced intersection of graphic and photographic forms, surreal and gothic, startling and soothing, makes me want to see much more. Photographs of Italian designer Isotta Dardilli's "Colors of Money" exhibition, with its purposeful naked wiring throughout the space as if influenced by the film *Brazil*, makes me wish I had actually seen the show. And Zoveck Estudio's electric "two-ring circus" chromo-orgiastic posters fill my eyes with psychedelic colour, and my head with hallucinogenic awe.

Designers must learn how to make new things, but not at the expense of the old. Therefore we look to the designers in this book to appreciate how far they've gone in that pursuit. We also look at their work enviously, covetously, and through this become inspired. We look so as to understand how they successfully play with, or even invent, visual and typographical languages. We look to see how they've built their individual view while supporting, framing and communicating a client's. I only have one question: I wonder whether 100 designers are a big enough pool to learn from?

# INTRODUCTION

*New Graphic Design* is an international round up of the
latest, most engaging and most thought-provoking work
of one hundred of the world's best contemporary graphic
designers. Some are established names, others are
not – innovation and excellence are the criteria used
for selecting the designers included in this book; so
alongside the work of well known practitioners like
Farrow, Sagmeister & Walsh, Irma Boom and Praline,
you will also find work by lesser known and younger
designers who have produced work that is visually
arresting, beautifully conceived and imaginatively
executed, or who have an undeniable compositional
eloquence that conveys content in thoroughly original
and thoughtful ways.

*James, Jennifer Georgina*
book design by Irma
Boom (Netherlands). A
collection of postcards
from parents
to their daughter.
Client: Erasmus
Publishing
Year: 2010

...ch designer has additionally contributed a statement of their personal philosophy, giving a unique insight into not only their own approach to graphic problem-solving, but also the ever-changing world of professional graphic design practice. Through this survey we have also set out to show the extraordinary breadth of graphic design today: from apps, websites and print ads, to infographics, signage and packaging.

Graphic design is an omnipresent feature of our daily media-driven world, even if most of the time we only register its messages subliminally. Every time we use a computer or a smartphone, read a book or a magazine, look at a billboard or unwrap packaging, we are interacting with the work of graphic designers. Their role is to convey a message, whether it is their own or someone else's. It isn't about creating work that shouts "I designed this!", quite the opposite: the graphic designer is more often than not a semi-anonymous conduit for ideas, but using the most direct ways possible. Ultimately the content of the message and its relevance remain at the heart of graphic design practice.

The processes involved in graphic design and its uses may change at an unpredictable rate, but perhaps because of its inherent nature, the creativity and originality of graphic design has not only kept pace, but exceeded expectation. What started with pen and ink, letterpresses and lithography, has seen digital technologies fundamentally shape the course of contemporary practice over the past 20 years. Today's designers need the same skills they have always depended on, such as a talent for compelling visual imagery, and increasingly these rely on having the necessary technical ability to use the digital tools at their disposal. This book's overview and selection of contemporary graphic design work not only reveals their creators' ambition to inspire, but demonstrates how recent developments within the digital domain have profoundly altered the way visual communications are delivered, from apps to banner ads. This influence will grow as technology continues to have a defining role within graphic design practice. This is not to forget, however, that what really lies at the heart of graphic design is the transmission of concepts, meanings and values; it is this aspect of functionality, generally for commercial purposes or societal agendas, that fundamentally sets it apart from fine art. In the past two or three years there has been a higher prominence of self-initiated work with a social dimension, which is not all about the hard-selling of a product – reflecting not only the current political climate and economically straitened times, but also the work of some pioneering teaching institutions and professional bodies, particularly the team at Fabrica who have brought social issues to the forefront of contemporary professional practice through their world-renowned workshops.

CD/LP cover artwork
created by NAM for
Sun Airway's 2012
album *Soft Fall*.
Client: Dead Oceans

Levi's billboard by
Sagmeister & Walsh
(USA). An installation of
constantly breaking down
and reforming typography.
Designer: Jessica Walsh
Production: Atomic Props
Client: Len Peltier, Levi's
Year: 2010

Graphic design was traditionally defined as a combination of imagery and typography whose aim is to deliver a message through visual means, but that doesn't mean that graphic design doesn't at times stray into the world of creative experimentalism for its own sake. Today this might seem to be a rather antiquated notion, as over the last 10 to 15 years the parameters of art, graphic design, film, animation, gaming and music have become increasingly blurred within the broader field of visual communication. The delivery platforms offered to today's graphic designers are startlingly broad in comparison with even a generation ago; as print mediums have given way to digital ones, so graphic design has moved from an essentially static medium to one that increasingly possesses a degree of movement and interactivity. The tools of the trade have shifted from ink, paper and Letraset, to graphics tablets and sophisticated image manipulation software and as a result, graphic designers have found they need to be more and more computer-savvy. But while the majority can design and build at least a simple website, far fewer can design and build an app. Digital competence will to this extent be the hallmark of any graphic designer's success, especially given that within the next few years the introduction of sophisticated 3-D modelling software will become commonplace. As Jürg Lehni said in a recent piece for *eye* magazine, "With the advent of programming platforms aimed at designers and artists, many new ways of working have emerged. This, however, has led to a gap between designers who are literate in code and those who are not."

The ability to continually update their digital skill set, and especially to write code proficiently, will ultimately have an impact on the career outcomes of the next generation of graphic designers. An especially stark indicator of this is that even today, around a third of what a computer animation undergraduate learns in the first year of their studies is likely to be obsolete by their third and final year — although this is perhaps the most extreme example within the creative arts, for graphic design students there are similar concerns. It is therefore crucial for graphic designers to embrace their inner geek (if they have one!) and get a good grounding in computer skills, so that as and when new digital platforms appear they can easily and happily make use of them — essentially hopping up to the next technological level.

Against this background of accelerating technological development, graphic design holds up a mirror, as it always has done, to wider political, social and economic change. In the last few years advertising budgets have shrunk, art schools closed and educational funding been squeezed as a result of the global recession. The impact of the economic downturn has certainly hit recent graduates hard, especially since within the creative industries protracted unpaid internships have become a common rite of passage into the world of work. However, the old adage "necessity is the mother of invention" holds true, and younger graphic designers are increasingly producing self-initiated work that often reflects a hand-made aesthetic, in contrast to the almost clinical precision of computer-generated imagery. For some designers, a new craft revival is underway, as practitioners aim to set themselves apart by creating work that connects emotionally with the viewer.

This can be seen in the return to more craft-based graphic media such as hand-printed fanzines, screen-printed posters, and hand-drawn type — all of which convey a sense of creative authenticity and quasi-nostalgia, and demand real hands-on skills. The newfound self-reliance among many young graphic designers, designing for themselves rather than for profit, means that much of their work is conceptual rather than commercially driven, which reflects a fundamental shift from graphic design practice of the 1990s and early 2000s. This kind of concept-driven work is often far closer to fine art than traditional "commercial art", as graphic design was once known; another example perhaps of the increasing convergence of the creative industries.

For most of its relatively short history, graphic design was a hands-on skill using print as a medium, and today's youthful designers are in some ways attempting to reconnect with the discipline's craft roots to create work that still retains the metaphorical fingerprints of its creator. It is this personalized element that often gives the resulting imagery a compelling and engaging "hand-crafted" quality, which in turn helps the work to resonate with an audience visually weary of the bland sameness of slick computer-generated perfection. As designers Staffan Forsman and Sven-Olof Bodenfors have said, "Outstanding craftsmanship has never been more relevant. It has a unique ability to break through in a media landscape that becomes more complex every day."

Although graphic designers have, historically, created self-initiated work as part of their roles as social and political commentators, there is a new fervour among young graduates to pursue a path of "designer as author" rather than taking the typical path as medium for a client's needs. The ease of disseminating this self-initiated work has increased, as design fairs, shops and online stores feature more and more products by graphic designers – if the designers don't distribute products themselves via their own websites. What's more, these beautifully produced and infinitely covetable hand-made products are an ideal advertisement for the designer's talents.

This craftsman-like method of authorship and distribution could seem to be at odds with the astounding variety of technology available to us now – but the two are not mutually exclusive, as many designers in this book prove.

The last few years have seen the introduction of tablet computers and smartphones, which have brought an unprecedented level of portability and accessibility to digital media. Meanwhile the web generation – those born around 1991 when the first website went online at CERN – is now coming of age and its members have a ready understanding and acceptance of the digital world. In fact a 2008 study at UCLA found that searching the internet increases brain function, at least among middle aged and older people; so it could well be that this new "web generation" has an altered brain chemistry thanks its ever increasing interaction with digital interfaces. Interestingly, according to a recent survey commissioned by Sky, 65% of all television viewers in Britain also like to surf the web at the same time as watching television programmes, while 60% like to also read and send emails, and another 47% browse social media sites. This digital multi-tasking has not only profoundly altered how people now access information on their own terms, but importantly for graphic design practice has also diminished viewers' attention spans, which means that today's visual communications need to make an immediate impact to hook a viewer's split-second interest as they browse their multi-screens. In such a climate it is essential for a message to be conveyed with utter clarity so that it is immediately understandable by the viewer, or for it to have a powerful visual or intellectual hook that will hold the viewer's attention long enough for them to receive and understand the message.

Although the Internet has been responsible for reducing viewers' attention spans, it has of course also facilitated the transmission of visual communication to a global audience, with one third of the world's population now online. At the end of 2011 there were approximately six billion mobile cellular connections worldwide, and according to Cisco global mobile data traffic is expected to increase 18-fold within the next five years. So for a computer-savvy and creatively talented graphic designer, this means the world truly is their big fat juicy oyster. Similarly some software programs, most notably Adobe Creative Suite, have democratized the practice of graphic design, putting the tools of creative graphic invention into the hands of the many rather than just the professional few. But just because someone might have the technical wherewithal to use Photoshop or Illustrator, it doesn't necessarily mean that their work will be as good as that produced by a professional graphic designer who has learned how to innovatively convey messages through visually engaging means, and who – most importantly – has the skill, experience and training to think and create in a unique and imaginative way. As the visual theorist and cultural commentator Johanna Drucker says in her book *Graphic Design History: A Critical Guide*, at the advent of the digital revolution "the tools of the designer were confused with the skills of the designer…The accessibility of production tools undercut the design profession since 'anyone' could make a flier or a brochure." This still holds true today, but just as there is good and bad art or bad music, so there is good and bad graphic design – and as a rule the

Opposite: marketing materials for Kiev's Arsenale 2012 by Barnbrook (UK). Client: Mystetskyi Arsenal Year: 2012

АРСЕНАЛЕ ~~ARSENALE~~ 2012 VIP

HOLA
※MEXICO※
FILM FESTIVAL
※ USA ☀ '10
www.holamexicoff.com

**Poster for a Mexican film festival by Zoveck Estudio (Mexico).**
**Client: Hola México Film Festival USA**
**Year: 2010**

former is the preserve of the professionally trained practitioner, while the latter is the work of the dabbling amateur. To this end Milton Glaser observed, "Computers are to design as microwaves are to cooking", by which he meant that the computer is a convenient means of producing a solution, and that ultimately it is the skill of the designer operating the computer and not the power of the software that is of most significance to the final outcome.

The digital revolution has also opened up graphic design practice on an international level – as revealed in the global selection of designers included in this book – with traditional centres of graphic design excellence such as Britain, Holland, Switzerland, France and the United States finding themselves vying on an international stage with progressive work coming out of Asia, Latin America and the Middle East. In China there were nearly 300,000 design students in 2008 studying at 1,259 different institutions, and it's fair to assume that a sizable number were being trained as graphic designers. And as the world's most populated country makes the transition from a manufacturing economy to a knowledge-based economy, this number is likely to increase.

In comparison to traditional arts subjects, the study of graphic design has also continued to grow in popularity in the West. For example, in Britain between 2002 and 2007 the number of graphic design students almost doubled from 4,645 to 8,190. Yet has the quality of the work produced got any better? Perhaps it has, as famous teaching institutions such as Central Saint Martins and the London College of Communication have recognized that in order to produce graduates fit for this brave new digital world, students still need to develop traditional "craft" skills from drawing to printmaking, and are encouraged to explore related disciplines such as photography, illustration and film-making. This is to equip their graduates with a practical, hands-on understanding of different techniques and materials, broadening their experience of visual media and giving them the ability to design creatively for almost any medium. This broader educational remit is aimed at giving students a greater adaptability within the jobs market, while also widening their creative horizons. A graduate who is proficient in traditional printing methods as well as coding is bound to be more hireable that one who isn't, while their work will probably be more interesting as well, since a knowledge of traditional techniques can inform innovative ways of approaching more recently developed processes of production. The importance of high-quality design education cannot be emphasized enough, as the Design Academy Eindhoven's motto reminds us: "When design frames life, education forms the future."

Although the Internet has provided a new arena for experimentation and dissemination, it has also inevitably spawned plagiarism at unprecedented levels, and designers frequently express a fear of "idea-theft" when posting their work on websites and blogs, often for good reason. Grabbing, dragging, cutting and pasting, a little Photoshop tweaking here and there, and who is to say an "homage" is not an original creative work? However, although it is vital for designers to be up to date with what is going on in their industry, they must guard against pastiche, and produce work with its own creative integrity. All too often graphic designers, and especially graphic design students, will look at a successful album cover or print ad and attempt to copy it, rather than use it as an inspirational stepping stone for the creation of something more innovative and original.

The surge in digital technology has also supposedly brought about the death of print – an assumption that is a little premature: in fact this book exemplifies the enduring relevance of the printed page, often still the best way to deliver relevant content because it demands a curatorial filtering authority. The Internet on the other hand is a never-ending sea of facts and fictions that almost defies navigation. The arrival of eReaders, far.from tolling the death knell of the printed book, is rather reincarnating it into a digital form. And a book, whether printed or digital, is still a work of a graphic designer. Likewise, the trend among younger graphic designers to create work crafted by hand is testament to the fact that the computer is not necessarily the answer for every design brief prayer, and that the world of print is still very much alive and kicking.

Love or hate it, digital technology is going to continue being a graphic design game-changer. Research in material science, neuroscience and artificial intelligence is likely to have a profound influence on the future delivery of visual communication. The advent of affordable 3-D desktop printers may well also transform graphic design into an increasingly physical medium. But it is the commercial application of graphene, now only a few years away, that will completely transform the digital trajectory and in its wake graphic design practice. Hailed as a miracle material, graphene, with its single plane of carbon atoms in a honeycomb-configuration, is a flexible yet super-strong two-dimensional film that possesses seemingly magical properties, being one thousand million times more conductive than copper. So what has this high-performance material got to do with the future of graphic design? Everything, because it will replace silicon in the manufacture of small hyper-fast transistors and computer processors, resulting in an exponential increase in computing power. Indeed Moore's Law, which states that the processing power of computer chips doubles every 18 months, is going to look decidedly outdated as and when graphene fuels the next digital revolution: super-smart, flexible electronic products, such as a new generation of paper-thin mobile computers that can be folded, even worn. Apart from changing the physical products used for the delivery of information, which will have a direct bearing on graphic design practice, graphene also promises to significantly increase processing power. The hardware and software that graphic designers will be using in the future will be faster and more powerful, allowing them as a consequence to create an unimaginable level of interactivity within their imagery. Yet even then, it will still be the message rather than the medium that is king.

The new media age has already profoundly changed the way we communicate with one another and how messages are transmitted. Graphic designers and interactive designers have been at the forefront of this new digital revolution. Many graphic designers however still have a deep-rooted affection for traditional processes that enable them to imbue their work with an engaging tactile quality. Perhaps in the future we will come to appreciate that traditional "analogue" methods and new "digital" mediums have different, yet unique qualities, and that both have validity within the realm of graphic design practice. Rather than a choice between either or, it will be a case of this as well as that, for digital and analogue media can and do complement each other, and can be synthesized to create wonderfully inspiring work that connects on a number of levels. Above all else, the graphic designer of the future will need to have creative adaptability, and to be technologically nimble enough to be able to hop from new platform to newer platform in a technologically accelerating world. But most important of all, no one should lose sight of what graphic design is ultimately all about: content. And as we often say to the graphic designers with whom we work personally, one of the best ways to deliver content is to use an approach based on the following dictum: the simpler, the bolder, the better. Remember, however, Paul Rand: "Simplicity is not the goal. It is the by-product of a good idea."

Yes We Can Mouse poster
by Krzysztof Domaradzki
of StudioKxx (Poland).
Client: self-initiated
Year: 2010

the Yes We Can.

wow.

MOUSE

# A IS A NAME

FRANCE

## A is a name, A is a rounded square, A is a god

**A is a Name**
www.a-is-a.name
Founded 2005

**Founding members**
Simon Renaud and
Jérémie Nuel (France
1981, France 1978)

**Education**
ESAD Strasbourg
(France)

**Philosophy**
We believe that everything in graphic design comes
back to typography — it's the only thing that we have
never questioned in our process, and the capital letter
A of our name is an icon that condenses this idea.
We wanted it to function almost as a mathematical
equation: A = everything. Since we came up with it,
we have constantly played with this: A is a name,
A is a rounded square, A is a god.

Good Times, Bad Times
typeface.
Client: *Dazed & Confused*
Year: 2011

BOOK OF
THE MONTH:
THE THING ABOUT
LIFE IS THAT
ONE DAY YOU'LL
BE DEAD
EXISTENTIAL MEANDERINGS
MADE FUN, FROM THE GENRE-
DEFYING AUTHOR

David Shields's superbly-titled new book is one of the best we've read since we went crazy over his last one, Reality Hunger, published in the UK early last year. "New" may be a tiny bit of a misnomer here however, in that The Thing About Life Is That One Day You'll Be Dead was originally published in the US in 2008. Sure, it actually pre-us, and new over here, shitting brilliant tha stuff really matters

Reality Hur busting, quot for the pri fiction, is an

190      Q&A / METRONOMY

# AFTER THE PARTY

The Totnes musician spills about his move to Paris, channelling the spirit of 1970s radio gods, and working with the ginger one from Girls Aloud

**TEXT TIM BURROWS**
**PHOTOGRAPHY AJ NUMAN**

Joseph Mount, the Devon-born mastermind behind Metronomy, has left recording on beaten computers in pokey bedroom him with the grou The Englis

# TIME
# IS
# MONEY

IN THE CURIOUS WORLD OF COUTURE, VALUE
IS NOT MEASURED BY PRICE
(WHICH NONE OF THE HOUSES WILL REVEAL)
BUT INSTEAD BY THE HUGE AMOUNT OF HOURS
IT TAKES TO PUT EACH PIECE TOGETHER

PHOTOGRAPHY ROE ETHRIDGE
STYLING KATIE SHILLINGFORD

Left and below: two
custom typefaces and
vinyl sleeve design.
Client: Marketing Music
Year: 2010

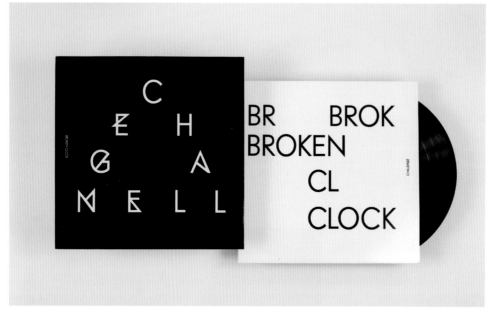

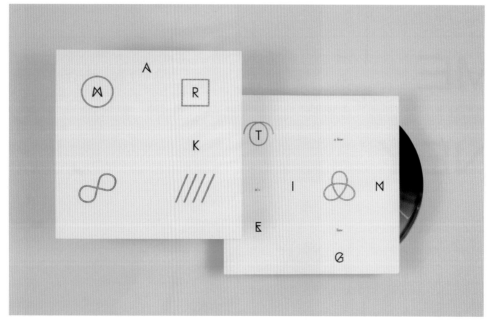

Right: poster for *We Were Undesirable in France* by Suzanne Leo-Pollack.
Client: Traces et Empreintes
Year: 2009

Below: *Imagination* by Batsheva Dagan, book design.
Client: Traces et Empreintes
Year: 2009

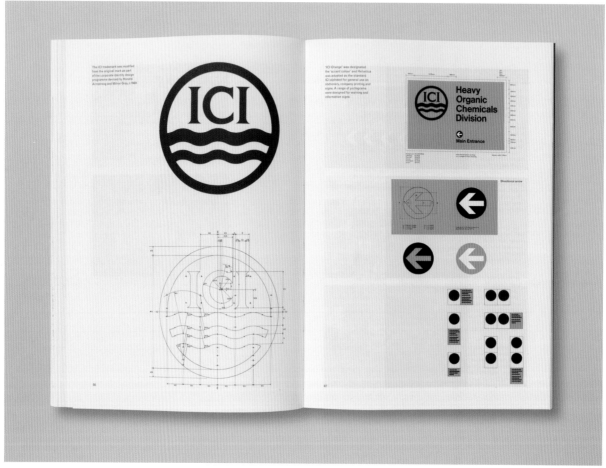

Above: *Design Research
Unit 1952–72* book design.
Client: Cubitt Gallery
Year: 2011

# A PRACTICE FOR EVERYDAY LIFE

UK

## We investigate, explore and experiment to draw together stories

---

**A Practice for Everyday Life**
www.apracticeforevery
daylife.com
Founded 2003

**Founding members**
Kirsty Carter and Emma
Thomas (both UK 1978)

**Education**
Graphic design at
University of Brighton,
communication art and
design at the RCA;
graphic design at
Camberwell College of
Art, London,
communication art and
design at the RCA (all
UK)

**Philosophy**
A Practice for Everyday Life is a design agency working with some of the world's most successful companies, galleries, institutions and individuals. We create a diverse range of work including brand identities, art direction, signage & wayfinding, exhibition design, print, editorial, publishing and websites, all from concept to production. We investigate, explore and experiment to draw together stories, which can translate and transform the ordinary into the extraordinary. This research-led approach, coupled with a sensitive and fastidious design sensibility, has always led to thoughtful and inspired solutions for our clients, and also earned us a reputation for crafting intelligent and innovative work. We have established an exceptional reputation through work for Architects' Journal, Art Dubai, British Council, Design Museum, Hayward Gallery, Hepworth Wakefield, ICA Boston, Tate Modern & Britain and the Wellcome Trust and are an increasingly sought-after partner for collaborations with architects, curators, creative directors and photographers.

Left: marketing materials
for the "Bauhaus: Art as
Life" exhibition at the
Barbican (London).
Client: Barbican
Year: 2012

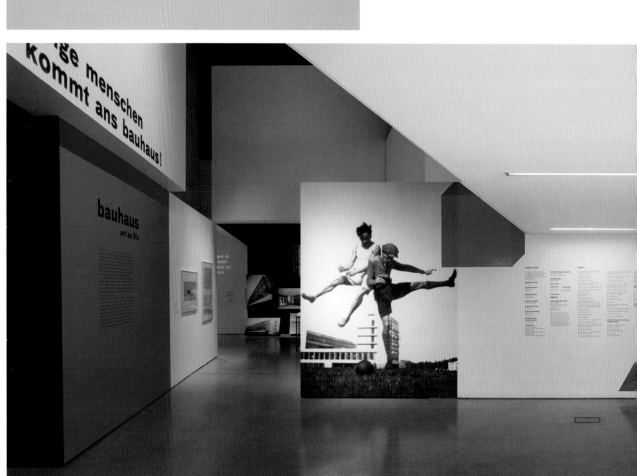

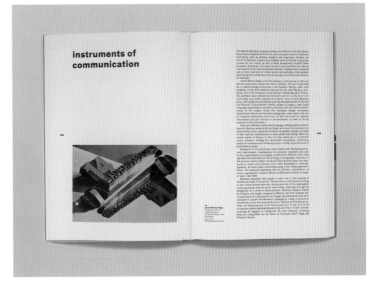

Above: exhibition design of "Bauhaus: Art as Life".
Architect: Carmody Groarke
Client: Barbican
Year: 2012

Right: exhibition catalogue for "Bauhaus: Art as Life".
Client: Barbican
Year: 2012

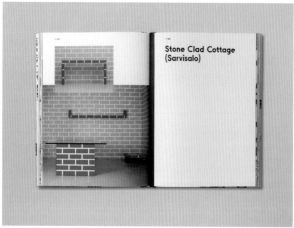

Stone Clad Cottage
(Sarvisalo)

Above: *The Art & Craft of
Richard Woods* book
design.
Client: Lund Humphries
Year: 2012

Right: publication design
for furniture designer
Faye Toogood's third
collection, Assemblage 3,
which she launched with
the auction house Phillips
de Pury & Company.
Client: Phillips de Pury
Year: 2011

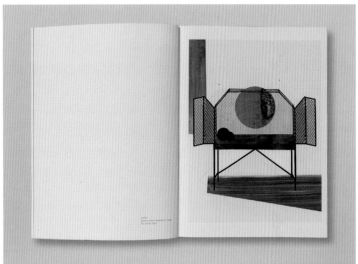

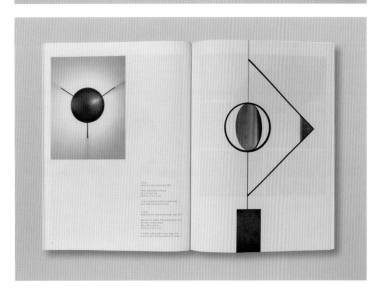

# REZA ABEDINI

IRAN

## Graphic works go out to be seen by people

**Reza Abedini**
www.rezaabedini.com
Born Iran 1967

**Education**
Diploma in graphic
design at University of
Tehran Art School,
painting at Tehran Art
University, printmaking
at Tehran University
(all Iran)

**Philosophy**
Throughout the history of human beings, the idea or symbol of a bridge was used to represent crossing from one world to another. Perhaps today the media, especially graphic design, plays this role of a bridge – in our time graphic design is an art form, and can play the role of this bridge between the visual, creative world and the real world very effectively. I come from a culture where mythology is very much alive. Graphic design is a sophisticated deformation of mythology through the ages – from a post-historical point of view, one can distinguish the reincarnation of myths in graphic works. And that's why we call the buttons and small images on our software "icons". Letters and words are other appearances of myths in our time. Writing is no longer just a means to save information. The forms and shapes of the letters and words have become very important, and so has the art of working with these forms, that is to say, typography and calligraphy, which is my favourite part of design. In graphic design, media and publications have focal importance. One can easily say that in the past, people went to see works of art but today, through media and publications, graphic works go out to be seen by people, and this is a secret that lies in the hands of the designer.

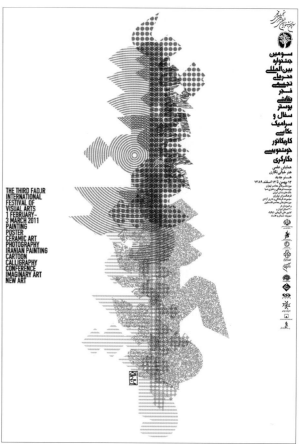

Above: poster advertising
the Azad Art Gallery,
Tehran (Iran)
Client: Azad Art Gallery
Year: 2010

Above: poster for the third
Fadjr International Festival
of Visual Arts.
Client: Ministry of Culture
and Islamic Guidance
Year: 2011

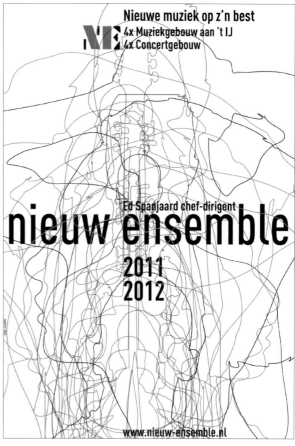

Above: poster for Italian
book festival Cartacanta,
celebrating 30 years of
book design in Iran.
Client: Cartacanta
Year: 2010

Above: poster for
Dutch orchestra Nieuw
Ensemble advertising
their new season of
concerts.
Client: Nieuw Ensemble
Year: 2011

PUBLICIDADE **CONCURSO**
AMBIENTALMENTE **DE IDEIAS**
RESPONSÁVEL

CANDIDATURAS

21—SET.
29—OUT

2010

A————————UTILIZAÇÃO
CONSCIENTE DA ÁGUA
COMO—UM—RECURSO
ESCASSO—E—GLOBAL

# ALVA

## PORTUGAL

## Alva believes in good ideas

**Alva Design Studio**
www.alva-alva.com
Founded 2008

**Founding members**
Diogo Potes and Ricardo
Matos (Portugal 1977,
Portugal 1974)

**Education**
Environmental
engineering at Instituto
Politécnico de Lisboa
and graphic gesign at
ETIC; graphic design at
IADE (all Portugal)

**Philosophy**
Alva: design, print and digital media. Alva operates as
a small studio with a focused team. Our projects range
from graphic design, art direction, identity and branding,
books, magazines, posters, typography, illustration,
websites, motion and environmental design. Alva is
Diogo Potes and Ricardo Matos. Alva's previous
clients include ModaLisboa, Area Store, Companhia
Nacional de Bailado, Instituto das artes, Vista Alegre,
Atlantis, and WearPlay. Alva believes in good ideas.
Alva believes in good design. Alva loves the detail.

Opposite: *Chicote*
magazine design.
Client: Smart Gallery

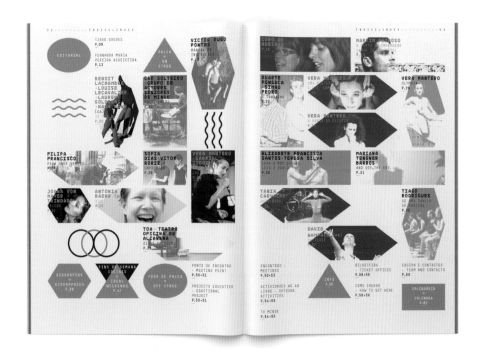

Above: visual identity and
publication design for the
Festival Materiais
Diversos.
Client: Materiais Diversos
Year: 2011

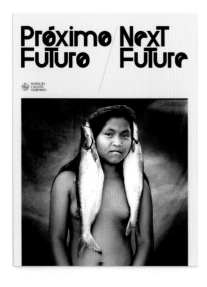

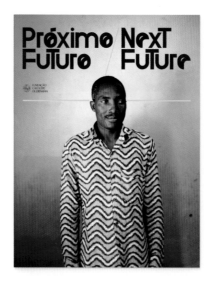

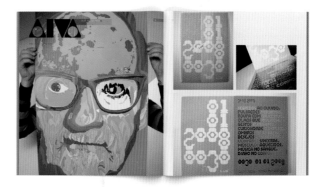

Opposite: magazine
design and visual identity
for Próximo Futuro, a
contemporary culture
programme dedicated to
instigating research and
creative projects Europe,
Africa, South American
and the Caribbean.
Client: Fundação Calouste
Gulbenkian

Above and right: design
festival catalogue.
Client: OFFF Design
Festival
Year: 2009

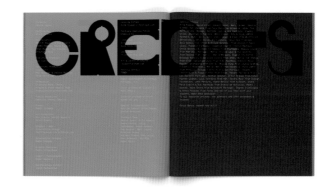

# BACHGÄRDE DESIGN & COMMUNICATION

SWEDEN

Opposite: *Typografins Väg, Specialupplagan* [Special Edition] book design.
Designer: Marcus Gärde
Bookbinder: Roger Johansson
Client: self
Year: 2010

## We are profoundly involved in the whole process from the very first idea to the final result

**BachGärde Design & Communication**
www.bachgarde.com
Founded 2007

**Founding members**
Marcus Gärde and Linnéa Bach Gärde (Sweden 1977, Sweden 1980)

**Education**
Forsbergs School of Graphic Design and Advertising, Berghs School of Communication, Stockholm Art School; Beckmans College of Design (all Sweden)

**Philosophy**
BachGärde is a creative design agency with focus on communication. We are profoundly involved in the whole process from the very first idea to the final result. Thanks to a broad international network, we offer full service solutions for both well established companies and up-and-coming brands. Regardless of form, fashion, lifestyle, art or culture, we strongly believe communication is a crucial part of brand building and concept development, for individuals as well as for companies.

EN TIDNING OM JORDEN

# FARM

NR 3 2010 | 79 KRONOR

Fett
Lyx
Gris
Internet
Invandrare
Soja
Drakar
Gösta

Opposite: *FARM*
magazine design.
Client: Eric Ericson,
Johan Lindskog
Designer: Marcus Gärde
Design assistant:
Pernilla Forsberg
Photographer [cover
image]: Gösta Reiland
Year: 2010

Right: *Nya Upplagan*
(no.50) newspaper design
Client: Lars Yngve,
Nya Upplagan
Graphic designer:
Marcus Gärde
Design assistant:
Pernilla Forsberg
Year: 2010

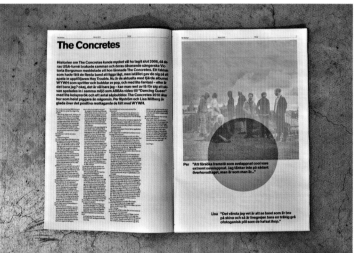

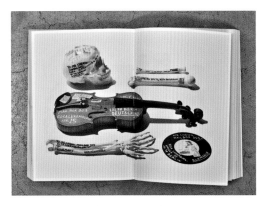

Left and below:
*Korrespondens* book
design.
Client: Eric Ericson and
Kartago
Designer: Marcus Gärde
Year: 2010

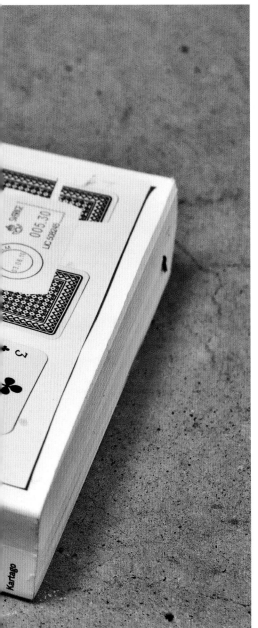

Above: *Typografins Väg,
volym II* book design.
Client: self
Designer: Marcus Gärde
Year: 2010

# MARIAN BANTJES

CANADA

Opposite: vector artwork
and design of magazine
cover for *GQ Italia*,
designed as one of
10 special covers for
the magazine's 10th
anniversary.
Client: *GQ Italia*
Year: 2009

## Detailed and lovingly precise

**Marian Bantjes**
www.bantjes.com
Born Canada 1963

**Education**
Didn't finish art school.

**Philosophy**
Although I am known for my organic forms and
custom typography, my interests lie more in the
juxtaposition of time, style and technology; precision
and structure; and of course patterning, systems and
obsessiveness. While perhaps half of my work is
vector-based, I also work in a wide range of physical
materials. My goals are to have my work surprise and
delight, intrigue, and promote exploration, discovery,
and perhaps result in satisfaction, contemplation or
the stirring of memory.

# GQ

ITALIA

**GENTLEMEN'S QUARTERLY**

Ottobre 2009, n. 121 / euro **3.00** (Italy only)

THE ANNIVERSARY ISSUE

10

THE ANNIVERSARY

ANNUMPLI STORE ASTYLE

Opposite: a tin foil artwork
responding to the brief
"The 00s", for the "End of
Decade" issue.
Client: *New York Magazine*
Year: 2009

Below: pencil typographic
piece illustrating the
theme "Relationships" for
UK illustration magazine
*Varoom*.
Client: *Varoom*
Year: 2010

Below: Chris Adrian's
*A Better Angel* book cover
vector artwork and design.
Client: Granta Publications
Art director: Michael Salu
Year: 2011

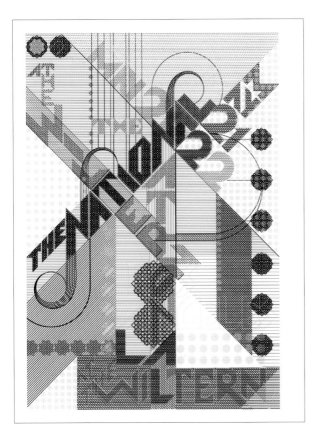

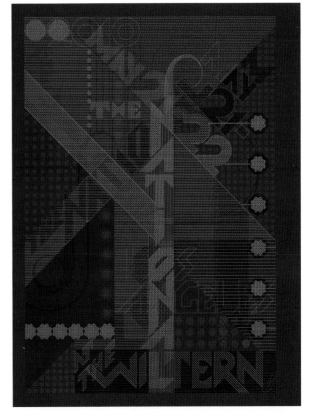

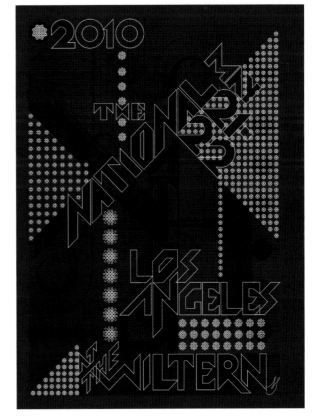

Opposite: vector art for a Laser sailing boat for part of the *Wallpaper*\* magazine exhibit at the Salone del Mobile, Milan.
Client: *Wallpaper*\*
Year: 2010

Right and above: artwork and design for a screen-printed poster. The three images show the poster in daylight, UV light, and in the dark – it is three posters in one.
Client: The National
Year: 2010

# BARNBROOK

UK

Opposite: poster which
formed part of the identity
for Kiev's Arsenale 2012.
Client: Mystetskyi Arsenal
Year: 2012

Left: logo for Occupy
London movement.
Client: Occupy London
Year: 2011

**Stop talking about design as an "industry", start using it as a way of instigating social change**

**Barnbrook**
www.barnbrook.net
Founded 1990

**Founding Member**
Jonathan Barnbrook
(UK 1966)

**Education**
Central Saint Martin's
(UK) and Royal College
of Art (UK)

**Philosophy**
Stop talking about design as an "industry", start using it as a way of instigating social change. Your voice makes a difference, in graphic design you have the tools to communicate to many, don't abuse this by telling people commercial things all the time. Graphic design is the tool of protest as much as the commercial world. If you can do that then at least try and express the beauty of the world and the wonder of your existence in everything you do.

# АРЅΞНΛЄ 2⬤
# AᴋSΞN▲Ʌⅼⅇ 1ⅼ2

**24.05.12 –
31.07.12**

## ПЕРША КИЇВСЬКА МІЖНАРОДНА БІЄНАЛЕ СУЧАСНОГО МИСТЕЦТВА

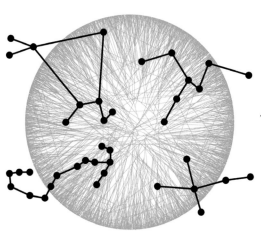

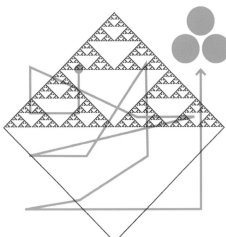

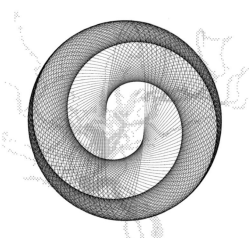

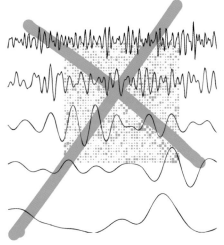

**НАЙКРАЩІ ЧАСИ, Н АЙГІРШІ ЧАСИ**
ВІДРОДЖЕННЯ ТА АПОКАЛІПСИС
У СУЧАСНОМУ МИСТЕЦТВІ

⊗ ARTARSENAL.GOV.UA
⊗ ARSENALE2012.COM

**МИСТЕЦЬКИЙ
АРСЕНАЛ**
MYSTETSKYI
ARSENAL

⊗ МІНІСТЕРСТВО
КУЛЬТУРИ УКРАЇНИ
⊗ КИЇВСЬКА МІСЬКА
ДЕРЖАВНА АДМІНІСТРАЦІЯ
⊗ МИСТЕЦЬКИЙ АРСЕНАЛ

SPECIAL PARTNERS

It was the best of times, it was the worst of times, it was the age of wisdom, it was the age of foolishness, it was the epoch of belief, it was the epoch of incredulity, it was the season of light, it was the season of darkness, it was the spring of hope, it was the winter of despair, we had everything before us, we had nothing before us, we were all going direct to heaven, we were all going direct the other way – in short, the period was so far like the present period...

This page: marketing
materials for Kiev's
Arsenale 2012.
Client: Mystetskyi Arsenal
Year: 2012

Right: book to accompany
exhibition of the Belgian
artist Wim Delvoye in an
Australian gallery.
Client: MONA
Year: 2011

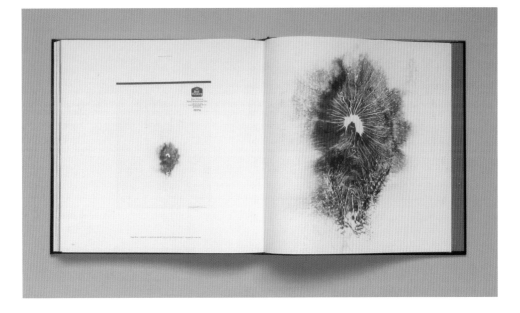

Left: CD and cover for
John Foxx and the Maths
album *The Shape of
Things*.
Client: Metamatic Records
Year: 2012

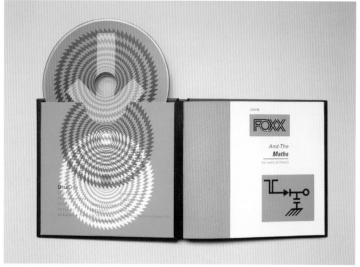

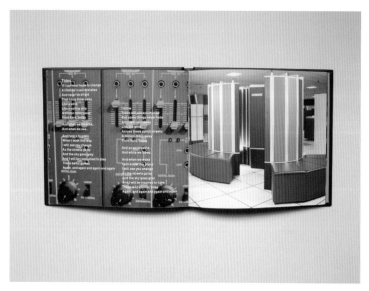

Below: identity for the
seventeenth Biennale of
Sydney including banners,
exhibition catalogue and
posters.
Client: Biennale of Sydney
Year: 2010

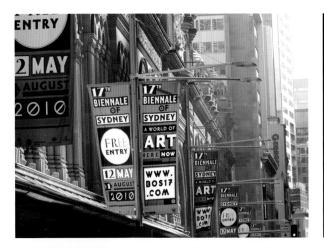

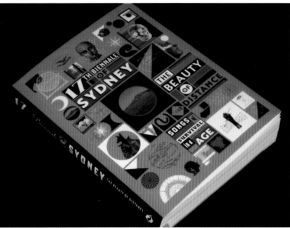

# CORALIE BICKFORD-SMITH

UK

Opposite: book covers
from the Cloth Bound
Classics series.
Client: Penguin Classics UK
Year: 2009

## Good design has to serve the purpose it was intended for

**Coralie Bickford-Smith**
www.cb-smith.com
Born UK 1974

**Education**
Typography and graphic
communication at
Reading University (UK)

**Philosophy**

Good design has to serve the purpose it was intended for. For me the book cover is there to serve the content, so the content has to be taken into consideration. How and to what extent the content is represented on the cover varies of course – sometimes it will be quite literal, other times more oblique, or even just a suggestion of mood and tone. For factual books, the title and the blurb can sometimes be enough to work with, whereas with fiction I like to read the whole book whenever possible. If something is well considered, it will entice. People want to explore it, feel it. That design shines through and connects. There are recurrent elements in some of my work, such as an Arts and Crafts influence, limited colour palette and a love of period detail, but I tend to approach each brief individually. That's the nature of cover design really – the designs are there to serve the writing, and there's such a range of material that we design for that a personal style isn't necessarily what you want the customer to see.

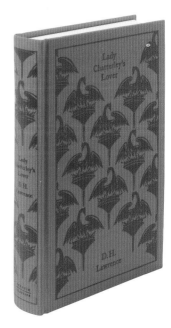

Left and below: book
covers for the F. Scott
Fitzgerald series.
Client: Penguin Classics UK
Year: 2010

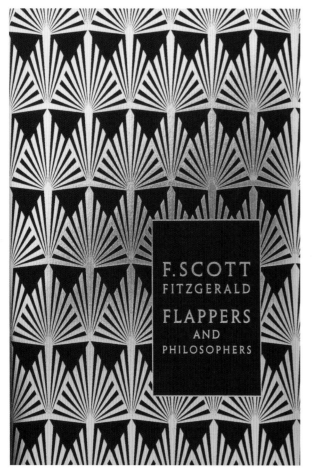

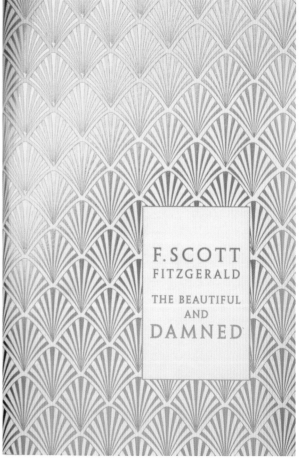

Left and below: book covers for the Penguin Great Food series.
Client: Penguin UK
Year: 2011

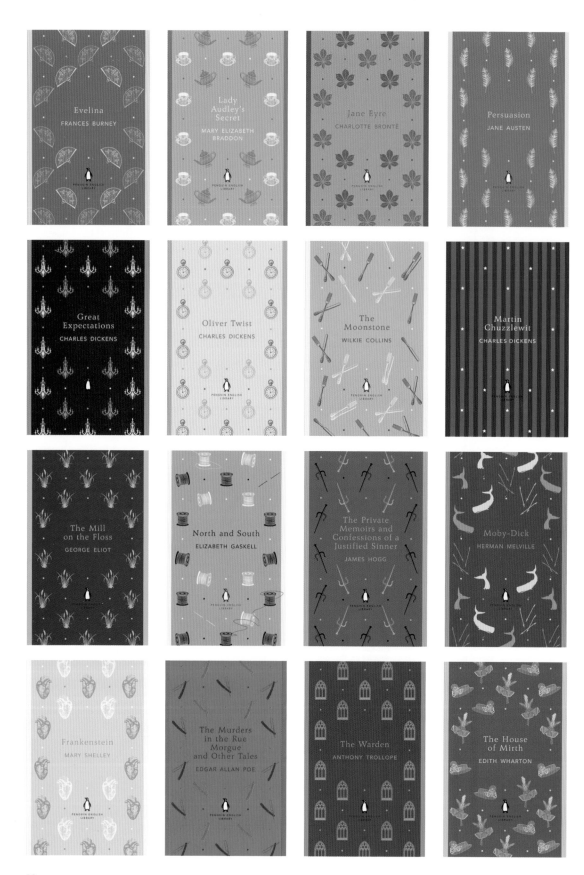

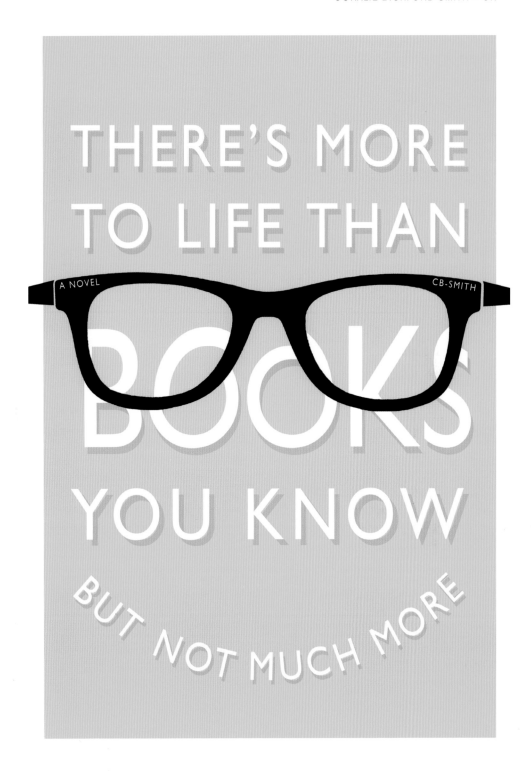

THERE'S MORE TO LIFE THAN BOOKS YOU KNOW BUT NOT MUCH MORE

A NOVEL

CB-SMITH

**Opposite: book covers
from the Penguin
English Library.
Client: Penguin Classics
Year: 2012**

**Above: self-portrait
book cover.
Client:** *Uppercase
Magazine*
**Year: 2010**

# BIG FISH

UK

Below: branding for
Belvoir cordial range.
Client: Belvoir
Year: 2010

# If it doesn't look lovely then it probably isn't

**Big Fish**
www.bigfish.co.uk
Founded 1994

**Founding Member**
Perry Haydn Taylor (UK)

**Education**
Graphic design at Central
Saint Martins, London
(UK)

**Philosophy**
The Big Fish design philosophy is remarkably simple:
if it doesn't look lovely then it probably isn't. And as for
how we do it? That would be telling…

Bottom: branding for
Clipper Classics range
of teas.
Client: Clipper
Year: 2009

Below: re-branding for
Dorset Cereals.
Client: Dorset Cereals
Year: 2012

Opposite: branding
for hand-made and
iced biscuit company,
Biscuiteers.
Client: Biscuiteers
Year: 2011

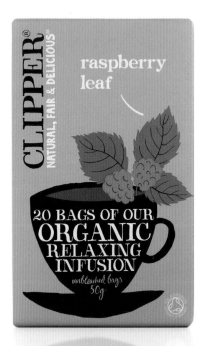

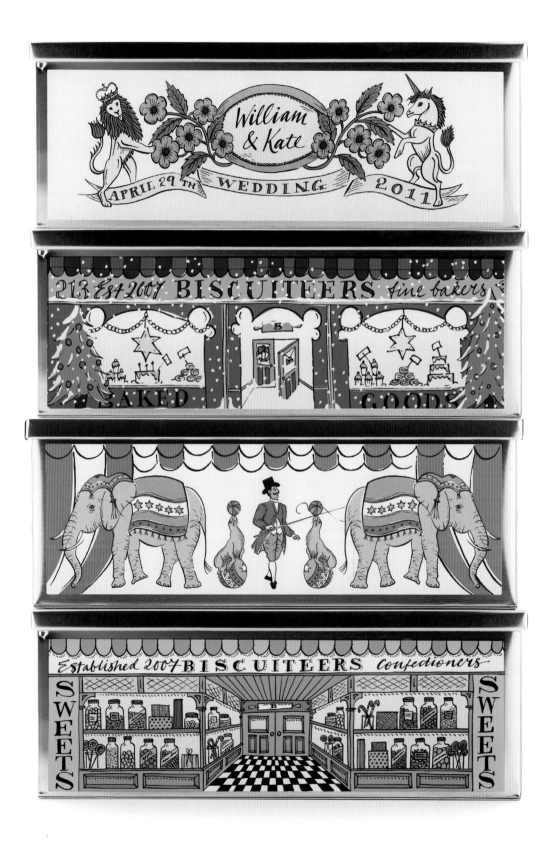

18

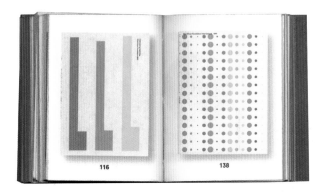

116          138

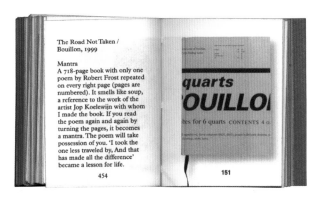

The Road Not Taken /
Bouillon, 1999

Mantra
A 718-page book with only one
poem by Robert Frost repeated
on every right page (pages are
numbered). It smells like soup,
a reference to the work of the
artist Jop Koelewijn with whom
I made the book. If you read
the poem again and again by
turning the pages, it becomes
a mantra. The poem will take
possession of you. 'I took the
one less traveled by, And that
has made all the difference'
became a lesson for life.

454                          151

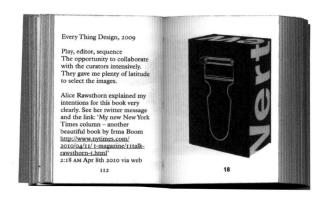

Every Thing Design, 2009

Play, editor, sequence
The opportunity to collaborate
with the curators intensively.
They gave me plenty of latitude
to select the images.

Alice Rawsthorn explained my
intentions for this book very
clearly. See her twitter message
and the link: 'My new New York
Times column – another
beautiful book by Irma Boom
http://www.nytimes.com/
2010/04/11/t-magazine/11talk-
rawsthorn-t.html'
2:18 AM Apr 8th 2010 via web

112                          18

# IRMA BOOM

NETHERLANDS

**Opposite:** *Biography in Books*, a miniature book containing a complete overview of Boom's work, designed by Boom for her retrospective exhibition at the Special Collections of the University of Amsterdam Library.
Client: University of Amsterdam
Year: 2010

**Right:** *Project Japan, Metabolism Talks...* book design.
Client: Taschen GmbH
Year: 2011

## My role in making books is to give another life to a story.

**Irma Boom**
www.irmaboom.nl
Born Netherlands 1960

**Education**
Graphic design at the AKI Art Academy, Enschede (Netherlands)

**Philosophy**

I honour the traditional book but do not want to stop there. My ambition is to develop the significance and the limits of the book. Structures that come from new media, the way text and images are treated, have given the book a new impulse. It is important to experiment and not to be afraid sometimes to create utter failures; the book can keep its vitality. There is a lot to explore in a technical way and even more importantly in terms of content and form. Happily through books, the past, present and future can take on profoundly contemporary results and become part of our everyday. My role in making books is to give another life to a story. Working with different worlds, exchanging thoughts and ideas is one of the most valuable ingredients in my practice. What has always been important to me is the complete trust of my commissioner. I immediately drop my "pen" if there is no collaboration and if I feel we're not on the same track, no use to continue. But if it works, then the object that we've collectively created hopefully pushes the boundaries of the definition of a book.

Right: *Every Thing Design* book design. An anthology of items from the Museum für Gestaltung, Zurich. Client: Hatje Cantz Verlag Year: 2009

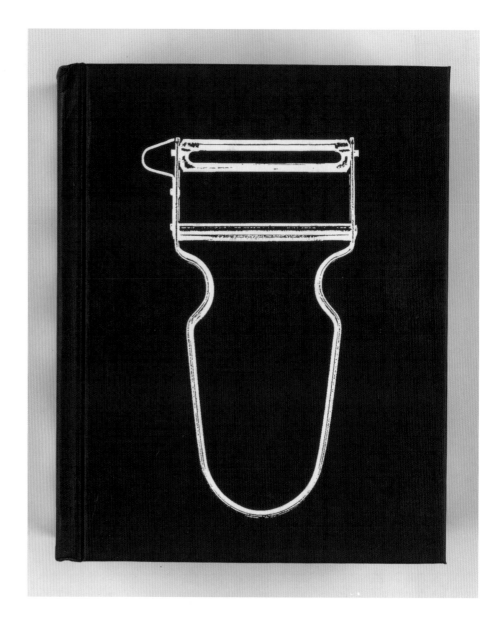

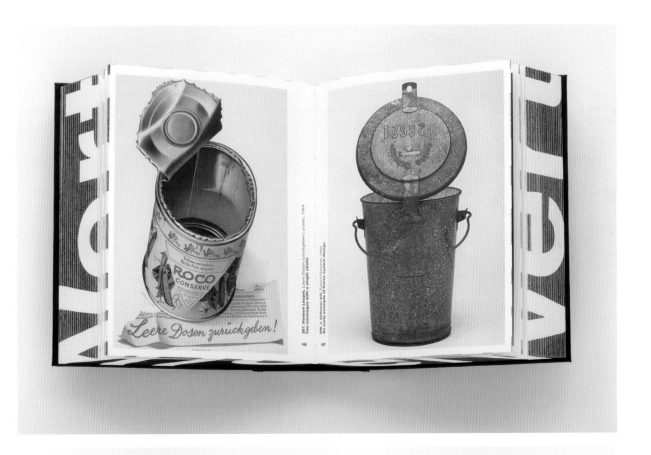

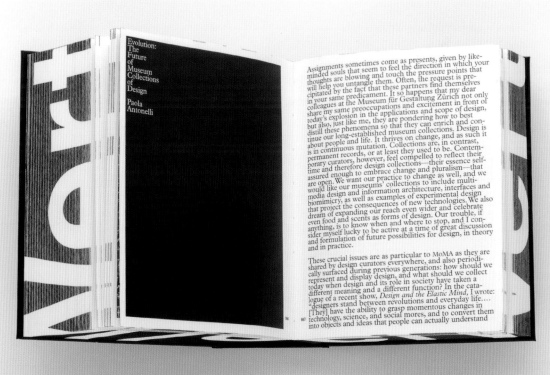

Evolution:
The
Future
of
Museum
Collections
of
Design

Paola
Antonelli

Assignments sometimes come as presents, given by like-minded souls that seem to feel the direction in which your thoughts are blowing and touch the pressure points that will help you untangle them. Often, the request is precipitated by the fact that these partners find themselves in your same predicament. It so happens that my dear colleagues at the Museum für Gestaltung Zürich not only share my same preoccupations and excitement in front of today's explosion in the applications and scope of design, but also, just like me, they are pondering how to best distill these phenomena so that they can enrich and continue our long-established museum collections. Design is about people and life. It thrives on change, and as such it is in continuous mutation. Collections are, in contrast, permanent records, or at least they used to be. Contemporary curators, however, feel compelled to reflect their time and therefore design collections—their essence self-assured enough to embrace change and pluralism—that are open. We want our practice to change as well, and we would like our museums' collections to include multimedia design and information architecture, interfaces and biomimicry, as well as examples of experimental design that project the consequences of new technologies. We also dream of expanding our reach even wider and celebrate even food and scents as forms of design. Our trouble, if anything, is to know when and where to stop, and I consider myself lucky to be active at a time of great discussion and formulation of future possibilities for design, in theory and in practice.

These crucial issues are as particular to MoMA as they are shared by design curators everywhere, and also periodically surfaced during previous generations: how should we represent and display design, and what should we collect today when design and its role in society have taken a different meaning and a different function? In the catalogue of a recent show, *Design and the Elastic Mind*, I wrote: "designers stand between revolutions and everyday life…. [They] have the ability to grasp momentous changes in technology, science, and social mores, and to convert them into objects and ideas that people can actually understand

Left and opposite:
volumes one and two of
*Dutch Heights*, an
illustrated annual of
design and art.
Client: Dutch Heights
Foundation
Year: 2010 and 2011

'Vervreemding van de werkelijkheid en het bevreemdende van de werkelijkheid zijn zeker geen onbekende thema's in de kunst van vandaag, maar Barbara Visser hanteert ze in haar werk op een heel eigen, creatieve wijze en met een grote visuele overtuigingskracht.
Het werk dat uit foto's, video's en installaties bestaat, wordt gekenmerkt door het ontregelen van verwachtingspatronen, soms heel direct, soms heel subtiel. De fotoserie *A Day in Holland / Holland in a Day* uit 2001 bijvoorbeeld toont op het eerste gezicht twee Japanse toeristen in een Hollands landschap met een molen. In werkelijkheid blijkt het om twee Nederlandse acteurs te gaan, die geschminkt zijn als Japanners en wandelen in Holland Village, een soort Madurodam op ware grootte in de Japanse stad Nagasaki. Grimmiger is de pseudo-documentaire fotoserie *The World Belongs to Early Risers* uit 2002. Ze toont een mediterraan kiezelstrand, met op de voorgrond een genietende zonnebader en op de achtergrond een fotograaf die met zijn team foto's maakt van een aangespoelde bootvluchteling – of van een actrice of fotomodel in die confronterende rol. In het werk van Visser is de gelaagdheid en de dubieuze betrouwbaarheid van beelden een terugkerend thema.
Van haar persoonlijke drijfveren achter haar werk weten we helemaal niets. Misschien is dat maar goed ook, want *Barbara Visser is er niet* (titel van de publicatie bij haar overzichtstentoonstelling in 2006, in Almere, red.). Haar werk zelf bleek al prijzenswaard zonder dat we als jury allerlei autobiografische ezelsbruggetjes nodig hadden'.

**Jury** H.W. van Os (vz), C.H. Blotkamp, R.H. Dijkgraaf, I.M. Veldman

De Dr. A.H. Heinekenprijs voor de Kunst – vernoemd naar de voormalige bestuursvoorzitter van het bierconcern – wordt sinds 1988 elke twee jaar toegekend aan een beeldend kunstenaar die woont en werkt in Nederland. De laureaten ontvangen de prijs (50.000 euro en een kunstwerk) vanwege hun grote verdiensten voor de Nederlandse kunst.

**Eerdere laureaten** Job Koelewijn, Daan van Golden, Aernout Mik, Guido Geelen, Marrie Bot e.a.

**Dr. A.H. Heinekenprijs voor de Kunst 2008**
Barbara Visser (1966)

110 • Beeldende kunst

Barbara Visser: A Day in Holland / Holland in a Day, 2001 (courtesy Annet Gelink Gallery / Stroom HCBK)

Barbara Visser doorliep tussen 1985 en 1991 de Gerrit Rietveld Academie in Amsterdam. Tussendoor bezocht ze de fameuze Cooper Union University in New York, en in 1998 de Jan van Eyck Academie in Maastricht. Vandaag de dag heeft ze zowel in Nederland als daarbuiten een grote naam opgebouwd. Haar werk is onder andere opgenomen in de collecties van het Stedelijk Museum Amsterdam, het Museum voor Moderne Kunsten in Arnhem, het Gemeentemuseum Den Haag, het Frans Hals Museum in Haarlem en Museum Boijmans Van Beuningen in Rotterdam. Ze exposeerde onder meer in Tokyo, Antwerpen, Berlijn en Sao Paulo. Eerder al kreeg Barbara Visser de Charlotte Köhler Prijs (1996), de Prijs Jonge Belgische Schilderkunst (1999) en de David Röell Prijs (2007).
www.barbaravisser.nl

111 • Dutch Heights

Film

Gouden Kalf (detail)

12 • Inhoud • Contents

13 • Dutch Heights

# BRIGHTEN THE CORNERS

UK

## We don't like dry work

**Brighten the Corners**
www.brightenthe
corners.com
Founded 1999

**Founding members**
Frank Philippin
and Billy Kiosoglou
(Germany 1967,
Greece 1973)

**Education**
Graphic design at
Camberwell College of
Arts, MA at Royal College
of Art (all UK) (both)

### Philosophy
We like simple design. We like to keep things clear
and enjoy editing out all the unnecessary bits that
cling to ideas, so you can call us minimalists, it's OK.
But we don't like dry work. We believe design should
be concept-driven, personally formed as well as
engaging and fun. Over the years, we've worked with
many clients including Anish Kapoor, the Goethe-
Institute, the British Council, Frieze Publishing, the
Department for Education, Bolles+Wilson Architects,
Accenture, and Laurence King Publishing, happily
switching between public sector, corporate and
cultural environments. All along we've resisted
specializing. This is important to us, as we feel that
doing the same thing over and over leads to formulaic
responses, and they never quite work. And it keeps us
on our toes, so that we don't become "those guys who
only do annual reports" or something equally scary.
And we like to keep our fingers in many pies: we
publish and sell work in our online shop and teach
graphic design at the University of Darmstadt – Frank
has the position of Professor there.

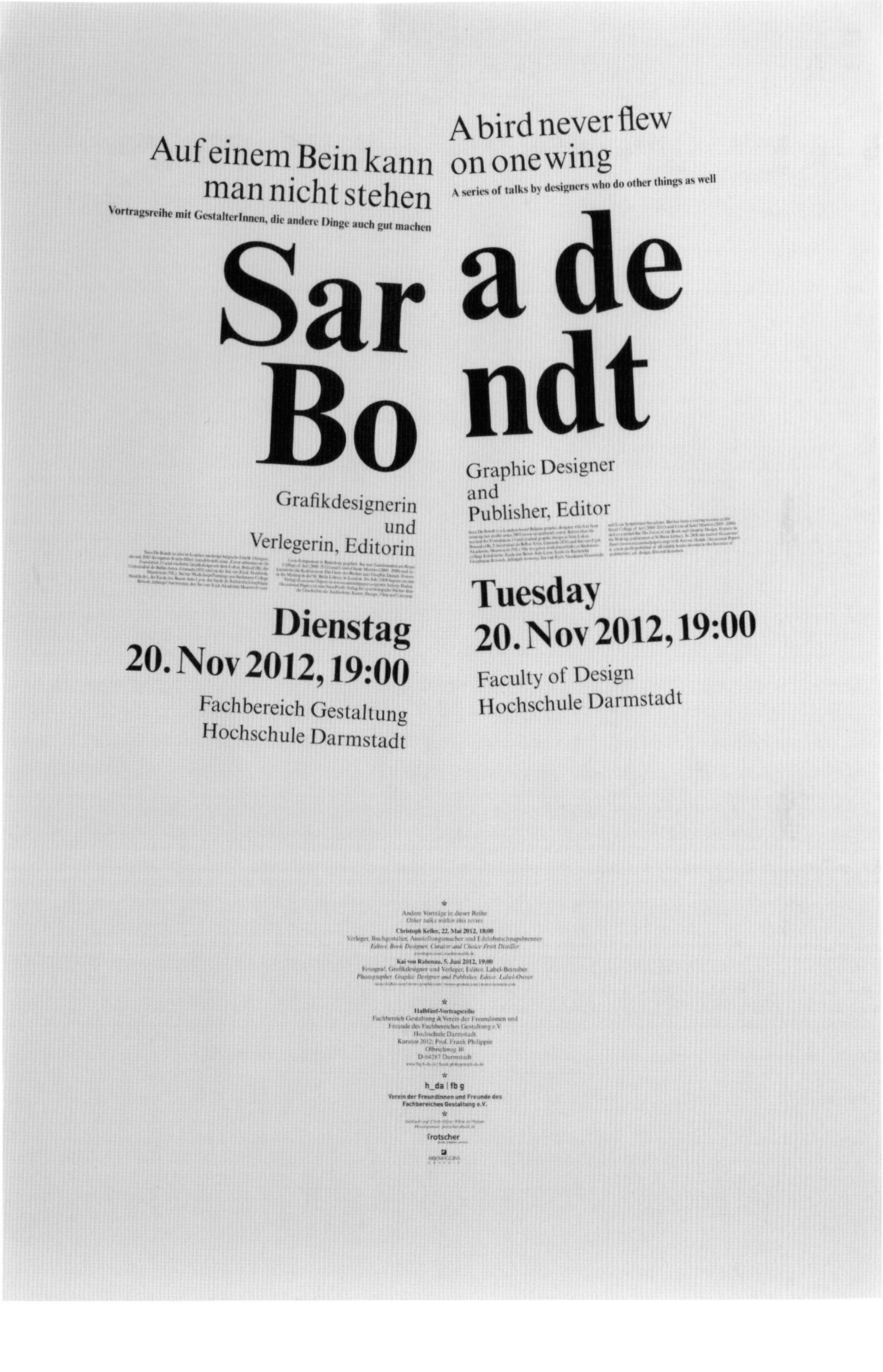

Auf einem Bein kann man nicht stehen

A bird never flew on one wing

Vortragsreihe mit GestalterInnen, die andere Dinge auch gut machen

A series of talks by designers who do other things as well

# Sar a de Bo ndt

Grafikdesignerin und Verlegerin, Editorin

Graphic Designer and Publisher, Editor

Sara De Bondt is eine in London ansässige belgische Grafik-Designer. [text too small to read reliably]

Sara De Bondt is a London-based Belgian graphic designer who has been teaching graphic design since 2005 [text too small to read reliably]

Dienstag
20. Nov 2012, 19:00

Fachbereich Gestaltung
Hochschule Darmstadt

Tuesday
20. Nov 2012, 19:00

Faculty of Design
Hochschule Darmstadt

Andere Vorträge in dieser Reihe
Other talks within this series

Christoph Keller, 22. Mai 2012, 19:00
Verleger, Buchgestalter, Ausstellungsmacher und Edelobstschnapsbrenner
Editor, Book Designer, Curator and Choice-Fruit Distiller

Kai von Rabenau, 5. Juni 2012, 19:00
Fotograf, Grafikdesigner und Verleger, Editor, Label-Betreiber
Photographer, Graphic Designer and Publisher, Editor, Label-Owner

Halbfünf-Vortragsreihe
Fachbereich Gestaltung & Verein der Freundinnen und
Freunde des Fachbereiches Gestaltung e.V.
Hochschule Darmstadt
Kuration 2012: Prof. Frank Philippin
Olbrichweg 10
D-64287 Darmstadt

h_da | fb g
Verein der Freundinnen und Freunde des
Fachbereiches Gestaltung e.V.

Frotscher

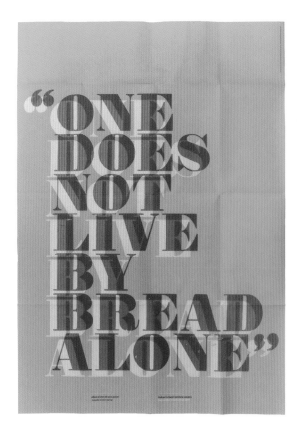

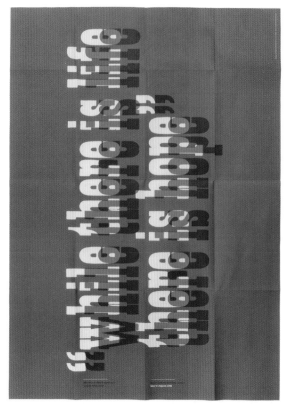

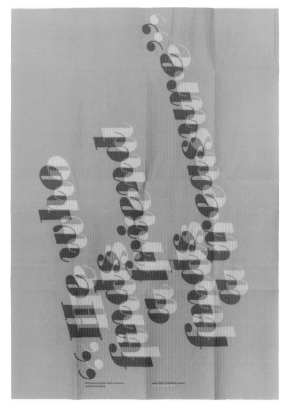

Opposite: posters for the
Italian Institute, London.
Client: Italian Institute
Year: 2009–10

Below: poster for a
screening of the Helvetica
documentary.
Client: Darmstadt
Hochschule Faculty of
Design
Year: 2010

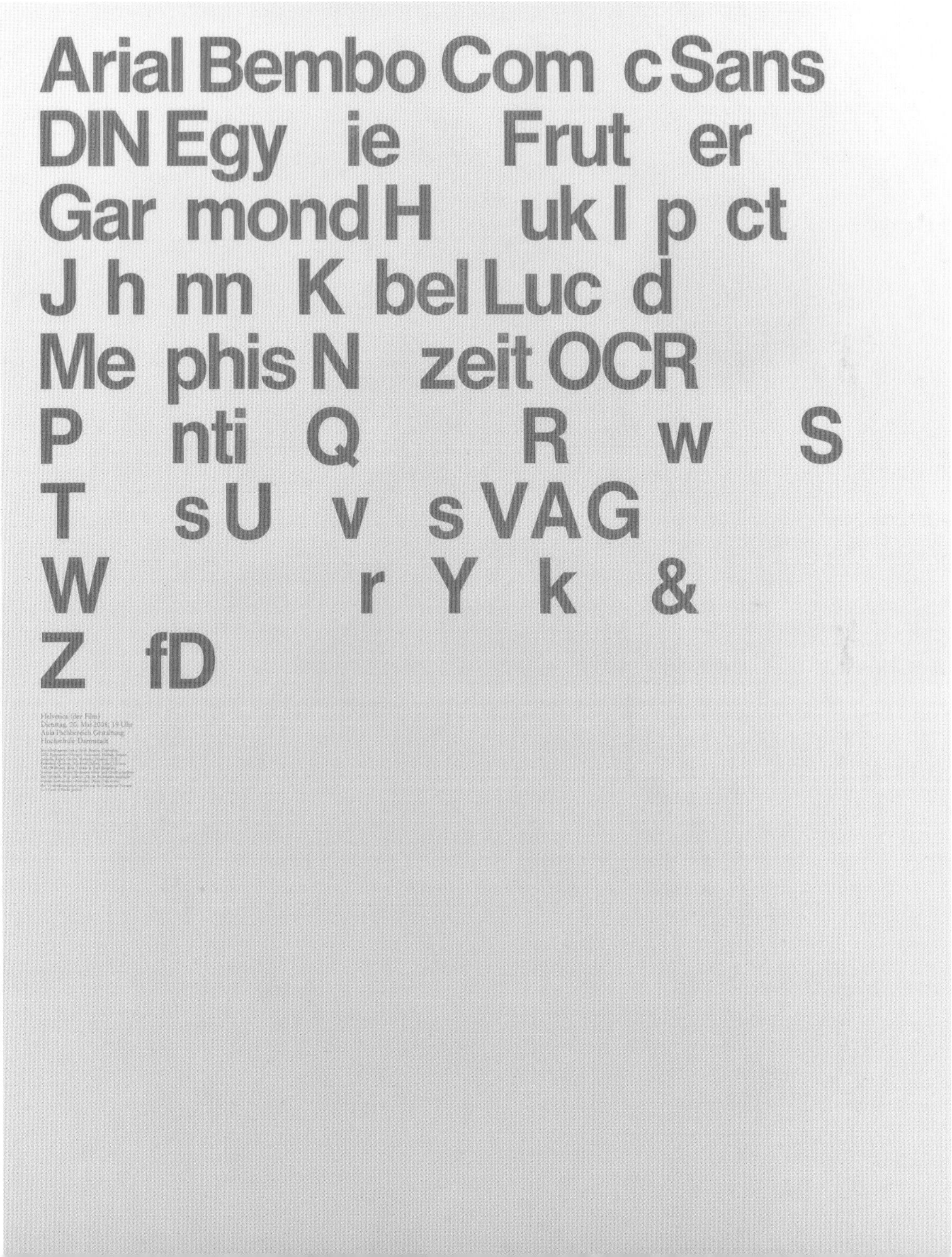

Arial Bembo Com c Sans
DIN Egy  ie    Frut  er
Gar  mond H    uk l p ct
J h  nn  K  bel Luc  d
Me  phis N   zeit OCR
P    nti  Q    R   w    S
T    sU   v   s VAG
W        r Y  k  &
Z  fD

# Leviathan/

**Anish Kapoor/**
**Grand Palais, Paris/**
**Monumenta 2011/**

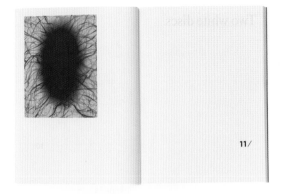

11/

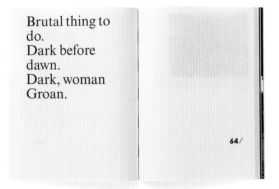

Brutal thing to
do.
Dark before
dawn.
Dark, woman
Groan.

64/

73/

107/

Above and right:
exhibition catalogue for
Anish Kapoor's *Leviathan*
installation at the Grand
Palais, Paris.
Client: Anish Kapoor
Year: 2011

Right: annual report for
a manufacturer of indoor
and outdoor lighting.
Client: Zumtobel Group
Year: 2012

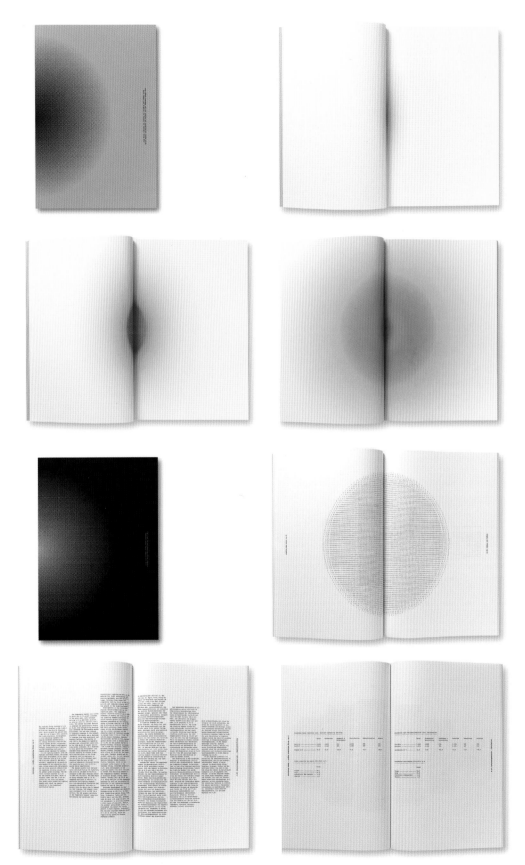

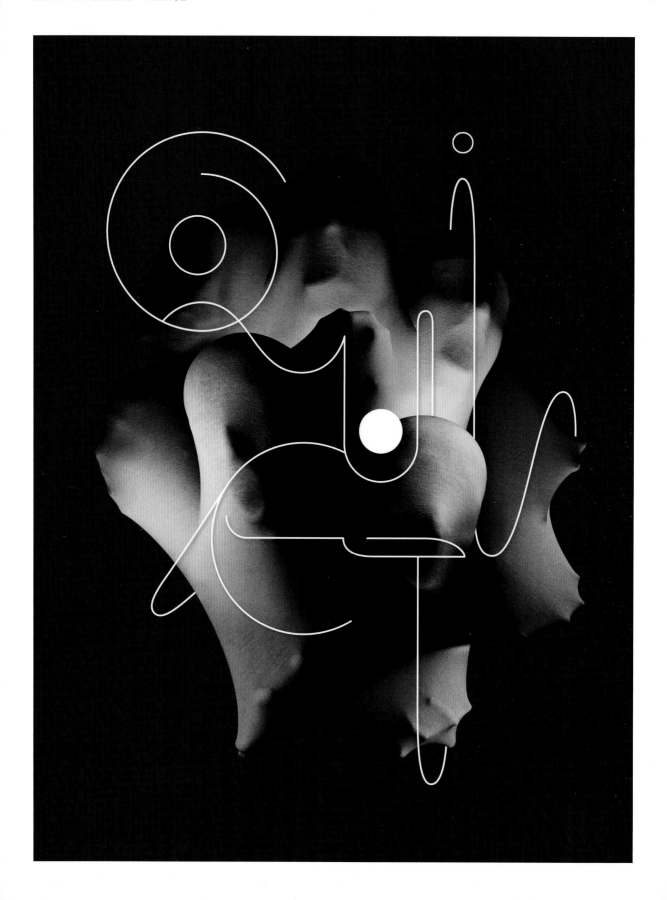

# JONATHAN BUDENZ

## FRANCE

Opposite: Quiet artwork
and design.
Client: *Querelle* magazine
Year: 2011

## Graphic alchemy

---

**Jonathan Budenz**
www.thisisjobudenz.com
Born Spain 1985

**Education**
Graphic design and
art direction at ESAG
Penninghen, Paris
(France)

**Philosophy**
Every kind of design that I see is interesting.
Everything people ask me to do is interesting. I am
in love with graphic design, typography, photography
and illustration. It's too hard to choose between them.
Whatever the project is, I'll always do my best. I can't
work without a goal of perfection. I'm always trying
to find ways to imbricate or mix all the design forms
that I know into a modern and graphic alchemy, and
if possible, make something unique. Trying to put
elements in order, disorder, break them and fix them.

Seeing what happens and finally getting a really good
composition. I like making weird but elegant images
– kind of "realist abstract". This is what gives my work
a personal style, and this is what I strive for through
personal or commissioned works. Being imaginative,
audacious, personal and productive is what I aim for.

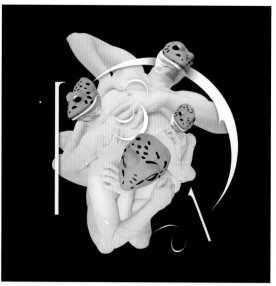

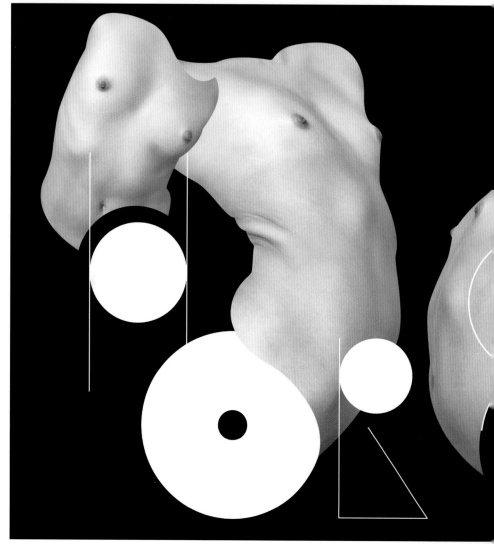

Right: Between 05, from
"In the Between 2.0"
exhibition at Gabriel &
Gabriel Gallery, Paris.
Client: self
Year: 2011

Far left: L'esquive, from
"Personne(s)" exhibition.
Client: self
Year: 2012

Left: Boa, from "In the
Between 2.0" exhibition at
Gabriel & Gabriel Gallery,
Paris.
Client: self
Year: 2011

Below: Between 02,
from "In the Between
2.0" exhibition at Gabriel
& Gabriel Gallery, Paris.
Client: self
Year: 2011

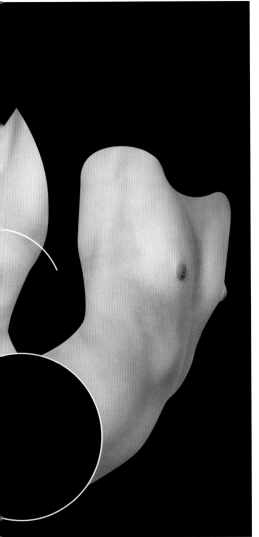

Left: We Are Maskswear
editorial design, art
direction and typography.
Client: self
Year: 2009

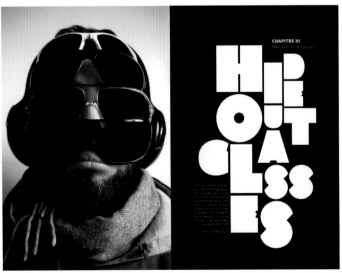

Opposite: promotional
poster.
Client: Rock and Culture
Year: 2009

# BUILD

UK

Opposite: identity for
*Objectified*,
a documentary about
product design, directed
by Gary Hustwit. The
identity was applied
across marketing
materials and packaging,
and the studio also
designed the menu
system and in-film
captions.
Client: Plexi Films
Year: 2009

## Design thinking for the real world

**Build**
wearebuild.com
Founded 2001

**Founding members**
Michael C. Place
and Nicola Place
(UK 1969, UK 1968)

**Education**
Graphic design at
Newcastle College
(left to follow his dream of
designing record sleeves);
graphic design and
illustration at Liverpool
Polytechnic (both UK)

**Philosophy**
We produce original, striking and mindfully executed
design for a wide range of clients, helping them to
articulate sometimes complex ideas about themselves
and their businesses – and to help them stand proudly
apart from their competitors. "Intelligent design,
exceptionally made" runs through everything we do.
Which means design thinking for the real world, with
an emphasis on detail and high quality production,
always with careful consideration for the way we do it.

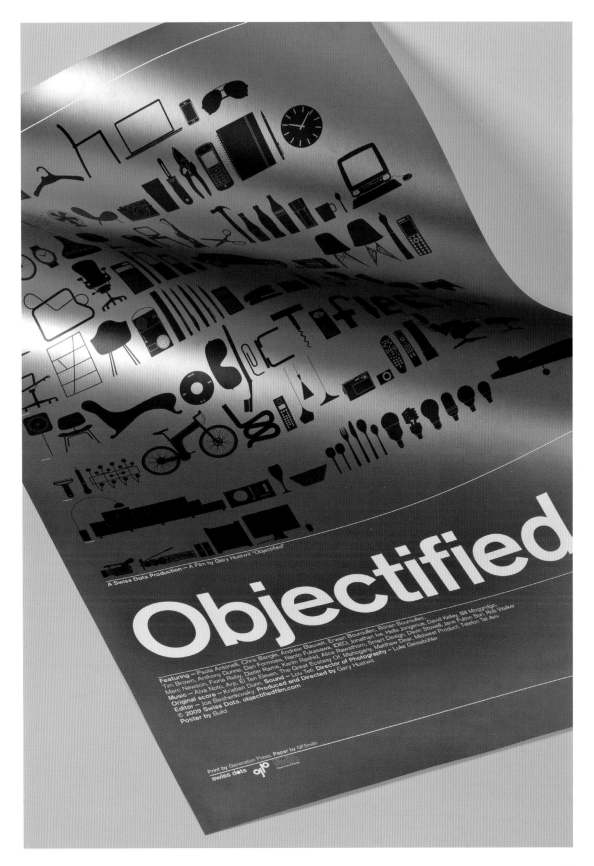

Left: identity for a new
café in Yorkshire, UK,
comprising stationery,
packaging, web and
signage.
Client: T&Cake
Year: 2011

Right: On-air and off-air
branding for PlusPlus,
a new Ukrainian children's
television channel.
Client: Natasha
Vashko/1+1 Ukraine
Concept, design and
direction: Build.
Original character design:
Edik Katykhin
Year: 2012

Left and below: identity for Brighton-based environmentally friendly printing company. The logo itself is based on paper moving through a printing press.
Client: Generation Press
Year: 2009

Opposite: typographic illustrations based around pangrams, Wordplay explores language and the written word – phrases that are familiar, funny, silly and thoughtful. Work comprises a postcard pack, posters, animation and app.
Client: Nokia
Year: 2012

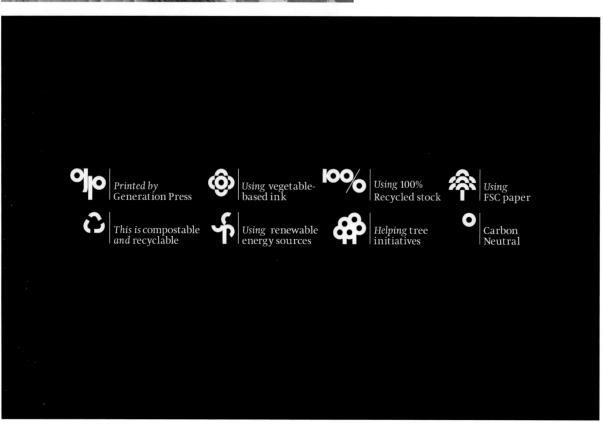

Printed by
Generation Press

Using vegetable-based ink

Using 100%
Recycled stock

Using
FSC paper

This is compostable
and recyclable

Using renewable
energy sources

Helping tree
initiatives

Carbon
Neutral

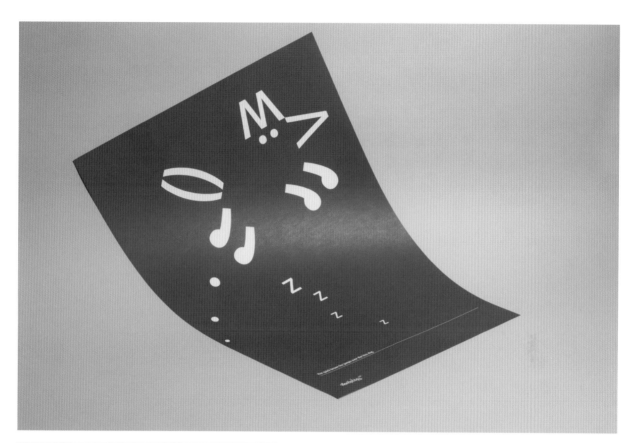

# BÜRO
# ACHTER
# APRIL

GERMANY

## We work to generate disorder

**Büro Achter April**
www.8apr.eu
Founded 2006

**Founding members**
Michael Fragstein, Marc Guntow, and Turan Tehrani (Poland 1972, Germany 1974, Germany 1979)

**Education**
Diploma in architecture and design at the Stuttgart State Academy of Art and Design; media and communication at HDM Media University (both Germany)

**Philosophy**
We work to generate disorder. By dismantling expectations, we hope to achieve a new path, a different perspective, or an unexpected breakthrough. While we avoid taking ourselves too seriously, we can also be uncompromising when it comes to realising concepts. We want to generate content, not just pixels. Moving content and bringing meaning into spaces are our overall design objectives. Space, interactive media, and film can all pursue a common goal, whether commercial or artistic. Either of these ends requires a concept – and a design that works in all aspects. We demand the highest standards when it comes to lighting, tempo, materials, perspectives, and colour, whether in illustration, stop motion, 3D animation or interior design.

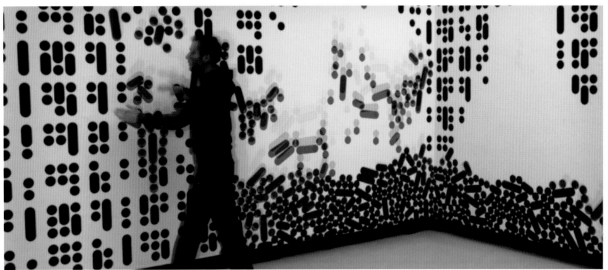

Below: didactic animation
and visual merchandising
presentation for runway
fashion show.
Client: Hugo Boss AG
Year: 2009

Right: animated music video for "Forget".
Client: Vania and the Master
Year: 2009

# BURO-GDS

FRANCE/USA

Below: identity for Women
in Islam, an organization
of professional and social
activist Muslim women
who are dedicated to the
empowerment of women
through knowledge and
practice of Islam.
Client: Women in Islam, Inc.
Year: 2012

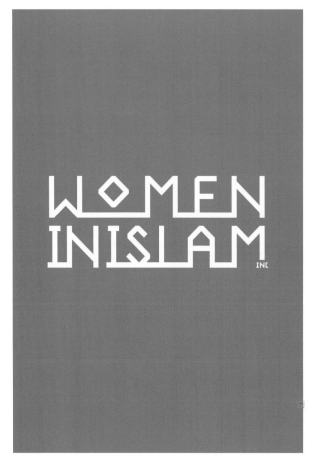

Below: New Spanish Books
(a guide to Spanish books
with translation rights
available) logo, folder
and postcards.
Client: ICEX (Spanish
Institute for Foreign Trade)
Year: 2010

# Design = Concept + Execution + Beauty

**Name**
www.buro-gds.com
Founded 2007

**Founding members**
Ellen Tongzhou Zhao and
Elamine Maecha (China
1981, Africa 1979)

**Education**
Cooper Union, New York (USA) and ENSAD,
Paris (France); ESAD Strasbourg (France) and
ANRT (France)

Below: Talents aux Arts
Décos! exhibition identity,
signage and graphic
communication.
Client: ENSAD
Year: 2009

Below: redesigning graphic
panels, wall text and labels
for the 25th anniversary
of the Institut du Monde
Arabe, Paris, and the
renovation of its museum
by Roberto Ostinelli.
Client: Institut du Monde
Arabe
Year: 2012

Bottom: animated and
printed New Year's card.
Client: ENSAD
Year: 2010

Below: In collaboration
with Mediacombo, an
interactive iPad guide for
the exhibition "Seeing
Gertrude Stein" at the
Contemporary Jewish
Museum, San Francisco
Client: Mediacombo
Year: 2010

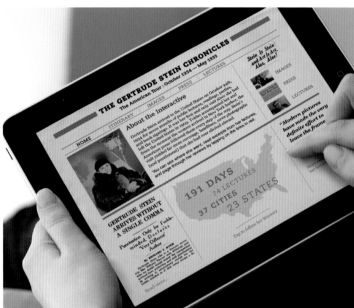

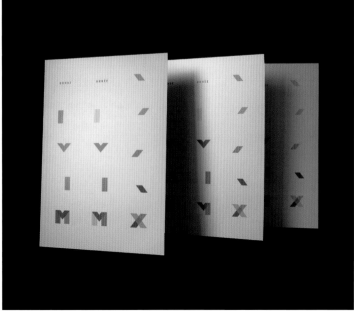

# CARNOVSKY

ITALY

## From light to dark, from reality to a dream

Below: *Animalia No.1.*
Client: self
Year: 2010

## Carnovsky

www.carnovsky.com
Founded 2007

### Founding members

Francesco Rugi and
Silvia Quintanilla (Italy
1977, Colombia 1979)

### Education

Art history, DAMS, at the
University of Bologna
(Italy), design at Domus
Academy (Italy); industrial
design at Universidad
de los Andes (Colombia),
design at Domus
Academy (Italy)

### Philosophy

We are a Milan-based artist/designer duo. Our latest work, RGB, is a work about the exploration of the "surface's deepness", and creating surfaces that mutate and interact with different chromatic stimuli. RGB's technique consists in the overlapping of three different images, each one in a primary color. The resulting images from this superimposition are unexpected and disorienting. Through a coloured filter it is possible to see clearly the layers in which the image is composed. We wanted to represent the theme of metamorphosis – we created a catalogue of natural motifs starting with the engravings from natural history's great European texts between the sixteenth and eighteenth century, from Aldrovandi to Ruysch, from Linnaeus to Bonnaterre. In each image three layers live together, three worlds that could belong to a specific natural kingdom, but that at the same time connect to a different psychological or emotional status that passes from the clear to the hidden, from light to dark, from reality to a dream.

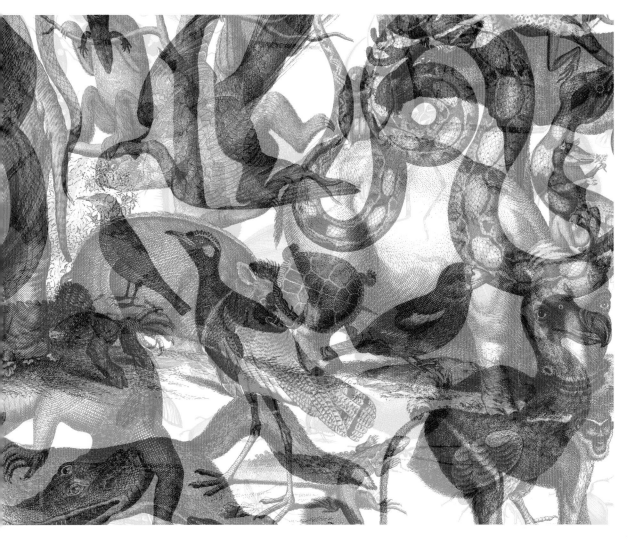

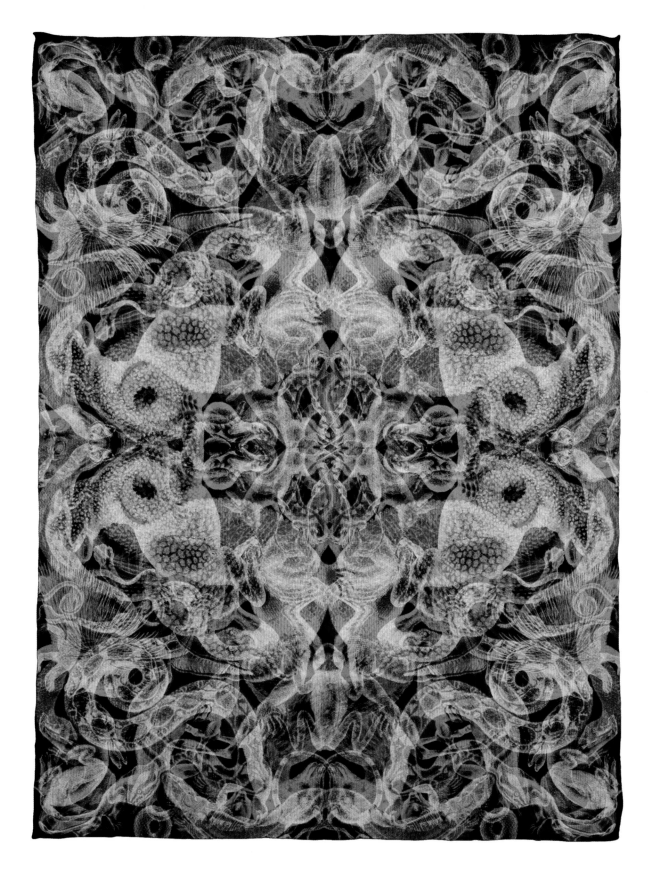

Above and opposite:
limited edition of 99
digitally printed silk
scarves.
Client: self
Year: 2012

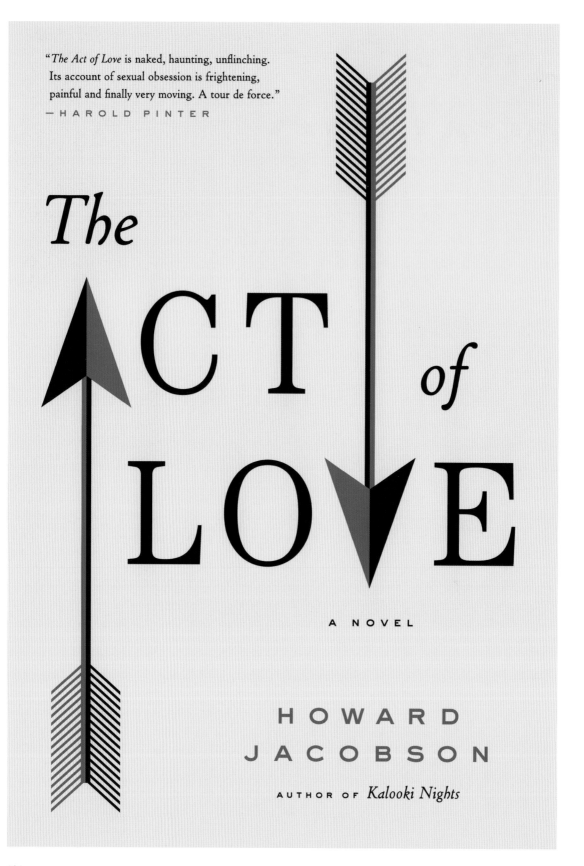

"*The Act of Love* is naked, haunting, unflinching.
Its account of sexual obsession is frightening,
painful and finally very moving. A tour de force."
— HAROLD PINTER

The
ACT
of
LOVE

A NOVEL

HOWARD
JACOBSON

AUTHOR OF *Kalooki Nights*

# CATHERINE CASALINO

USA

Opposite: *The Act of Love*
by Howard Jacobson,
hardcover book jacket.
Client: Simon & Schuster
Year: 2009

## I want the reader to understand what the book is about, before they even read a word of it

**Catherine Casalino**
www.catherinecasalino.com
Born USA 1981

**Education**
The College of William
and Mary, NYU Publishing
Institute, SVA Continuing
Education, FIT Continuing
Education (all USA)

**Philosophy**
I see every book I work on as a chance to push myself
in a new creative direction. I don't strive to have a style
or look, but to let each individual book dictate the design.
The variety of books I get to work on – from biographies
to zombie novels – really keeps me on my toes
and allows me not only to push my own skills, from
photography to hand-lettering, but also to collaborate
with talented artists and photographers. I love doing
very conceptual design with ideas that come right out
of the text. I want the reader to understand what the
book is about, before they even read a word of it.

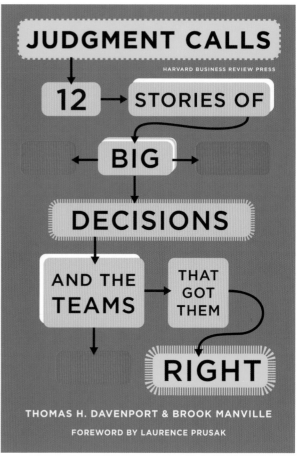

Above: *The Middlesteins*
by Jami Attenberg, book
jacket and photography.
Client: Grand Central
Publishing
Year: 2012

Above: *Judgment Calls* by
Thomas H. Davenport and
Brook Maville, book jacket
design and illustration.
Client: Harvard Business
Review Press
Year: 2012

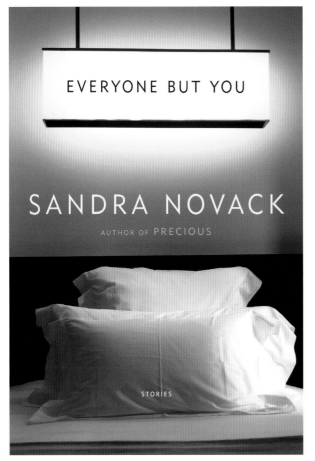

Above: *Everyone But You*
by Sandra Novack,
hardcover book jacket
design.
Client: Random House
Year: 2011

Above: *21st Century
Motherhood* by Andrea
O'Reilly, paperback book
jacket design.
Client: Columbia
University Press
Year: 2010

# ALVIN CHAN

NETHERLANDS

Below: *Durian: King of Fruits* poster submission for an exhibition, inspired by the love-it-or-hate-it flavour of this exotic fruit.
Client: Makanlah Buah-Buahan Tempatan
Year: 2011

Below: *Mangosteen: Burst of Taste* abstract poster submission for an exhibition.
Client: Makanlah Buah-Buahan Tempatan
Year: 2011

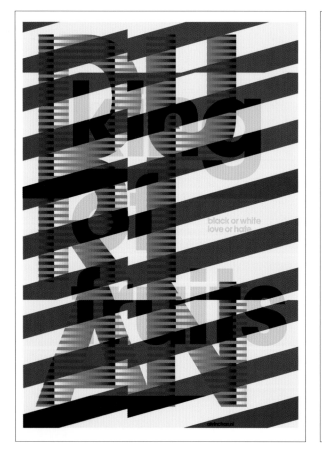

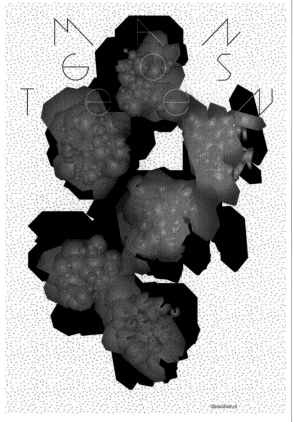

**Alvin Chan**
www.alvinchan.nl
Born Malaysia 1971,
moved to Australia

**Education**
Graphic design at Curtin
University of Western
Australia

**Philosophy**
My unique cultural and lingual background plays an important role in my design process. I am a Malaysian-born Australian graphic designer, living and working in the Netherlands. I started my career at Emery Vincent Design in Melbourne. For five years, I produced work in the field of cultural and corporate projects, specifically in identity and environmental graphics. I then moved to the Netherlands to work for Studio Dumbar. This move proved crucial to my development as a creative, as my work became more expressive and experimental. I later worked at Brown KSDP, then became creative director at Koeweiden Postma Amsterdam. Seeking a new challenge, I took a role at Nike as Creative Director of Brand Design in Europe and later the Global Creative Director of Nikefootball. Most recently, I was the Creative Director of TBWA Paris and started my own practice in June 2011. My work has received international recognition both in awards and publications. In 2007, I was accepted as a member of Alliance Graphique Internationale, representing the Netherlands.

# My unique cultural and lingual background plays an important role in my design process

Below: poster to support
the Japan earthquake
relief effort.
Client: self
Year: 2011

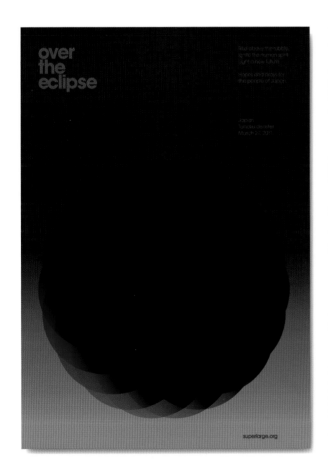

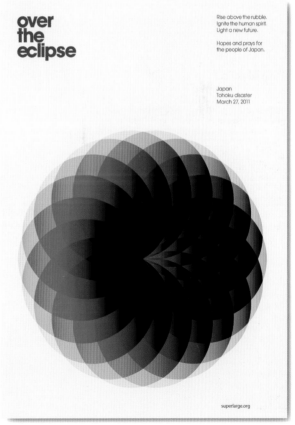

**Above and opposite:
Identity for a search
engine optimisation
company based in
Australia.
Client: Soft Rocks
Year: 2011**

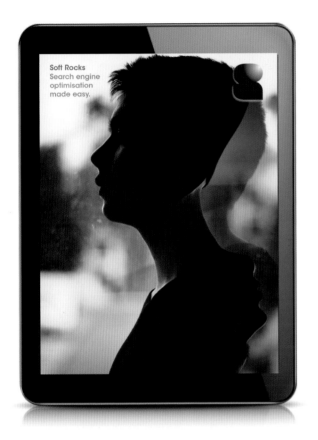

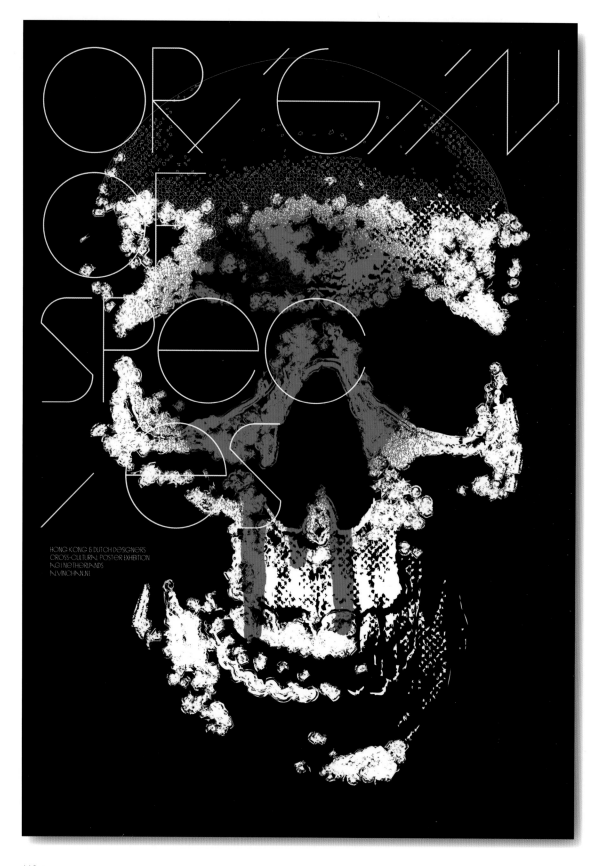

ORIGIN OF SPECIES

HONG KONG & DUTCH DESIGNERS
CROSS-CULTURAL POSTER EXHIBITION
AGI NETHERLANDS
N.VINCHAN.NL

Opposite: *Origin of Species* poster design. 20 designers from the Netherlands and Hong Kong designed posters on set themes.
Client: Hong Kong Design Association.
Year: 2011

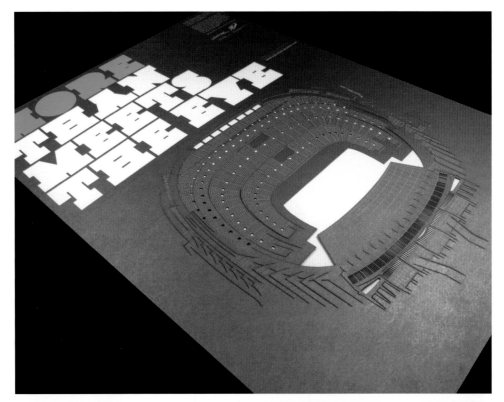

Right: an A2 size folded invitation which reveals the Camp Nou football stadium completely created from one piece of paper. Entitled: "More than Meets the Eye" it references the club's motto: "More than a Club".
Client: Nikefootball
Designed while working at: Nike Brand Design
Paper architecture: Ingrid Siliakus
Year: 2009

# CONOR
# & DAVID

IRELAND

Opposite: a special
centenary edition of the
annual UCD Architecture
yearbook. The wrap-
around cover unfolds as
a print with images from
the 100-year history of
the school.
Client: UCD Architecture
Year: 2012

Left: Identity and website
for a dance theatre
company. A stationery
suite was created without
a logo applied – each
month, the client was sent
a new stamp to be applied
to all stationery items.
Client: Fabulous Beast
Year: 2011

## We seek out clients who love what they do and we venture to produce work that we love for them

**Conor & David**
www.conoranddavid.com
Founded 2006

**Founders**
Conor Nolan and David
Wall (Ireland 1979, Ireland
1980)

**Education**
Visual communication at
National College of Art &
Design, Dublin (Ireland)
(both)

**Philosophy**
The focus of Conor & David's work is to create useful,
beautiful, content-driven graphic design for print and
screen, which we do for a diverse range of clients.
Each project is considered as an opportunity to inject
craft and a sense of play into the brief. We love
creating systems and relish testing them. We stretch
them as far as we can across a variety of media, using
the myriad skills we have at our disposal to seek the
broadest range of implementations. We seek out
clients who love what they do and we venture to
produce work that we love for them.

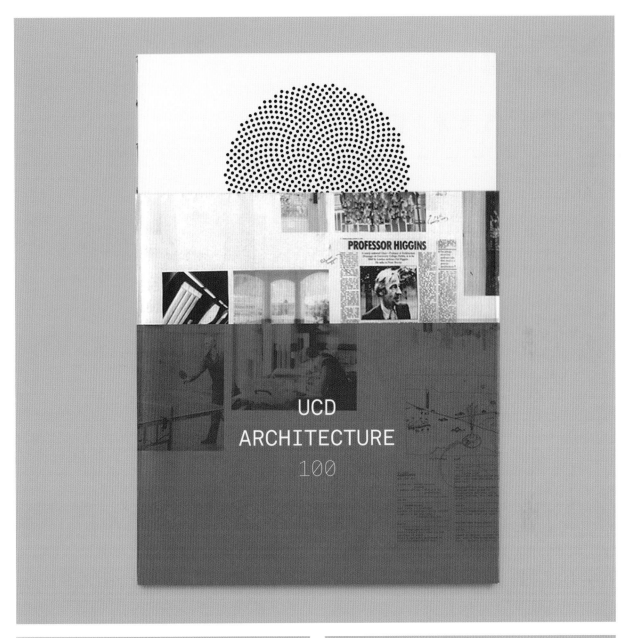

Below: redesign of a
masthead and magazine
reviewing books for children
and teenagers.
Client: Children's Books
Ireland
Year: 2011

Below: magazine editorial
design.
Client: Children's Books
Ireland
Year: 2011

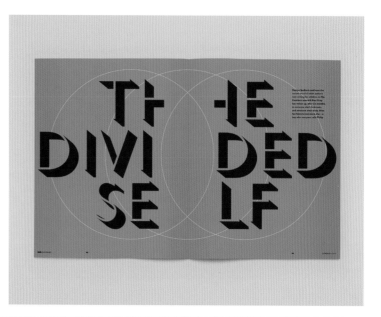

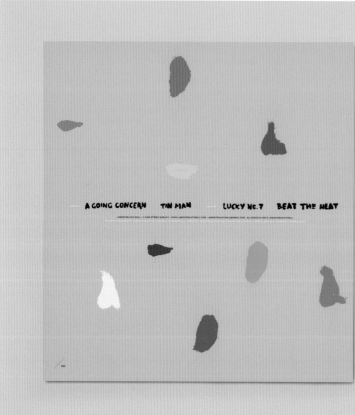

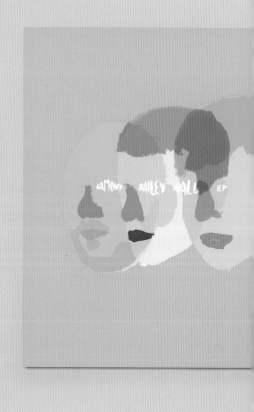

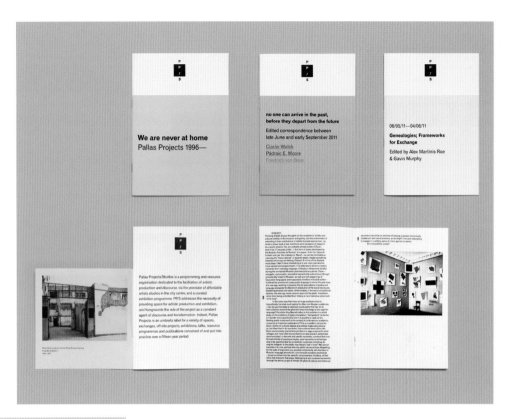

Left: limited edition vinyl album for an electronic-influenced pop trio.
Client: Lamont/Bailey/Wall
Year: 2012

Above: a series of exhibition catalogues for a gallery and studio space in Dublin.
Client: Pallas Projects/ Studios
Year: 2011

Left: a one-stop
architecture handbook
encouraging undergraduate
students to think of design
and technology as an
integrated whole. The
book is case-bound in a
durable yellow PVC cover.
Client: UCD
Year: 2011

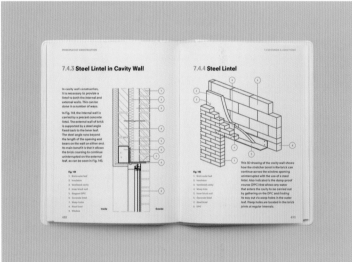

Opposite: a limited edition
lithographic print (which
viewed upside down
reveals a message) to
accompany an exhibition
of work by German
product designer Dieter
Rams entitled "Less But
Better".
Year: 2011
Client: Curate and Design

**HOW TO SURVIVE 33¾ YEARS IN ADVERTISING**

*The ramblings of M.Denton Esq.*

# COY!
# COMMUNICATIONS

UK

Opposite: *Stabbed in the Back* poster promoting an inspirational talk by Mark Denton, founder of Coy! Client: self Year: 2011

## The fruits of the subtle hand can be a delicate delight

---

**Coy! Communications**
www.coy-com.com

**Founder**
Mark Denton
Born UK 1956

**Education**
Graphic design at
Ravensbourne
College of Design
and Communication

**Philosophy**
The fruits of the subtle hand can be a delicate delight. I have a deep admiration for exponents of graphic works that are sensitive and display both nuance and restraint. That said, given the choice, I'd always go for the slightly hefty touch. A lead fist in a reinforced concrete glove if you like. It's a decision that is as much for practical reasons as it is about aesthetic preference. With all of the visual noise out there nowadays why try to communicate with a whisper?

The way I see it is a well-aimed chainsaw will probably do the job more effectively (and possibly more spectacularly) than a rapier. I just don't like having my work ignored. In fact I genuinely believe it's better to produce creative stuff that is reviled and debated than have it overlooked due to its invisibility… now, where's my sledgehammer?

Above: dancing
gravestone for the cover
of the D&AD 2012 Annual.
Client: D&AD
Year: 2012

Above: Ethel's Brew
product design, marketing
materials and advertising.
Client: DDB Worldwide
Year: 2012

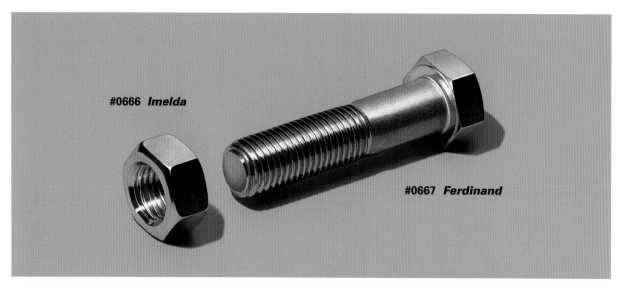

#0666 *Imelda*

#0667 *Ferdinand*

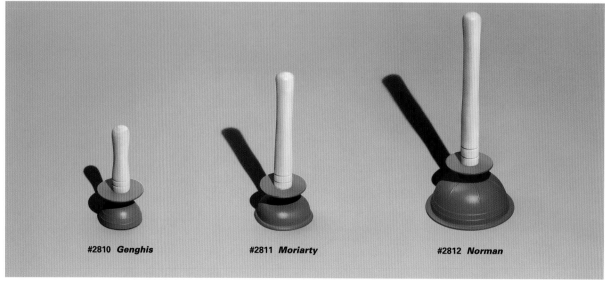

#2810 *Genghis*

#2811 *Moriarty*

#2812 *Norman*

Above: "evil" plungers, nuts and bolts as part of branding for A Large Evil Corporation.
Client: A Large Evil Corporation
Year: 2011

Opposite: *Old Mod* promotion for exhibition on British youth culture.
Client: self
Year: 2011

# LOTTIE CRUMBLEHOLME

UK

Opposite: *Madame Prunier's Fish Cookery Book* by Madame Prunier and *Modern Cookery for Private Families* by Eliza Acton jacket designs. Part of the Classic Voices in Food series, a set of contemporary editions of classic food literature books
Client: Quadrille Publishing
Year: 2011

## Educating, informing, explaining, inspiring and campaigning

**Lottie Crumbleholme**
lottiecrumbleholme.com
Born UK 1982

**Education**
Communication art and design at the Royal College of Art (UK)

**Philosophy**
I'm a freelance graphic designer and research associate at the Helen Hamlyn Centre for Design at the Royal College of Art. This means that although my background is in print-based graphic design, I now spend as much time involved in design research, teaching and running workshops as I do in designing books. Ultimately, my interest lies in educating, informing, explaining, inspiring and campaigning; working on a diverse range of projects spanning everything from making classic food literature accessible to a wider audience, to engaging employees with sustainability in the workplace.

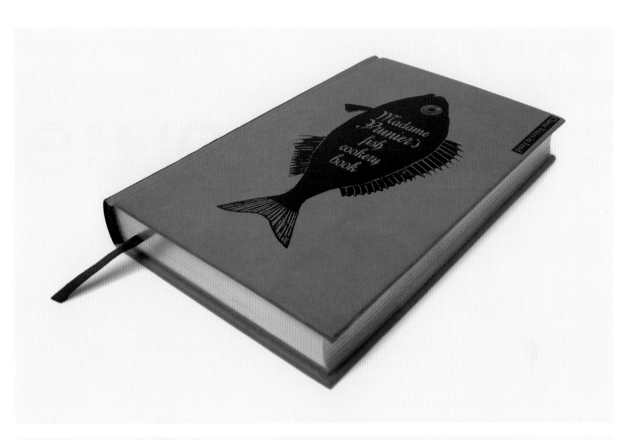

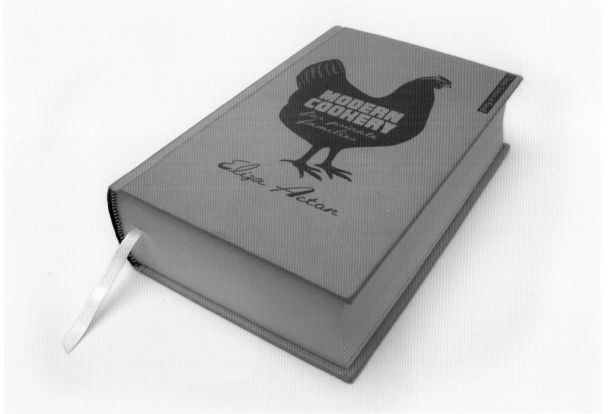

Below: Doing Your Bit –
posters promoting a
letter-writing campaign,
asking politicians for help
to tackle climate change.
Client: Barbican Centre
Year: 2009

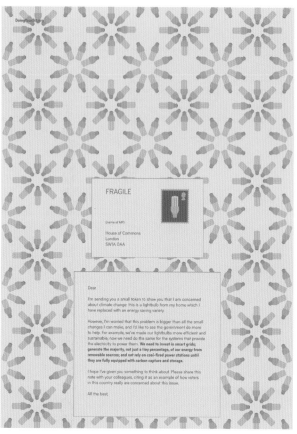

Right: More or Less a
Cookbook, helping people
think about changing their
diets to make less of an
environmental impact —
including book and dinner
party invitations. Made
in collaboration with
illustrator Emma Löfström.
Client: self
Year: 2009

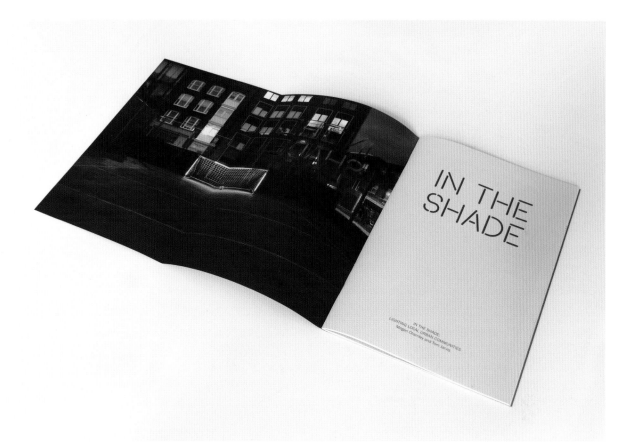

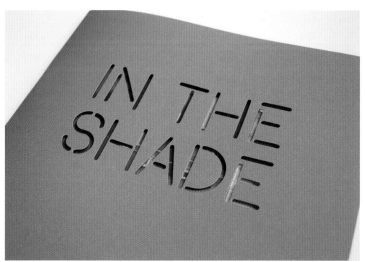

Left and above: *In The Shade*, a publication describing a research project in lighting design on the Boundary Estate in East London, undertaken by Helen Hamlyn Research Associates Megan Charney and Tom Jarvis from the Royal College of Art. Client: Helen Hamlyn Centre for Design
Year: 2012

# ISOTTA DARDILLI

ITALY

Opposite: *27* Installation
at Galleria Browning,
Treviso, Italy.
Client: self
Year: 2009

## Today's biggest challenge is to keep graphic design alive

**Isotta Dardilli**
www.isotype.it
Born Italy 1971

**Education**
Graphic design at
Academy of Fine Art,
Venice, and research at
Fabrica, Treviso (both
Italy)

**Philosophy**
Graphic design surrounds us, it is everywhere, giving us the chance to take a real look at things around us and kind of getting into them. I believe the right way to do a good job is to talk to clients on many subjects, to have a liking for them, to embrace them in order to structure the meaning of their project – and to love it. I do not believe in "nice graphics". Yes, it does exist, but to me it is and will always be just an exercise in style, leading to nothing but boredom and standardization. You often see really nice work that is just a copy of someone else's, and the style has no reference to the aim of the project. Today's biggest challenge is to keep graphic design alive, in a world where graphics seem to just be the smallest part of much more complex projects, often causing its importance to be put in the background, in a world where communication tools are made available to everybody. I know it's not easy, but to me the main thing is to keep on having fun doing my job!

Above: poster promoting
a temporary gallery.
Client: Fuel
Year: 2010

Above: *Neu* poster for
a conference at Fabrica,
Benetton's design
research centre.
Client: Fabrica
Year: 2009

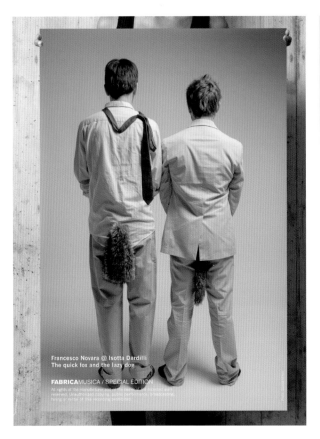

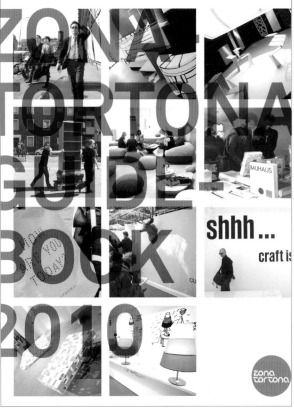

Above: poster for "The
quick fox and the lazy dog"
conference at Fabrica.
Client: Fabrica.
Year: 2009

Above: the official guide
for the Zona Tortona section
of Milan Furniture Fair.
Client: Design Partners
Year: 2010

Colors
of Money

From 3.7 2009 to 1.11 2009
Wed - Sun 14-19h  Thu until 21h

1, rue de l'Aciérie L-1112 / Luxembourg-Hollerich

T +352 2662 2007
exit07@rotondes.lu
www.rotondes.lu

Above: "Colors of Money"
poster for exhibition
at CarréRotondes,
Luxembourg.
Client: Fabrica
Year: 2009

Opposite: "Colors of
Money" exhibition at
CarréRotondes, Luxem-
bourg, curation and
design direction.
Client Fabrica.
Year: 2009

# ODED EZER

ISRAEL

Left: an experimental "typo-ritual" scheme for futuristic, typographic religion.
Client: self
Year: 2009

Opposite: I ❤ Milton poster – an homage to Milton Glaser's famous I ❤ NY logo.
Client: self
Year: 2009

Overleaf: New American Haggadah, a newly translated Haggadah, complete with essays and commentary from some of the brightest Jewish literary and intellectual voices. Edited by Jonathan Safran Foer and translated by Nathan Englander.
Client: Little, Brown & Co.
Year: 2011–12

## Be honest

**Oded Ezer**
www.odedezer.com
www.ezerfamily.com
www.logotype.co.il
Born Israel 1972

**Education**
Bezalel Academy of
Art & Design (Israel)

**Philosophy**
Good typography delivers the content in a perfect way;
Extraordinary typography becomes the message itself.
Be honest. Play, don't work. Design should be easy,
both by concept and production.

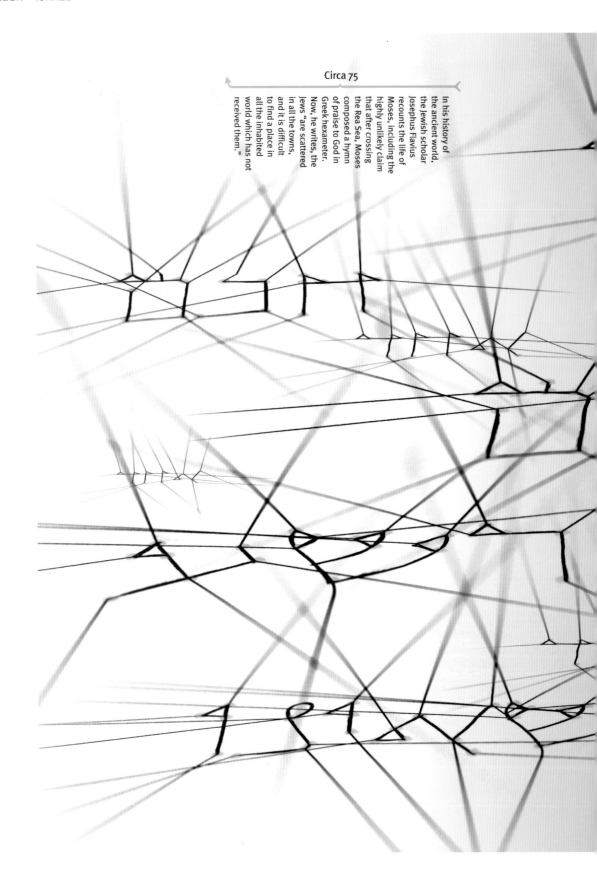

Circa 75

In his history of,
the ancient world,
the Jewish scholar
Josephus Flavius
recounts the life of
Moses, including the
highly unlikely claim
that after crossing
the Rea Sea, Moses
composed a hymn
of praise to God in
Greek hexameter.
Now, he writes, the
Jews "are scattered
in all the towns,
and it is difficult
to find a place in
all the inhabited
world which has not
received them. »

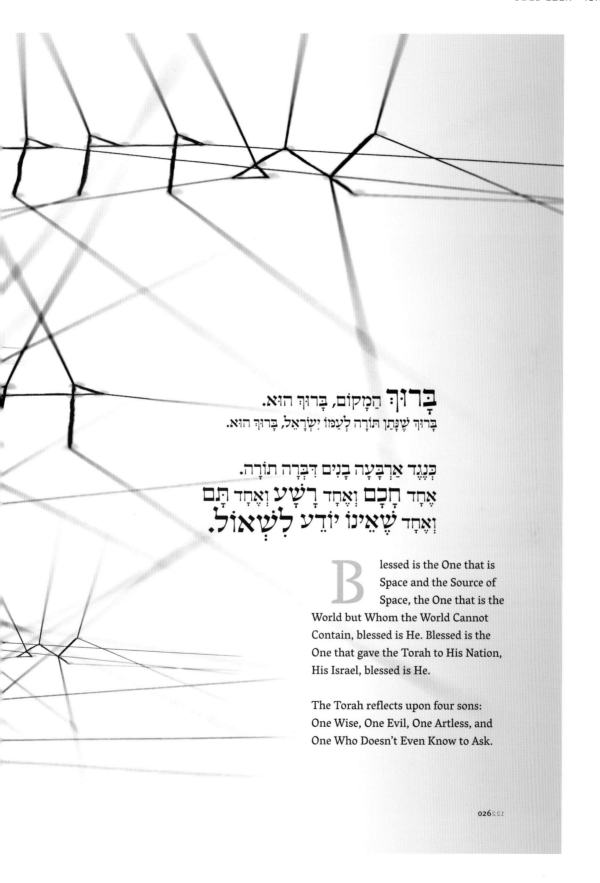

בָּרוּךְ הַמָּקוֹם, בָּרוּךְ הוּא.
בָּרוּךְ שֶׁנָּתַן תּוֹרָה לְעַמּוֹ יִשְׂרָאֵל, בָּרוּךְ הוּא.

כְּנֶגֶד אַרְבָּעָה בָנִים דִּבְּרָה תוֹרָה.
אֶחָד חָכָם וְאֶחָד רָשָׁע וְאֶחָד תָּם
וְאֶחָד שֶׁאֵינוֹ יוֹדֵעַ לִשְׁאוֹל.

**B**lessed is the One that is
Space and the Source of
Space, the One that is the
World but Whom the World Cannot
Contain, blessed is He. Blessed is the
One that gave the Torah to His Nation,
His Israel, blessed is He.

The Torah reflects upon four sons:
One Wise, One Evil, One Artless, and
One Who Doesn't Even Know to Ask.

026

Below: One-off shoe and poster design and a short video performance produced for a charity exhibition in aid of the Center for Victims of Sexual Assault, and the Shufuni Shoes Fair (Ezer pictured wearing his "type mohawk").
Client: Shufuni
Year: 2010

Below: Charles Dickens's
*Great Expectations*.
Taking a 1955 Hebrew
translation of the novel
and translating it back into
English on the internet,
the result is incorrect and
unreadable, questioning
the relationship between
English and Hebrew.
Client: GraphicDesign&
Year: 2012

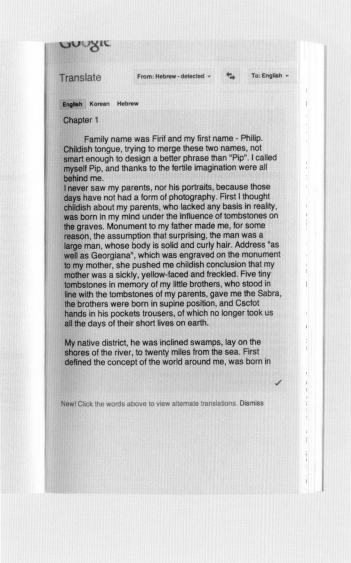

Translate  From: Hebrew - detected ▾  ⇄  To: English ▾

English  Korean  Hebrew

Chapter 1

Family name was Firif and my first name - Philip.
Childish tongue, trying to merge these two names, not
smart enough to design a better phrase than "Pip". I called
myself Pip, and thanks to the fertile imagination were all
behind me.
I never saw my parents, nor his portraits, because those
days have not had a form of photography. First I thought
childish about my parents, who lacked any basis in reality,
was born in my mind under the influence of tombstones on
the graves. Monument to my father made me, for some
reason, the assumption that surprising, the man was a
large man, whose body is solid and curly hair. Address "as
well as Georgiana", which was engraved on the monument
to my mother, she pushed me childish conclusion that my
mother was a sickly, yellow-faced and freckled. Five tiny
tombstones in memory of my little brothers, who stood in
line with the tombstones of my parents, gave me the Sabra,
the brothers were born in supine position, and Cscfot
hands in his pockets trousers, of which no longer took us
all the days of their short lives on earth.

My native district, he was inclined swamps, lay on the
shores of the river, to twenty miles from the sea. First
defined the concept of the world around me, was born in

New! Click the words above to view alternate translations. Dismiss

# KIKO FARKAS/ MÁQUINA ESTÚDIO

## BRAZIL

Opposite: poster
designed for a Chinese
printing company
representing impressions
of China after visiting the
Icograda Congress.
Client: Artron
Year: 2010

Right: surfboards.
Assistant designer:
Mateus Valadares
Client: BMW
Year: 2010

## Passionate about beauty

**Kiko Farkas/Máquina Estúdio**
www.kikofarkas.com.br
Born Brazil 1957

**Education**
Architecture at
Universidade de São
Paulo (Brazil)

**Philosophy**
The fundamental tools for the studio's work are
drawing and a passion for colour. The tendency to
garner inspiration from anything that crosses Kiko's
path is a strong characteristic of his work. Most
important of all, Kiko is passionate about beauty, and
strives always to achieve it with his design and
illustration work. Founded by Kiko in 1987, Máquina
Estúdio has grown to be one of the most prolific

Brazilian design studios with an international client
base. In the studio's work for cultural institutions and
publishing, we have created a range of printed media,
from children's books to art books, annual reports and
exhibition catalogues. We recently won a national bid
to create Brazil's trademark for tourism.

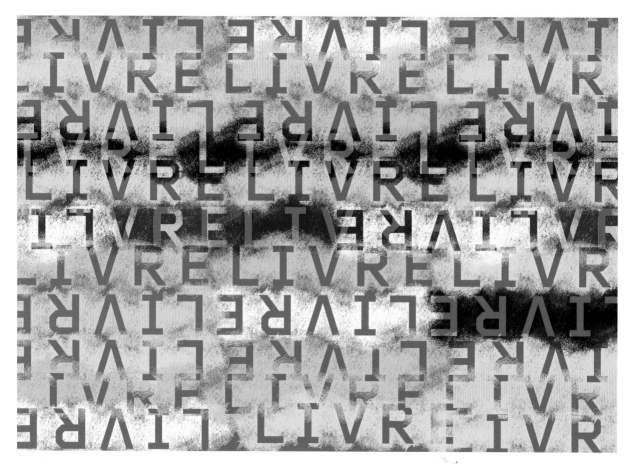

Above and right: identity
for LIVRE: conteúdo e
cultura (LIVRE: content
and culture).
Assistant designer:
Mateus Valadares
Client: Livre, 2010

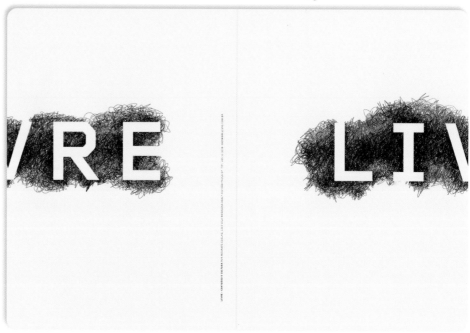

Above: *o sol do meio dia*
film poster.
Client: Bananeira Filmes
Year: 2009

Above: CD packaging.
Client: Biscoito fino record
company
Year: 2010

# FARROW

UK

Opposite: packaging for a
limited edition vinyl version
of the Pet Shop Boys
album *Yes*. Consisting
of the album tracks split
over 11 separate records,
each in a coloured sleeve,
housed in a smoked
perspex case.
Client: The Vinyl Factory
Year: 2009

Left: *British Baking* book
design. An illustrated
recipe book for renowned
restaurateur Oliver Peyton's
Peyton and Byrne brand.
Client: Square Peg
Year: 2011

Opposite bottom:
Spiritualized's *Sweet
Heart, Sweet Light*
album artwork.
Client: Spiritualized
Year: 2012

## The aesthetic is inherent

**Farrow**
www.farrowdesign.com
Founded 1995
Mark Farrow
Born UK 1960

**Education**
Self-taught

**Philosophy**
There is no manifesto in place within the studio.
We just work hard to produce the most appropriate
and very best solution we can for each project we
are asked to design. The aesthetic is inherent.

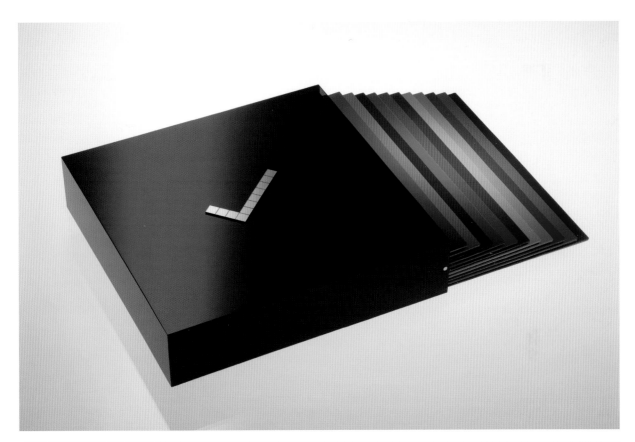

Above and opposite:
Volvo Ocean Race yacht.
Nine sails were designed,
which are used in different
combinations depending on
the conditions. Images of
the boat were used as
Camper's global advertising
campaign and the graphic
patterns were used in
stores and applied to
commercial footwear
and clothing.
Client: Camper
Year: 2010

Opposite: graphic lighting design for pan-Asian restaurant Chan, located in Thessaloniki, Greece. Produced in collaboration with architects Andy Martin Studios.
Client: Chan
Year: 2011

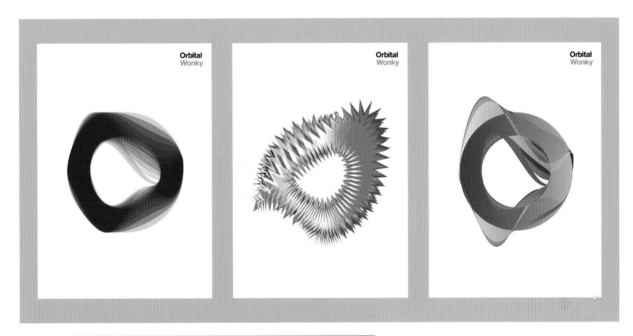

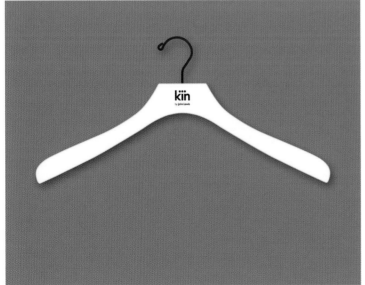

Left: identity for Kin, a family fashion label for John Lewis.
Client: John Lewis
Year: 2012

Above: set of limited edition posters produced for sale on the band Orbital's "Wonky" tour.
Client: Orbital
Year: 2012

# LOUISE FILI

USA

Below: subway poster.
Client: School of Visual
Arts, New York
Year: 2011

Below: Love stamp.
Client: United States
Postal Service
Year: 2012

# Never sit around and wait for the phone to ring

**Louise Fili**
www.louisefili.com
Born USA 1951

**Education**
Studio art at Skidmore
College (USA)

**Philosophy**
My two rules of graphic design:
1. Never depend on any one type of work, or any one client.
2. Never sit around and wait for the phone to ring. Every designer needs to have personal projects – it's the only way to find one's design voice.

**Below:** *Scripts* **book jacket design, and authorship with Steven Heller. Client: Thames & Hudson Year: 2011**

**Overleaf: book jacket designs and typography. Client: Rizzoli International Year: 2011**

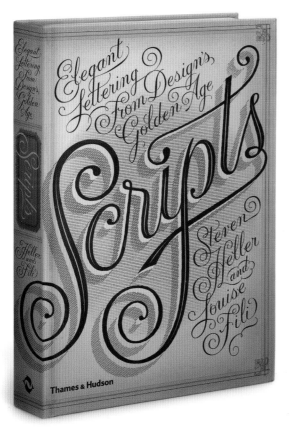

**Below:** *Elegantissima* **book design and authorship. Client: Princeton Architectural Press Year: 2012**

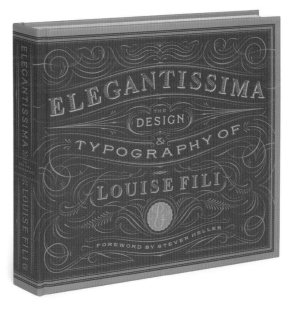

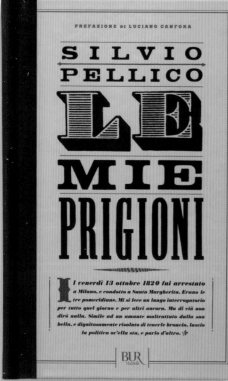

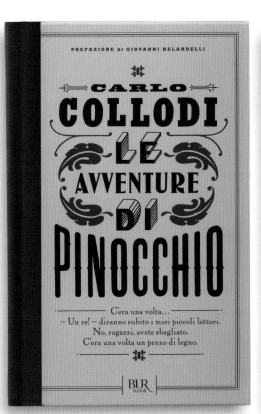

PREFAZIONE DI GIOVANNI BELARDELLI

## CARLO
# COLLODI
## LE
## AVVENTURE
## DI
# PINOCCHIO

C'era una volta…
– Un re! – diranno subito i miei piccoli lettori.
No, ragazzi, avete sbagliato.
C'era una volta un pezzo di legno.

BUR
rizzoli

PREFAZIONE DI GUSTAVO ZAGREBELSKY

# GIOVANNI
# VERGA
# I MALA
# VOGLIA

Un tempo i Malavoglia erano stati numerosi come i sassi della strada
vecchia di Trezza; ce n'erano persino ad Ognina, e ad Aci Castello,
tutti buona e brava gente di mare, proprio all'opposto di quel che
sembrava dal nomignolo, come dev'essere.

BUR
rizzoli

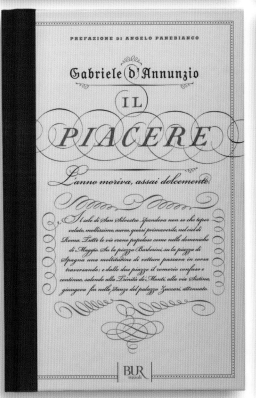

PREFAZIONE DI ANGELO PANEBIANCO

Gabriele d'Annunzio
IL
# PIACERE

L'anno moriva, assai dolcemente.

Il sole di San Silvestro spandeva non so che tepor
velato, mollissimo, aureo, quasi primaverile, nel ciel di
Roma. Tutte le vie erano popolose come nelle domeniche
di Maggio. Su la piazza Barberini, su la piazza di
Spagna una moltitudine di vetture passava in corsa
traversando; e dalle due piazze il romorio confuso e
continuo saliva alla Trinità de' Monti, alla via Sistina,
giungeva fin nelle stanze del palazzo Zuccari, attenuato.

BUR
rizzoli

PREFAZIONE DI ANDREA RICCARDI

ALESSANDRO
MANZONI
# I PROMESSI
# SPOSI

Quel ramo del lago di Como, che volge a mezzogiorno, tra due
catene non interrotte di monti, tutto a seni e a golfi, a seconda
dello sporgere e del rientrare di quelle, vien, quasi a un tratto a
ristringersi, e a prender corso e figura di fiume, tra un promon-
torio a destra, e un'ampia costiera dall'altra parte.

BUR
rizzoli

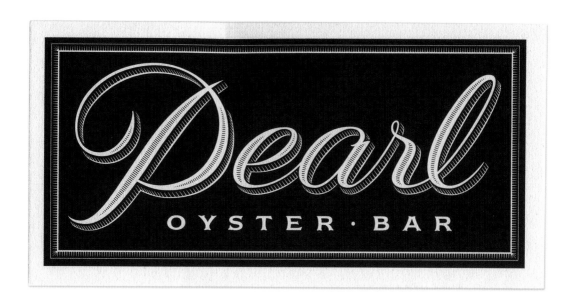

Above: logotype.
Client: Pearl Oyster Bar
Year: 2012

Right: tea tins.
Client: Ambessa Teas
Year: 2012

Opposite: presentation
box for book of work
by the graduates of
the graphic design
department at SVA.
Client: School of Visual
Arts, New York
Year: 2011

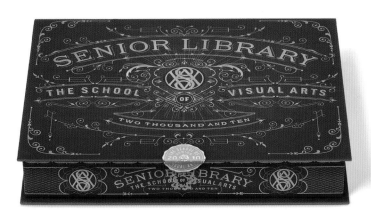

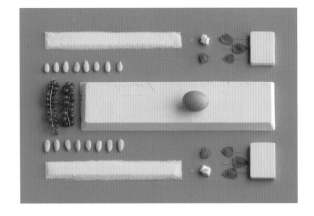

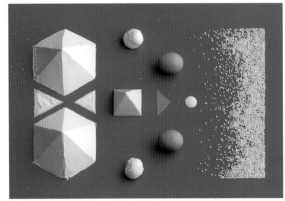

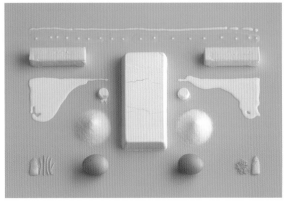

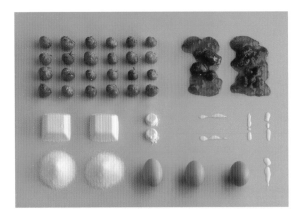

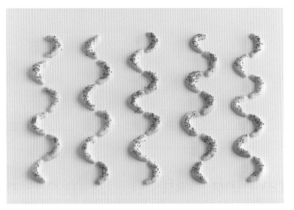

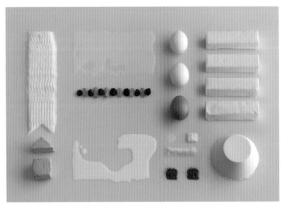

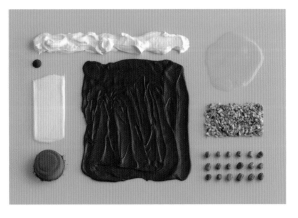

# FORSMAN & BODENFORS

## SWEDEN

## Outstanding craftsmanship has never been more relevant

**Forsman & Bodenfors**
www.fb.se
Founded 1986

**Founding members**
Sven-Olof Bodenfors,
Staffan Forsman, Mikko
Timonen and Jonas
Enghage (Sweden 1946,
Sweden 1946, Finland
1951, Sweden 1959).

**Education**
Industrial design at
College of Art & Crafts
University Gothenburg;
art direction at College of
Art & Crafts University
Gothenburg; graphic
design at College of Art
& Crafts University in
Gothenburg; unfinished
and irrelevant studies.

**Philosophy**
Outstanding craftsmanship has never been more
relevant. It has a unique ability to break through in a
media landscape that becomes more complex every
day. Design bridges the gap between digital and
analogue. Design turns interesting ideas into powerful
concepts. We're not a design agency. But design is at
the very heart of what we do.

Proud partner of the LGBT Festival.

Opposite: poster
promoting sponsorship
by Västtrafik, a public
transport company,
of the LGBT festival.
Client: Västtrafik
Year: 2011

Above: XC Travels
website and iPhone app.
Client: Volvo Cars AB
Year: 2011

Above: calendar for a
charity street paper.
Client: Faktum
Year: 2011

Opposite: poster for the
Brit Insurance Designs
of the Year awards.
Client: Design Museum
Year: 2011

Above: sea weather
website and iPhone app.
Client: Swedish Sea
Rescue Society
Year: 2010

# MICHAEL
# FREIMUTH

USA

Opposite: design and
illustration of magazine
cover, "Building A Green
Economy", an issue
featuring an extensive
piece by *New York Times*
columnist Paul Krugman
on environmental policy
Client: *The New York
Times Magazine*
Design director:
Arem Duplessis
Designer: Kyle Poff
Year: 2010

## Far greater opportunity and reward lie in the unknown

**Michael Freimuth**
www.michaelfreimuth.
com
Born USA 1980

**Education**
Washington University,
RISD (both USA)

**Philosophy**
Our personal design philosophy is to put ourselves in
frightening and new situations, then solve the
challenges we face. It's incredibly easy to acquiesce to
what is familiar, easy or known – the far greater
opportunity and reward lie in the unknown and the
accompanying success or failure at the end of the
given endeavour. We seek projects and clients with
similarly open minds and budgets, so that we may
collectively create rich and compelling brand
experiences, memorable cultural experiments and
impactful, meaningful and socially responsible
communications.

# BUILDING A GREEN ECONOMY

BY PAUL KRUGMAN

Left and below: creative direction, art direction and design of *Matériel Magazine 001*, an annual, short-run publication developed to unearth and showcase emerging artists, designers and writers.
Client: *Matériel Magazine*
Art Director: Kyle Poff
Year: 2009

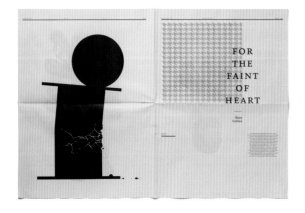

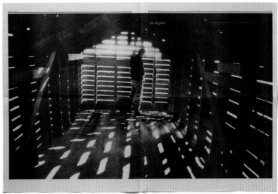

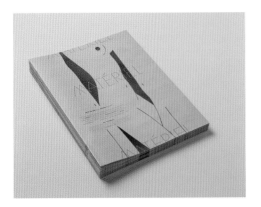

Left and below: creative
direction, art direction
and design of *Matériel
Magazine 002.*
Client: *Matériel Magazine*
Art director: Kyle Poff
Year: 2011

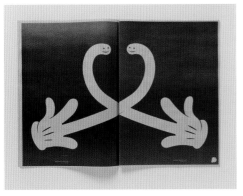

Left and below: identity for a new coffee shop in Brooklyn's Crown Heights neighborhood, Glass Shop, seeking to establish itself by communicating its local, neighborhood commitment and high quality product.
Client: Glass Shop
Year: 2009

Above: Solar Clock – an interactive screensaver inspired by the unique and innovative "Polar Clock" – a time-keeping model consisting of concentric circles as units of time, and based on the millennia-old technology of Greek analemmatic sun-dials.
Motion-designer: Kurt Lawson
Developer: Bill Woodruff
Client: self
Year: 2011

# HILARY GREENBAUM

USA

Below: editorial design of
"Who Made That?" features.
Client: *The New York
Times Magazine*
Year: 2012

# The content is the design, the design is the content

**Hilary Greenbaum**
hilarygreenbaum.com
Born USA 1979

**Education**
Communication design
at Carnegie Mellon
University, New York,
graphic design at the
California Institute of the
Arts (both USA)

**Philosophy**
The content is the design. The design is the content.
I believe that design is both the process and the result
of giving form to an idea, even if the idea is the form
itself. Throughout the development of any particular
project, I seek to generate a structure that can both
house and reinforce the narrative that it conveys,
while engaging the viewer and challenging visual
conventions. My practice is a combination of rigour,
intuition and play.

Overleaf: "Decision
Fatigue" editorial design.
Client: *The New York
Times Magazine*
Year: 2011

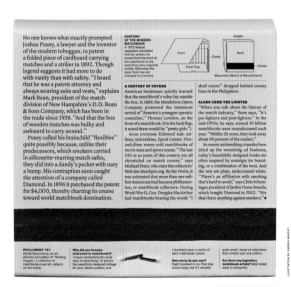

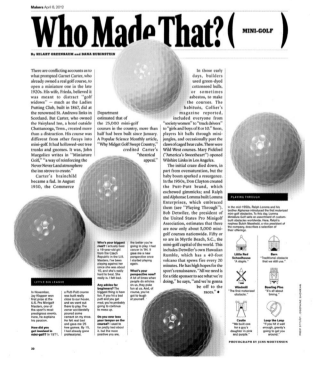

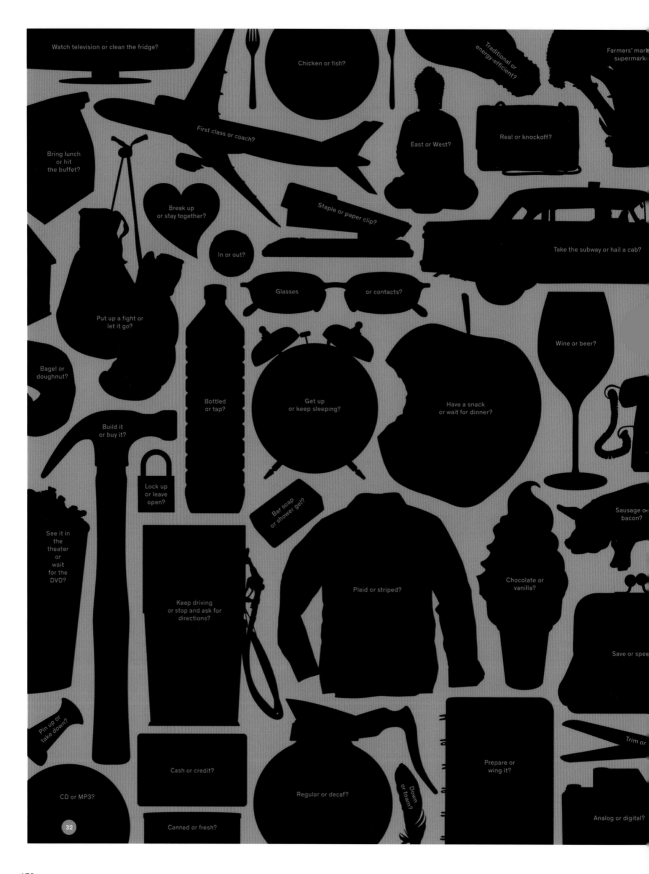

Watch television or clean the fridge?

Chicken or fish?

Traditional or energy-efficient?

Farmers' mark supermark

First class or coach?

East or West?

Real or knockoff?

Bring lunch or hit the buffet?

Break up or stay together?

Staple or paper clip?

Take the subway or hail a cab?

In or out?

Put up a fight or let it go?

Glasses

or contacts?

Wine or beer?

Bagel or doughnut?

Bottled or tap?

Get up or keep sleeping?

Have a snack or wait for dinner?

Build it or buy it?

Lock up or leave open?

Bar soap or shower gel?

Sausage or bacon?

See it in the theater or wait for the DVD?

Plaid or striped?

Chocolate or vanilla?

Keep driving or stop and ask for directions?

Save or spe

Pin up or take down?

Trim or

Prepare or wing it?

Cash or credit?

CD or MP3?

Regular or decaf?

Down or foam?

32

Canned or fresh?

Analog or digital?

# TO CHOOSE IS TO LOSE

The very act of making decisions depletes
our ability to make them well.
So how do we navigate a world of
endless choice?

**BY JOHN TIERNEY**

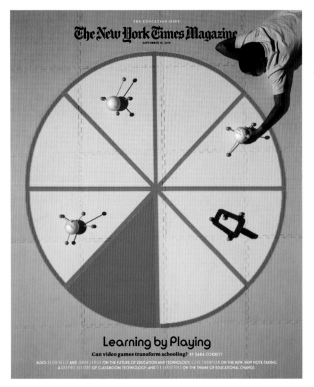

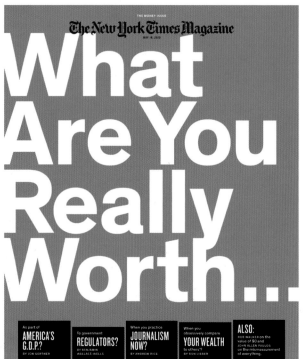

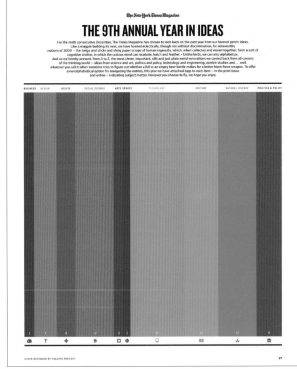

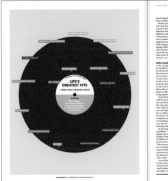

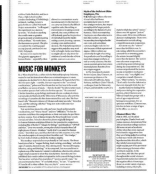

Opposite: magazine covers.
Client: *The New York
Times Magazine*
Year: 2009 – present

Above: "The Year in Ideas"
issue cover and editorial
design.
Client: *The New York
Times Magazine*
Year: 2009

# CATHERINE GRIFFITHS

NEW ZEALAND/FRANCE

Opposite: The Trestle Leg Series installation. The brief was to take eight writings from prominent New Zealand poets and authors, and an oratory, or "korero", of a local Maori chief, and apply them to eight columns beneath the Auckland Harbour Bridge as part of a wider park restoration project
Client: New Zealand Transport Agency
Year: 2012

## The materiality of things

**Catherine Griffiths**
www.catherinegriffiths.co.nz
Born New Zealand 1966

**Education**
Visual communication design at the School of Design, Wellington (New Zealand)

**Philosophy**
I live and work near Auckland (in a forest), and Paris (on a boat). My design practice spans visual communication, self-published artist books, typographic installations and public sculpture, and occasionally writing on design, giving lectures, and working with students. My response as a typographer, designer and artist is shaped by circumstance, an appreciation for content and meaning, the written word, and the image. Space, light and sound, the materiality of things, and the landscape are recurring elements in my design and art-based practice.

Left: AEIOU, a site-specific typography and sound installation for a new block of apartments with the practical objective of providing a screen of privacy for the residents.
Client: Cubana Apartments, New Zealand
Year: 2009

Above: *I Must Behave*, an artist book designed in collaboration with Bruce Connew, and in response to his photographs and to Connew's intent.
Client: Bruce Connew
Year: 2009

Opposite: the "letter-crumbs" of this wayfinding, or losing, system responds to the existing logo of Athfield Architects Limited with a "hillside intervention".
Client: Athfield Architects
Year: 2011

# H55

SINGAPORE

Opposite: identity system,
store cards and notebook
design.
Client: Kapok
Year: 2009

## Identifying and actualizing

**H55**
www.h55studio.com
Founded 1999

**Founding Member**
Hanson Ho
Born Singapore 1974

**Education**
Diploma in visual
communication at
Temasek Polytechnic
(Singapore)

**Philosophy**
Design is about identifying and actualizing an idea
that is relevant to the intention of the project.

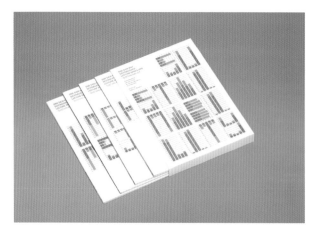

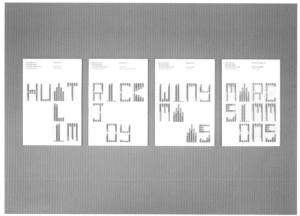

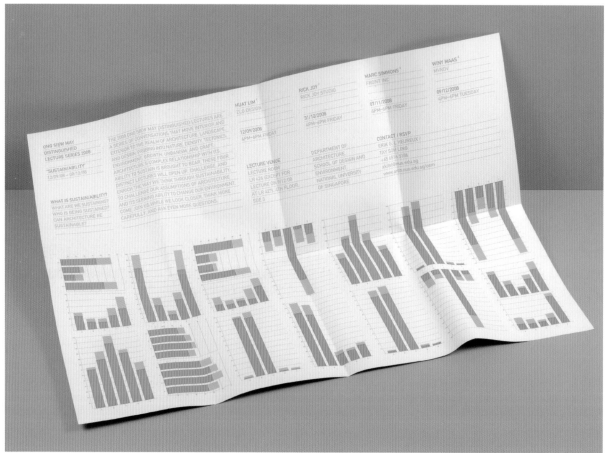

Above: Ong Siew May
Distinguished Lecture
Series identity, poster
and book design.
Client: National University
of Singapore
Year: 2009

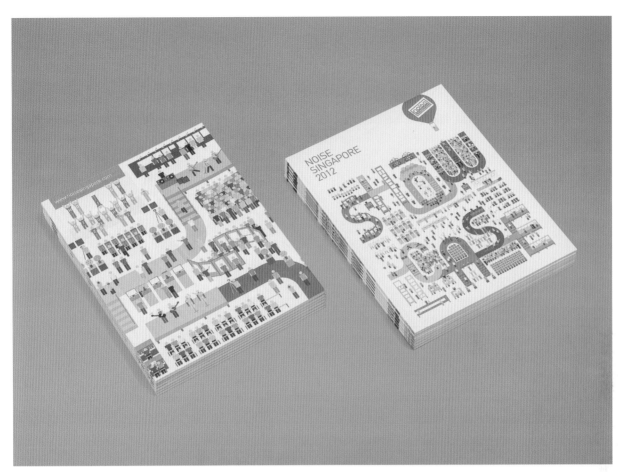

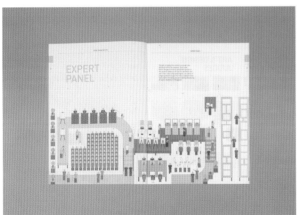

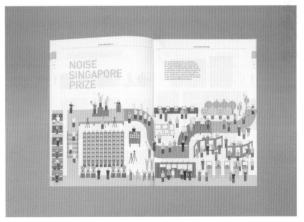

Above: Noise Singapore
campaign graphic system,
illustration and publication
design.
Client: National Arts Council
Year: 2012

# CHARLOTTE HEAL

UK

Opposite: *Contemporary
Lingerie Design* by Katie
Dominy, book design.
Client: Laurence King
Publishing
Year: 2010

## My design education instilled in me the importance of ideas and conceptual design

**Charlotte Heal**
charlotteheal.com
Born UK 1982

**Education**
Graphic design at
Brighton University,
communication art and
design at the Royal
College of Art (both UK)

**Philosophy**
My design education at Brighton University and the
RCA instilled in me the importance of ideas and
conceptual design. This philosophy continues in my
practice today. I like to have a reason to support a
piece of design and this is dependent on the subject
matter. I am here to solve a client's problem and it
is my role as the designer to listen to the client and
communicate their personality or message. By treating
each project as a unique exercise I don't have a
repetitive "style" to my work, nor is it trend-led.
Being concept-driven I do a great deal of investigation
before I even begin the work – this sets the tone
for my response. I believe graphic design is a team
effort to produce a solution that communicates well.
Each job gives me a new opportunity to learn and
new constraints from which my ideas can form.

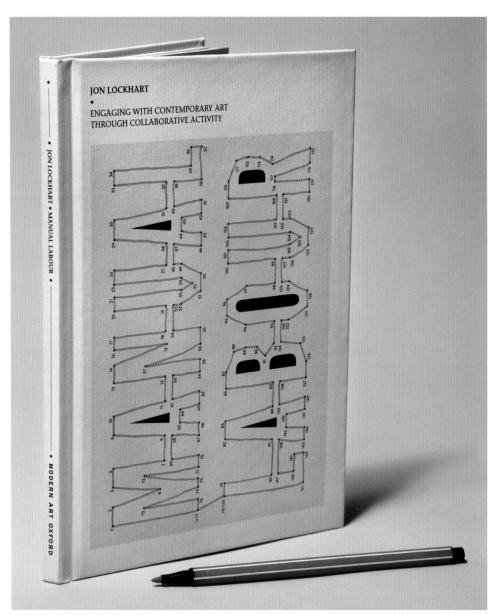

Left and below: *Manual Labour* by Jon Lockhart, book design.
Client: Modern Art Oxford
Year: 2010

Right and below: *Baked in America* by David Lesniak and David Muniz, book design.
Client: Random House Group
Year: 2011

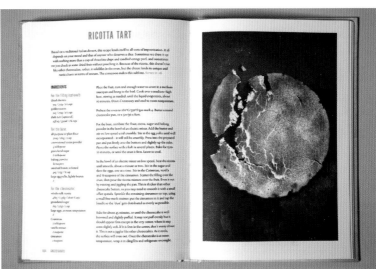

Above: *Textile Designers
at the Cutting Edge* book
design.
Client: Laurence King
Publishing
Year: 2009

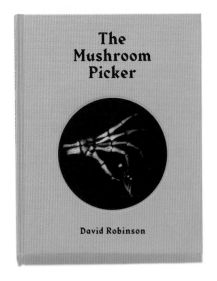

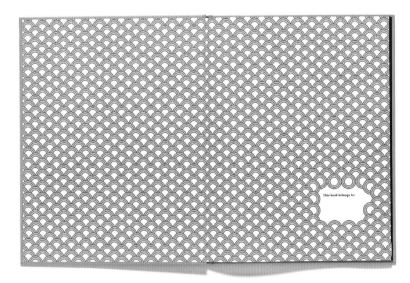

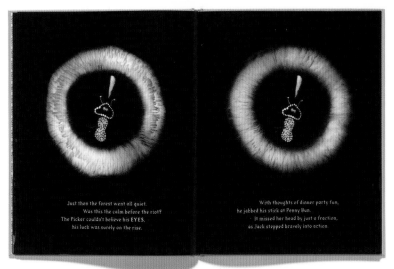

**Above and right:** *The Mushroom Picker* by David Robinson, book design.
Client: Violette Editions
Year: 2012

# LISA HEDGE

USA

Below: *History in Circles & Squares*, illustration and custom type in printed visual concept journal
Client: self
Year: 2011

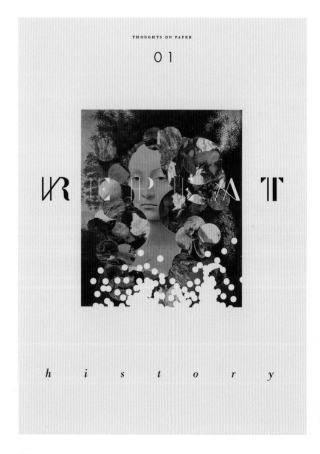

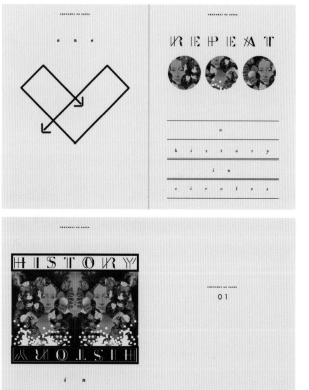

# Tell visual stories

**Lisa Hedge**
www.lisahedge.com
Born New Zealand 1984

**Education**
Fine art at University
of Southern California
(USA)

**Philosophy**
My practice as a designer involves various methods of image-making through illustration, typography, collage and photography. My work attempts to overlay these techniques to understand and realize ideas in a visual form, and craft narratives that are vibrant yet subtle. I'm drawn to design with materiality, concept and colour, and like to break apart letterforms, rework images and construct ideas that tell visual stories with these qualities. I'm interested in the mutable role of style in the design process, and the capacity for form to amplify or conceal any meaning that might be inherent or implied by the textual or visual content.

Below: *Elizabeth: In 21 Acts*, excerpts from printed book.
Client: self
Year: 2011

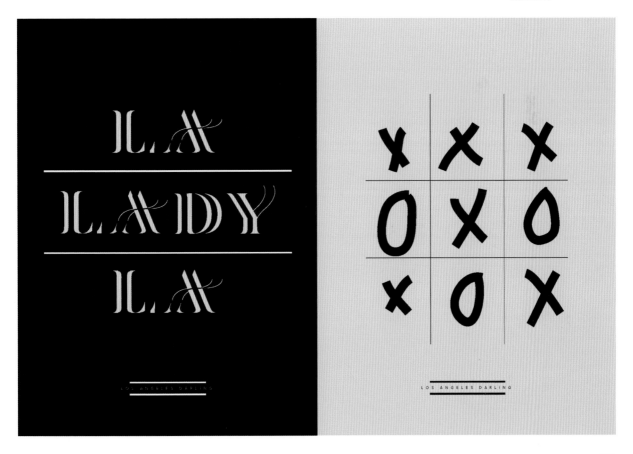

DARK ROADS AND ROLLING HILLS
THE PERSISTENCE OF SELECTIVE MEMORY
2009

Left: The Persistence
of Selective Memory,
illustration.
Client: self
Year: 2011

Left: Charcoal & Wine,
digital illustration.
Client: self
Year: 2011

Opposite: Modern Day,
illustrated prints and
postcards.
Client: self
Year: 2011

MARCEL
DUCHAMP

1917

JOSEF
ALBERS

1959

FRANK
STELLA

1958

LARRY
BELL

1966

JASPER
JOHNS

1974

RENE
MAGRITTE

1964

ROY
LICHTENSTEIN

1963

ON
KAWARA

1966

FELIX GONZALEZ
-TORRES

1991

SOL
LE WITT

1975

GEORGIA
O'KEEFFE

1923

JEFF
KOONS

1985

ED
RUSCHA

1966

HENRI
MATISSE

1952

LUCIO
FONTANA

1960

CY
TWOMBLY

1971

PABLO
PICASSO

1907

PIET
MONDRIAN

1921

ALEXANDER
CALDER

1937

DONALD
JUDD

1965

DAN
FLAVIN

1963

VAN
GOGH

1989

JACKSON
POLLOCK

1950

SALVADOR
DALI

1937

WILLEM
DE KOONING

1952

ANDY
WARHOL

1962

RICHARD
SERRA

1959

ROBERT
RYMAN

1961

ALBERTO
GIACOMETTI

1960

BARNETT
NEWMAN

1950

MODERN IN GREEN

# HELMO

FRANCE

## Complex but not complicated

**Helmo**
www.helmo.fr
Founded 2006

**Founding members**
Thomas Couderc,
Clément Vauchez
(France 1977,
France 1978)

**Education**
ISBA Besançon (both);
DSAA typographie in
École Estienne Paris
(both France)

**Philosophy**
We don't have a "design philosophy" so to speak, we
try to explore visual language in (new) and unusual
ways. A major part of our work is designing posters
for cultural events. We take care to create images that
are complex but not complicated, sometimes slightly
strange and which contain several possible meanings
and interpretations. We believe that a poster has to
invite people in the street to think, to question
themselves about the subject of the poster and the
graphic language used. Seeing a poster in the street
is like meeting somebody by chance, it has to be an
unusual meeting for you to notice it and for it to stand
out in the flow of everyday life.

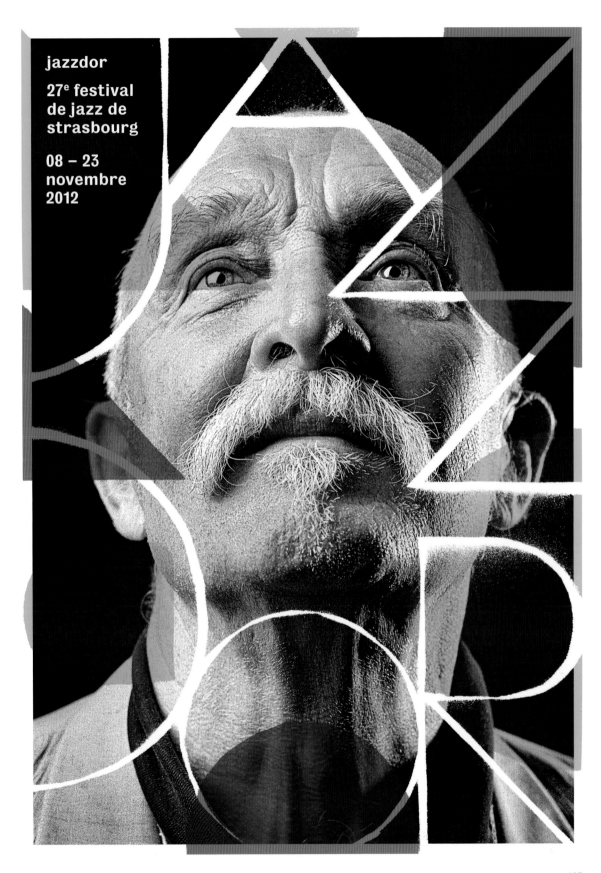

jazzdor

27e festival
de jazz de
strasbourg

08 – 23
novembre
2012

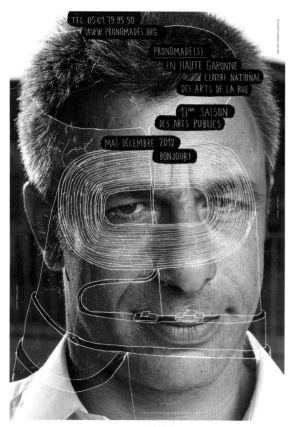

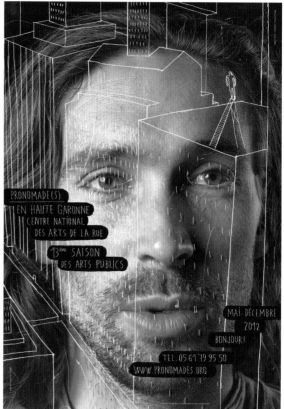

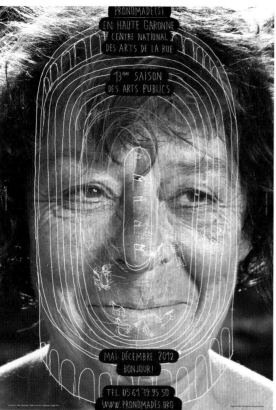

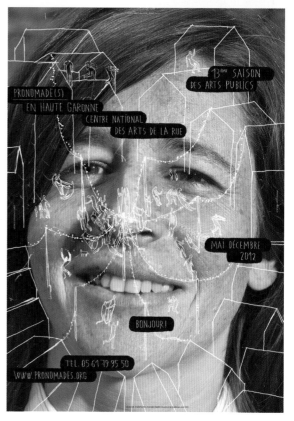

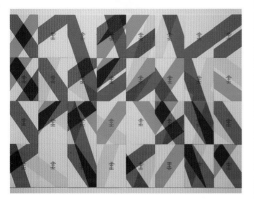

Right and above: town
signage and street
furniture design for an
international poster and
graphic design festival
in Chaumont, France.
Client: Chaumont
Year: 2010

Opposite: posters for
an arts center for theatre,
dance and performance
in Haute Garonne, South
of France.
Client: Pronomades
Year: 2012

# Le Lieu du Design

Exposition
du 8 octobre 2010
au 8 janvier 2011

# Good Design, Good Business

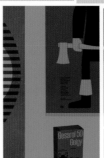

Design graphique
et publicité par Geigy
1940-1970

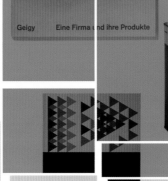

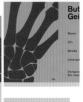

Du mardi au vendredi de 13h à 18h
Le samedi de 11h à 18h
Accès libre

Exposition conçue par
le Museum für Gestaltung Zürich.

Sur www.lelieududesign.com retrouvez
le programme complet des conférences
et des ateliers pour enfants.

Le Lieu du design,
74 rue du Faubourg Saint-Antoine
75012 Paris
www.lelieududesign.com

Le Lieu du Design est une initiative
du Conseil Régional d'Île-de-France.

L'exposition Good Design, Good Business
a reçu le précieux soutien de:
la Mairie de Paris, le Museum für Gestaltung Zürich,
Pro Helvetia · Fondation suisse pour la culture,
le Centre Régional du Tourisme Paris Île-de-France,
J.C. Decaux, le Festival international
de l'affiche et du graphisme de Chaumont
et l'agence 14 Septembre.

Partenaires média:
Les Échos, Les Inrockuptibles, Télé Obs Paris,
Challenges, Intramuros, Nova et parisART.

Opposite: publicity for
a retrospective of graphic
design produced for
Swiss pharmaceutical
company, Geigy.
Client: Le Lieu du Design
Year: 2010

Right: publicity for art
and sound festival.
Client: Sonorama
Created with: Alice Guillier
Year: 2009

# ALBERTO HERNÁNDEZ

UK

Below: Imaginary Friends
poster.
Client: Self
Year: 2011

Below: *Étapes* magazine
issue 10 front cover and
font.
Client: Gustavo Gili
Year: 2010

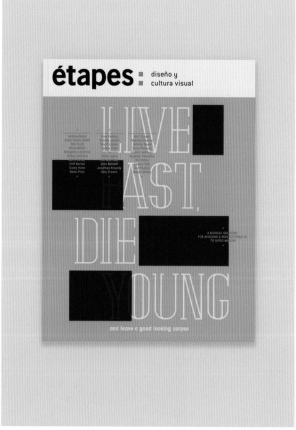

# Everything should be made as simple as possible, but no simpler.

**Alberto Hernández**
www.hereigo.co.uk
Born Spain 1985

**Education**
Graphic design at
Escuela de Arte número
10, Madrid (Spain),
MA graphic design
at London College
of Communication

**Philosophy**
I'm a Spanish designer based in London. My main interests are design for print and experimenting with typography, but my portfolio is diverse, taking inspiration from many sources.
I believe in the words of Albert Einstein, that "everything should be made as simple as possible, but no simpler".

**Above and right: Is
Shepard Fairey Stealing?
essay and editorial
design/folding poster.
Client: self
Year: 2009**

19 June 2011 / #worldrevolution / #globalrevolution

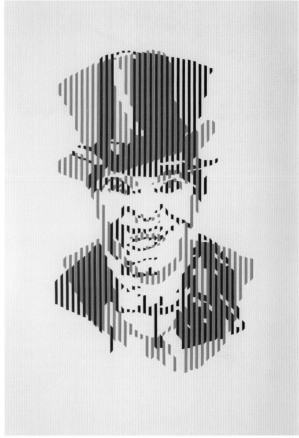

**Above: Get the Trap**
**Ready! poster.**
**Client: Voices with Futura**
**Year: 2011**

**Above: Jekyll and Hyde**
**letterpress poster. Client:**
**self**
**Year: 2009**

**Above: Hybrid Novels
editorial design.
Client: self
Year: 2009**

# HEY

SPAIN

Below: Laus campaign
branding.
Client: adg FAD
Year: 2010

# We usually prefer looking forward

**Hey**
www.heystudio.es
Founded 2007

**Founding members**
Verónica Fuerte,
Tilman Solé (Spain
1980, Spain 1975)

**Philosophy**
We are a design studio based in Barcelona. We mostly work in brand identity, illustration and editorial design. But if someone asks us to do, for example, a lamp, we will also do it. We always wanted to have our own style, and we believe we achieved it. Geometry, colour, direct typography. Let's say purity. When we look back to all our work we feel it is consistent, but we usually prefer looking forward. Our personal projects are almost as important as the commercial ones. They let us explore, innovate, travel to other dimensions and meet nice people. We are small. We like it that way because it lets us stay close to our clients, be flexible and take care of every single detail in every step of the process. We're sure you've read that before somewhere else, but we mean it. Work with us and you'll see.

Below: Projecta't
identity and branding.
Client: Generalitat de
Catalunya
Year: 2010

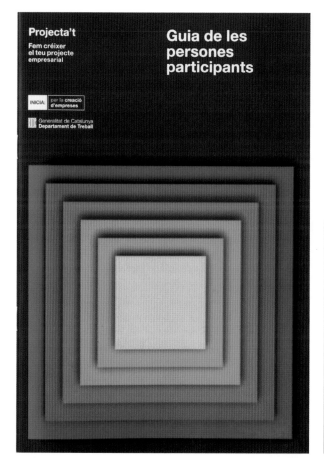

Below: Gandules'12
identity and branding
Client: CCCB
Year: 2012

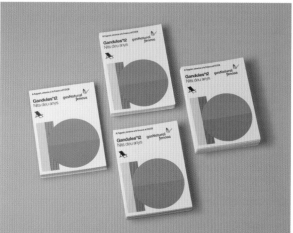

Opposite top: identity and
branding.
Client: Film Commission Chile
Year: 2012

Above: ArtFad campaign
branding.
Client: A FAD
Year: 2011

Opposite bottom:
Teatre CCCB identity
and branding.
Client: CCCB
Year: 2011

# HEYDAYS

NORWAY

Below and opposite:
poster for the annual
Design Versus Music
event part of the Insomnia
festival held in Tromsø.
Client: Insomnia
Year: 2009

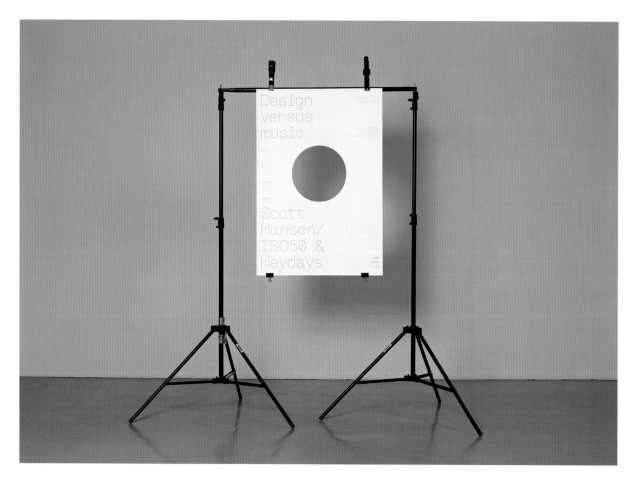

# We remove noise to add value

**Heydays**
heydays.no
Founded 2008

**Founding Members**
Mathias Hovet, Martin
Sanne, Lars Kjelsnes,
Thomas Lein, Stein
Haugen (all Norway)

**Education**
Westerdals School of
Communication (Norway)

**Philosophy**
Heydays is a design studio that creates strong visual
concepts, which trigger curiosity, create excitement
and show ambition. We listen, research and challenge.
We remove noise to add value.

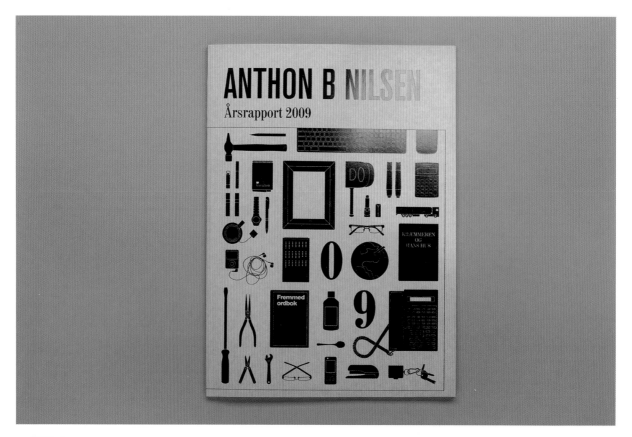

Opposite and right: annual
report for a company that
operates in the fields of
property development,
paper recycling and
private education.
Collaboration with Berit
Bakkerud & Martine
Holmsen.
Client: Anthon B Nilsen
Year: 2010

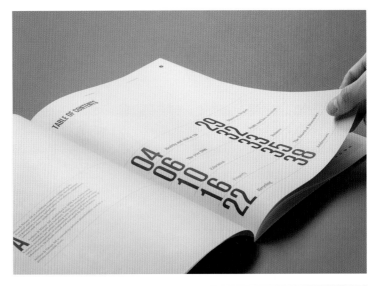

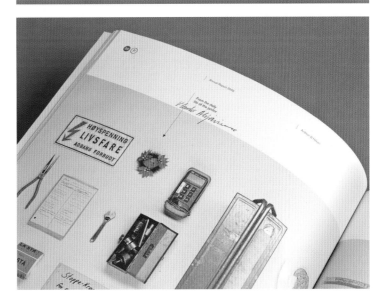

# HYATT ASSOCIATES

FRANCE

## A challenge to the conventional

**Hyatt Associates**
hyattassociates.co.uk
Founded 2006

**Founding member**
Kelly Hyatt (UK 1971)

**Education**
Graphic design at
Leicester De Montfort
University (UK)

**Philosophy**
The essence of Hyatt Associates is in creating solutions that not only answer a brief but which draw on stimulus and inspiration from a very broad creative backdrop. Sometimes this acts as a challenge to the conventional or expected response but more often than not, it results in a progressive solution that adds something unexpected. Drawing on experience from a diverse range of categories from private jet hire to greetings cards with everything in between, our solutions have included corporate literature and communication, websites, brand identities, signage, exhibitions and editorial. Whatever the brief, we'll explore and bring the solution to life.

Below: branding and
website design.
Client: Lagom Design
Year: 2011

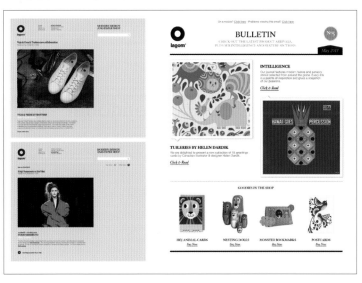

Opposite: branding and
illustration.
Client: Family Investments
Year: 2011

Right: branding and
website design.
Collaboration with D3R.
Client: Vintage Seekers
Year: 2010

# PEDRO INOUE

BRAZIL

## There is no point in doing work that you don't believe in or working for people you don't admire

**Pedro Inoue**
www.coletivo.org/pedro
Born Brazil 1977

**Education**
Never graduated, but
I can easily say that I
got a BA from working
at Barnbrook (2001–07)

**Philosophy**
"Nothing else matters if you don't have the strength
to keep fighting for something truthful" – J. Cortázar.
There is no point in doing work that you don't believe
in and there is no point in working for people you don't
admire. The financial bottom line ("we all have bills to
pay") ends up ruling our lives and excusing us, both as
professionals and as citizens, from committing to the
real problems the world faces today. Please let us not
make this the bottom line that defines us: "making
money" is an old formula that has got humanity into
this current environmental, social, and economic crisis.
If we keep repeating the same mistakes, we are likely
to end up where we are headed right now.

DE
DENTRO
DENTRO
DE
DE FORA

INSIDE OUT / OUTSIDE IN

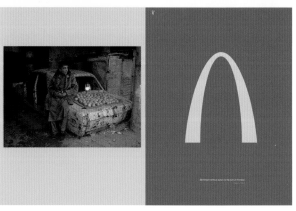

Opposite top: magazine
covers.
Client: Adbusters
Year: 2012

Right: Stephan Doitschinoff
monograph book design
Client: Gestalten
Year: 2009

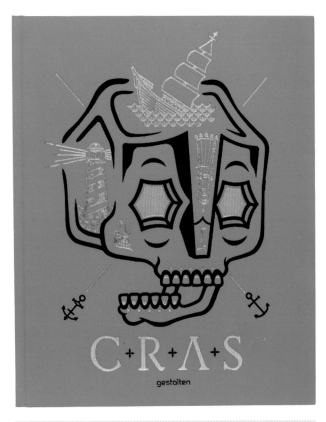

Opposite below:
magazine editorial design
and art direction.
Client: Adbusters
Year: 2010

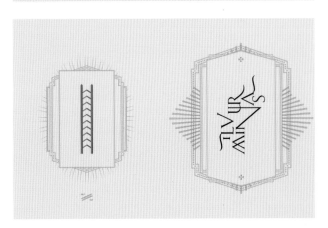

Left: CD and 12-inch
artwork for DJ MIXHELL.
Client: Boysnoize Records
Year: 2012

Opposite: Philip K. Dick
series book jacket design.
Client: Aleph Publishers
Year: 2012

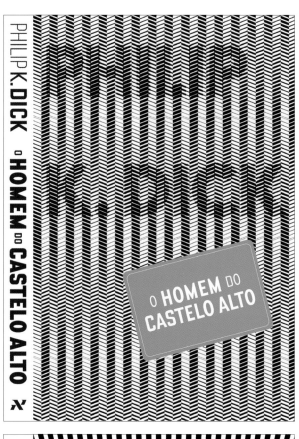

PHILIP K. DICK

O **HOMEM** DO **CASTELO ALTO**

O **HOMEM** DO
**CASTELO ALTO**

PHILIP K. DICK

FLUAM, MINHAS LÁGRIMAS, DISSE O POLICIAL

**FLUAM,**
MINHAS LÁGRIMAS,
DISSE O POLICIAL

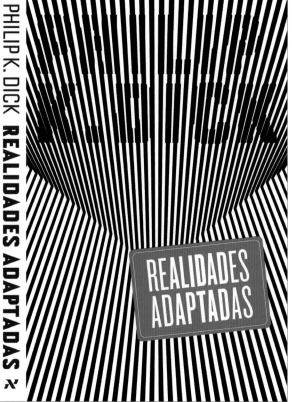

PHILIP K. DICK

**REALIDADES ADAPTADAS**

**REALIDADES
ADAPTADAS**

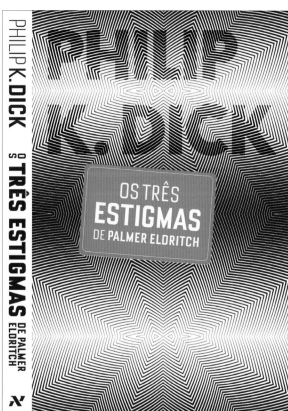

PHILIP K. DICK

OS **TRÊS ESTIGMAS** DE PALMER ELDRITCH

OS TRÊS
**ESTIGMAS**
DE PALMER ELDRITCH

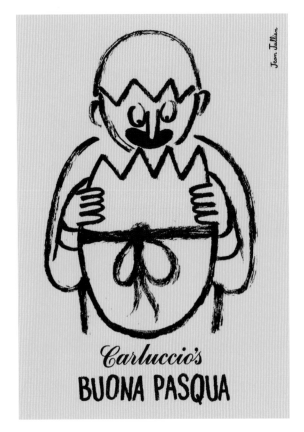

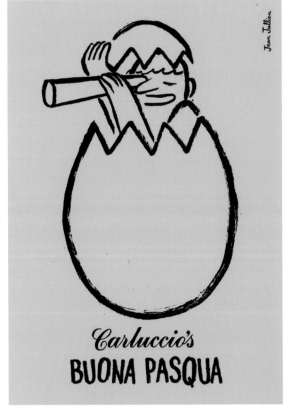

# IRVING & CO

UK

Opposite: poster
promotion for restaurant.
Client: Carluccio's
Illustration: Jean Julien
Year: 2012

Right: carrier bags
for restaurant and
delicatessen.
Client: Carluccio's
Year: 2010

## Big thinking with a human touch

---

**Irving & Co**
www.irvingandco.com
Founded 2008

**Founding Member**
Julian Roberts (UK 1968)

**Education**
University of Central
Lancashire (UK)

### Philosophy

Irving & Co have a highly crafted and astute approach. We deliver design excellence, underlined with a strategic capacity to help our clients develop new design concepts or define existing strengths. We bring authenticity and substance to our work – it's not just about style, but a marriage of sharp thinking and conviction of invention. Our core principles: big thinking with a human touch – we identify what it is that makes our client's ideas different, and help bring them to life through inspiring and creative work; instinctive creative vision – we have a strong intuitive sense of what is right in creating a visual language for the brand; honest and level-headed – an unfussy hands-on approach, with a creative intelligence that

embodies our design work; we are thorough but keep it simple working hand in hand with our clients so there is a collective ownership of the project in hand; creativity is more than just design – permeating every facet of the design approach from gathering knowledge through to specialist know how of printing processes; natural emotional intelligence – we are attuned to the different cultural sensitivities of organizations and markets which is why you will not see a fixed house style; we respect that each client has a different set of aspirations and qualities – with incisive thinking and clarity we develop successful ideas and craft them with passion into original work to produce outstanding success.

**Above: packaging design
for Christmas food range.
Client: Carluccio's
Year: 2010**

Above: skincare range
packaging.
Client: Rapha
Year: 2010

Below: formal glassware
packaging.
Client: John Lewis
Year: 2012

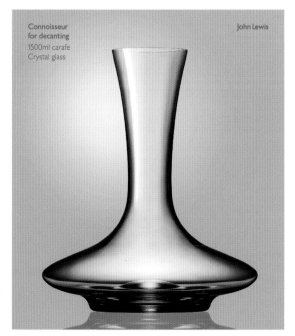
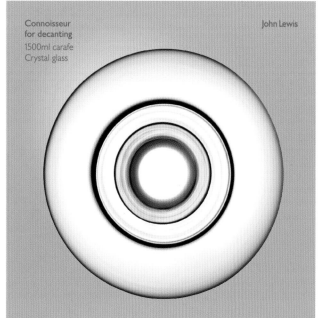

# ISHAN KHOSLA DESIGN

INDIA

## We find the ordinary, the discarded and the unusual exciting and inspiring

**Ishan Khosla Design**
www.ishankhosla.com
Founded 2008

**Founding member**
Ishan Khosla
(India 1976)

**Education**
MFA design at the
School of Visual Arts,
New York (USA)

### Philosophy

At Ishan Khosla Design, we find the ordinary, the discarded and the unusual exciting and inspiring. We are avid collectors and documentarians of culture and try to bring in the lateral thinking from our collections into our design practice. This makes our work experimental, unexpected and yet professional. We are a four-year-old boutique design firm specializing in brand identities, websites, print collaterals, books and catalogues. We also pride ourselves in working in new areas of interest such as fashion, furniture and rugs. We like projects that are conceptual and relate to the culture of India – where the design is meaningful and has a story. Our continued interest in creating distinct, personal and "handmade" work for our clients integrates with the idea of collaborating with other creatives. We aren't just graphic designers anymore but "inter-disciplinarians" – and have worked with hoarding painters, henna artists, Kaavad craftsmen, calligraphers and fashion and product designers to create work that is conceptual and fresh, yet meaningful. Our work has been published widely, and has been shown at the Venice Biennale and the Alliance Française.

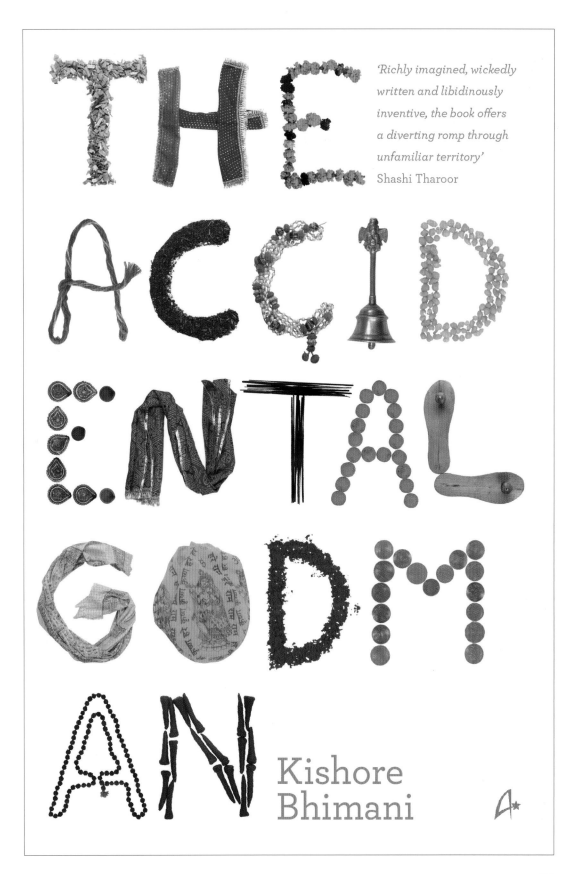

THE
ACCID
ENTAL
GODM
AN

'Richly imagined, wickedly written and libidinously inventive, the book offers a diverting romp through unfamiliar territory'
Shashi Tharoor

Kishore
Bhimani

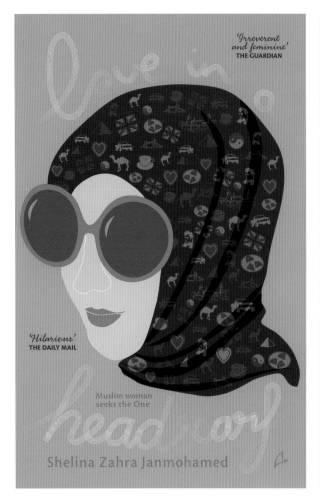

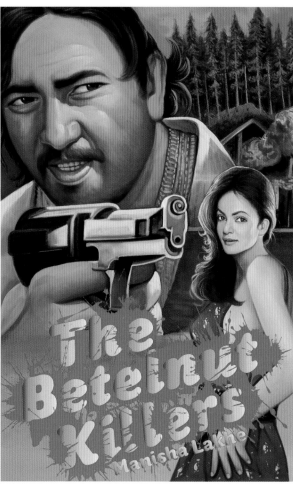

Above: *Love in a
Headscarf* by Shelina
Zahra Janmohamed,
book jacket design.
Client: Amaryllis
Year: 2011

Above: *The Betelnut
Killers* by Manisha Lakhe,
book jacket design.
Client: Random House
Year: 2009

Opposite: interactive
website design.
Client: Wrap
Year: 2012

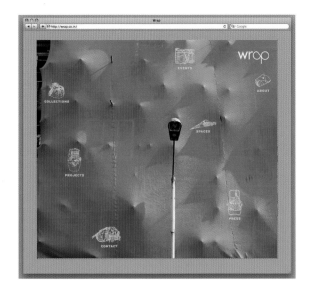

FADE
AWAY

Jancsó Áron

# ÁRON JANCSÓ

HUNGARY

## I'm searching for the unexplored

---

**Áron Jancsó**
www.aronjancso.com
Born Hungary 1986

**Education**
Started three degrees,
finished none.

**Philosophy**
I make letters: type design, calligraphy, or graffiti hand-styles, I love them all. I'm searching for the unexplored, so I spend most of my time experimenting with whatever comes to mind – I make my own tools and inks, and when working with vectors I prefer to create my own systems, structures, and colour schemes. It's best when I have time to work from scratch, and work without using other designers' products like fonts or stock photos. Different cultures inspire me a lot too, I like to blend their styles into each other using geometric or modernist styles as a foundation.

Above: Modernism Meets
The Streets poster.
Client: self
Year: 2009

Above: exhibition poster.
Client: self
Year: 2010

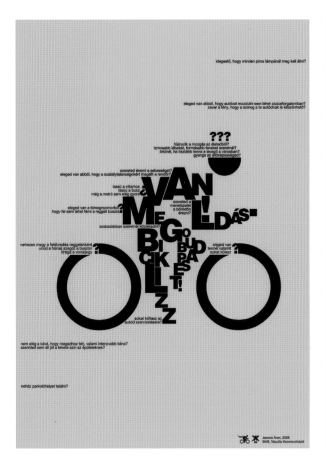

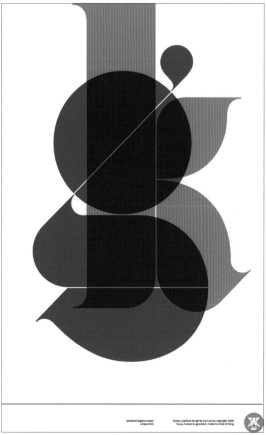

Above: Cycle Budapest
poster.
Client: self
Year: 2009

Above: Ogaki typeface
poster.
Client: self
Year: 2009

# LUCAS JATOBA

BRAZIL

## Ideas that are universal and can be understood by every single person on the Earth

**Lucas Jatoba**
www.lucasjatoba.com
Born Brazil 1981

**Education**
Social communication
(advertising) at ESPM
(Brazil)

### Philosophy

I started my career working as a graphic designer at various design agencies in São Paulo, Brazil. I then moved to the advertising business, working at Lowe São Paulo as a Junior Art Director for clients such as Renault, National Geographic, Stella Artois and Johnson & Johnson. My next stop was Barcelona, Spain, where I worked for three years as a Conceptual Art Director at Contrapunto BBDO, winning 15 awards. The itch for adventure struck again at the beginning of 2011, when I decided to move to Sydney. In my first month there I started freelancing for Leo Burnett, then moved to Ogilvy, Droga5, and am now at Havas Worldwide. My last personal project, Adéu, Barcelona! got 500,000 views on YouTube in three weeks. 80,000 people shared it on Facebook and I was interviewed by ABC News (USA), NHK (Japan) and SBT (Brazil). I like to work on ideas that will touch people, make them laugh, make them cry, or make them love someone. Ideas that are universal and can be understood by every single person on the Earth.

Above: poster advertising
a typography course.
Client: Complot Creativity
School
Year: 2009

Above: poster advertising
a typography course.
Client: Complot Creativity
School
Year: 2009

Opposite: posters
campaigning against
female genital mutilation.
Client: Association of
Women Against Genital
Mutilation
Year: 2011

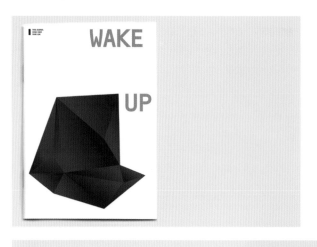

Discovery of oil and gas peaked in the 1960s. Production is set to peak too, with the Middle Eastern countries regaining control of world supply. Almost two-thirds of the world's total reserves of crude oil are located in the Middle East, notably in Saudi Arabia, Iran and Iraq. An assessment of future world oil supply and its depletion pattern shows that between 1980 and 1998 there was an 11.2 per cent increase in world crude oil production, from 59.6 to 66.9 million barrels of oil per day. Current world production rates are about 25 Gb (billion barrels) per year. A simple calculation shows that if consumption levels remain constant, world crude oil reserves, at approximately 1 trillion barrels, could be exhausted around 2040.

**GLOBAL WARNING & FINITE OIL**

The oil crises of the 1970s when the Organisation of Petroleum Exporting Countries (OPEC) states reined in their production have passed into folk memory. However, they were accompanied by massive disruption and global economic recession. The same happened in 1980 and 1991.

Colin J. Campbell, a pre-eminent oil industry analyst, believes that future crises will be much worse. "The oil shocks of the 1970s were short-lived because there were then plenty of new oil and gas finds to bring on stream. This time there are virtually no new prolific basins to yield a crop of giant fields sufficient to have a global impact. The growing Middle East control of the market is likely to lead to a radical and permanent increase in the price of oil, before physical shortages begin to appear within the first decade of the 21st century. The world's economy has been driven by an abundant supply of cheap oil-based energy for the best part of this century. The coming oil crisis will accordingly be an economic and political discontinuity of historic proportions, as the world adjusts to a new energy environment".

**IN THE NEAR FUTURE THE COMPETITION FOR OIL WILL BE RAW AND REAL.**

The three main purposes for which oil is used worldwide are food, transport and heating. In the near future the competition for oil for these three activities will be raw and real. An energy famine is likely to affect poorer countries first, when increases in the cost of paraffin, used for cooking, place it beyond their reach. Following the peak in production, food supplies all over the world will begin to be disrupted, not only because of price increases but because the oil will no longer be there.

"THE COMING OIL CRISIS WILL ACCORDINGLY BE AN ECONOMIC AND POLITICAL DISCONTINUITY OF HISTORIC PROPORTIONS, AS THE WORLD ADJUSTS TO A NEW ENERGY ENVIRONMENT"

# BEN JEFFERY

UK

Opposite: Wake Up,
editorial design high-
lighting the dangers of
the oncoming oil crisis.
This journal documents
the intrinsic nature of oil
within our food system.
Client: self
Year: 2012

## Complex simplicity

**Ben Jeffery**
benjeffery.net
Born UK 1987

**Education**
Graphic design at Leeds
College of Art (UK)

**Philosophy**
Complex simplicity: both aesthetically and
conceptually, simplicity is always the most effective
philosophy in solving complex design problems.

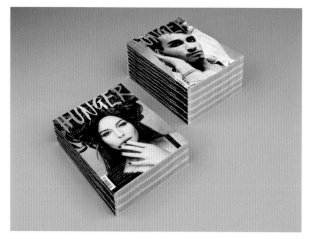

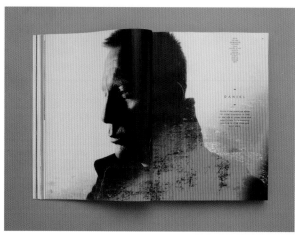

Above: editorial design of
issue two of *The Hunger*,
photographer Rankin's
magazine.
Client: *The Hunger*
Year: 2012

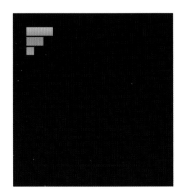

Above: branding for
a creative company
specializing in creating
annual reports and
branding projects for
major corporations.
Client: Further Creative
Year: 2012

241

# JOHN MORGAN STUDIO

UK

Below: *The Jet Age Compendium: Paolozzi at Ambit* book design.
Client: Four Corners Books
Year: 2009

Below: The AA Files journal design.
Client: Architectural Association
Year: 2009

# The more you practise the less articulate you become

**John Morgan Studio**
www.morganstudio.co.uk
Founded 2000

**Founding member**
John Morgan (UK 1973)

**Education**
Typography and graphic
communication at the
University of Reading
(UK)

**Philosophy**
The more you practise the less articulate you become,
or more specifically there is less desire to be articulate
about your practice. To borrow from Turner,
"atmosphere is my style".

**Below: Hilary Lloyd poster.**
**Client: Raven Row gallery**
**Year: 2011**

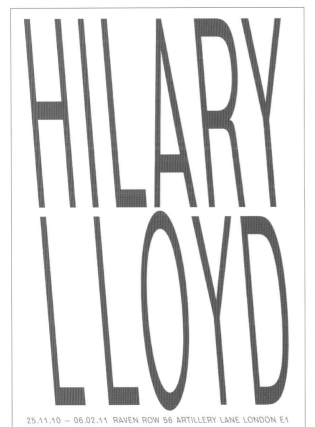

**Below: business card design.**
**Client: Raven Row gallery**
**Year: 2009**

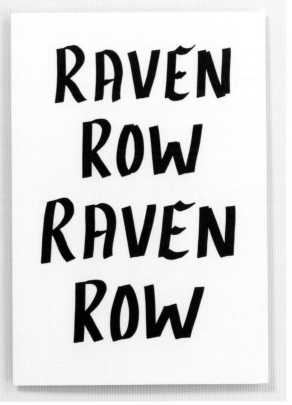

Opposite: *Vanity Fair* from the Four Corners Familiars series, book design.
Client: Four Corners Books
Year: 2010

Left: *A Stick of Green Candy* from the Four Corners Familiars series, book design.
Client: Four Corners Books
Year: 2009

Below: postcards, business cards and invitations for Ray Johnson exhibition.
Client: Raven Row
Year: 2009

# KARLSSON WILKER

USA

Right: One of two posters for a Danish lecture series. Client: Lynfabrikken Year: 2009

## We do not tend to adhere to any "design philosophy"

**Karlsson Wilker**
www.karlssonwilker.com
Founded 2000

**Founding Members**
Hjalti Karlsson and Jan
Wilker (Iceland 1976,
Germany 1972)

**Education**
Parsons School of
Design, NYC (USA);
Stuttgart State Academy
of Art and Design
(Germany)

**Philosophy**
We do not tend to adhere to any "design philosophy".
All we can say is that after 12 years, no one superior
process has crystallized from our daily practice. We
operate "organically", which seems to be the natural
way for us, in a studio of four, albeit obviously being
inefficient and time-consuming.

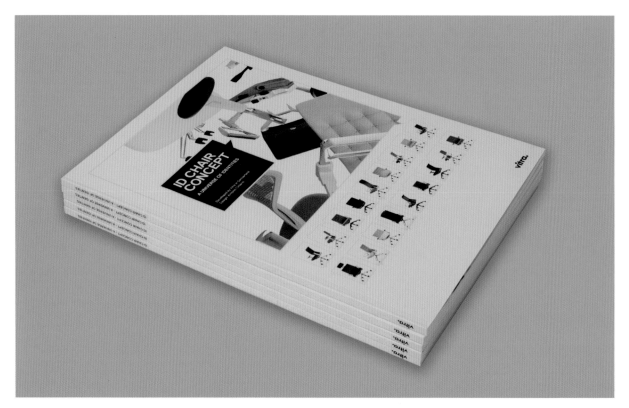

Opposite: catalogue
forming part of the
campaign for Vitra's
*ID Chair Concept.*
Client: Vitra
Year: 2010/11

Top: interactive terminals
at the Museum of the
Moving Image, NY.
Client: Museum of
the Moving Image, NY
Year: 2011

Above: covers for the
China-based *NewGraphic*
design publication.
Client: *NewGraphic*
magazine
Year: 2009

# KELLENBERGER-WHITE

UK

## Each design problem deserves its own particular formal solution

**Kellenberger-White**
www.kellenberger-white.
com
Founded 2009

**Founding members**
Eva Kellenberger
and Sebastian White
(Switzerland 1982,
UK 1985)

**Education**
Graphic design at
Camberwell College of
Arts (UK), communication
art and design at the
Royal College of Art;
textile design at Central
Saint Martins College
of Art and Design (UK),
communication art and
design at the Royal
College of Art (UK)

**Philosophy**
We create identities, publications, exhibitions and
digital applications for cultural institutions, businesses
and individuals. We believe each design problem
demands its own particular formal solution. This
case-by-case approach relies on exploration and
enquiry, and therefore our final design solutions are
appropriate and considered. It is our ambition to
create unique solutions that subvert expectations and
challenge preconceptions. Central to our approach is
a desire to unlock the poetic potential of a wide range
of materials and craft techniques (both in digital and
print), producing a visually diverse and tactile range of
work. As a small-team studio we often work with
specialists and collaborating partners, such as
programmers, 3D designers, writers and editors, font
developers, and photographers and illustrators. Many
of our clients are in the field of the arts and culture.

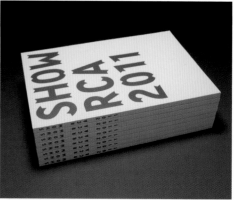

Left and above: catalogue, invites and promotional material, banners, signage and way-finding for Show RCA 2011.
Client: Royal College of Art
Year: 2011

Opposite: exhibition graphics for the Saint-Etienne Design Biennale, France.
Client: Dunne & Raby
Year: 2010

# NEIL
# KELLERHOUSE

USA

Below: poster design and
art direction for *The Social
Network*, directed by
David Fincher.
Client: Sony/Columbia
Pictures
Year: 2010

Below: art direction,
design and copy concept
for *The Social Network*.
Client: Sony/Columbia
Pictures
Year: 2010

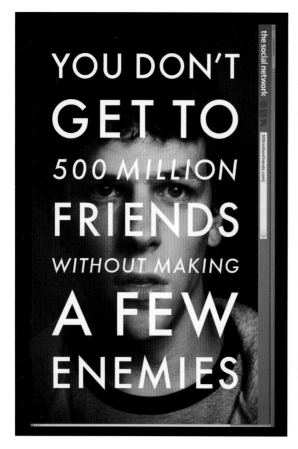

# The solution comes from the problem

**Neil Kellerhouse**
www.kellerhouse.com
Born USA 1965

**Education**
Visual communication at
California Institute of the
Arts (USA)

**Philosophy**
I learned this from Lou Danziger: the solution comes
from the problem. All the decisions – the type, the
image, the metaphor – come from whatever it is I'm
selling or the message I'm trying to convey. It's not
about making a pretty picture, it's about serving
whatever it is I'm trying to communicate. This dictates
what it looks like.

Below: artwork for *The
Killier Inside Me*, a film by
Michael Winterbottom.
Client: Magnolia Pictures
Year: 2010

Below: artwork for the film
*The Girl With the Dragon
Tattoo.*
Client: Sony/Columbia
Pictures
Year: 2010

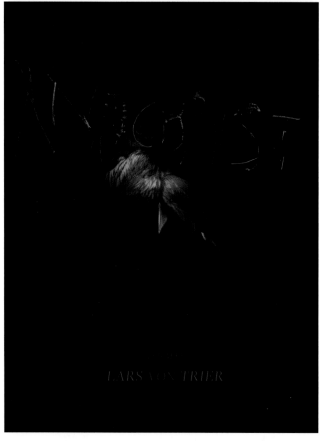

Opposite: artworks for
*Antichrist*, a film by Lars
Von Trier.
Client: The Criterion
Collection
Art directed with:
Sarah Habibi
Year: 2010

Right: poster for
*Gomorrah*, a film by
Matteo Garrone.
Client: The Criterion
Collection
Art directed with:
Sarah Habibi
Year: 2010

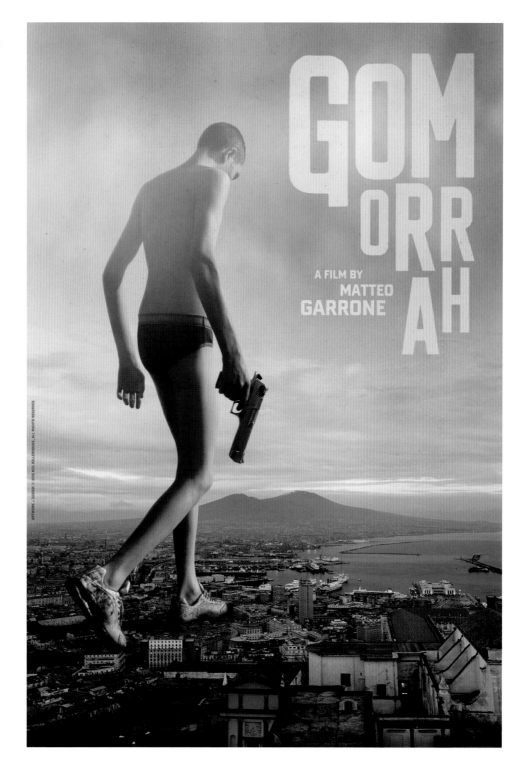

FROM THE DEAD WALL ASSOCIATED ON THOSE HOUSELESS NIGHTS WITH THIS TOO COMMON STORY, I CHOSE NEXT TO WANDER BY BETHLEHEM HOSPITAL; PARTLY, BECAUSE IT LAY ON MY ROAD ROUND TO WESTMINSTER; PARTLY, BECAUSE I HAD A NIGHT FANCY IN MY HEAD WHICH COULD BE BEST PURSUED WITHIN SIGHT OF ITS WALLS AND DOME.

HOUSE LESS

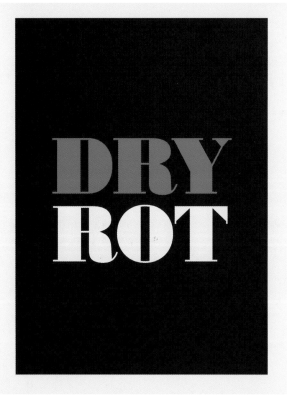

DRY ROT

Walking the streets under the pattering rain, Houselessness would walk and walk and walk, seeing nothing but the interminable tangle of streets, save at a corner, here and there, two policemen in conversation, or the sergeant or inspector looking after his men. Now and then in the night—but rarely—Houselessness would become aware of a furtive head peering out of a doorway a few yards before him, and, coming up with the head, would find a man standing bolt upright to keep within the doorway's shadow, and evidently intent upon no particular service to society. Under a kind of fascination, and in a ghostly silence suitable to the time, Houselessness and this gentleman would eye one another from head to foot, and so, without exchange of speech, part, mutually suspicious. Drip, drip, drip, from ledge and coping, splash from pipes and water-spouts, and by-and-by the houseless shadow would fall upon the stones that pave the way to Waterloo-bridge; it being in the houseless mind to have a halfpenny worth of excuse for saying *'Good night'* to the toll-keeper, and catching a glimpse of his fire.

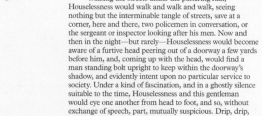

DRIP

# KENT LYONS

UK

Opposite: identity for
a global campaign
celebrating the life and
legacy of Charles Dickens.
Client: Dickens 2012
Year: 2012

## Committed to communication that is beautiful and useful

**Kent Lyons**
www.kentlyons.com
Founded 2004

**Founding Members**
James Kent and
Noel Lyons (UK 1974,
UK 1972)

**Education**
Graphic design at
Ravensbourne; English
literature and philosophy
at Wolverhampton (both
UK)

**Philosophy**
As an agency, we are committed to making
communication that is beautiful and useful – that
looks great and functions excellently – and we don't
compromise on either element. This is self-evident in
our work, and means that when we produce something,
it not only looks and feels engaging and attractive,
it works effectively and communicates the message,
as intended. We are a full service agency – we work
across print, branding, digital, advertising and marketing,
and we bring award-winning excellence to all these
fields. As a result we are able to take on broad-scope
projects to develop a single unified campaign that
delivers a compelling and consistent message across
a range of media, and to a range of audiences.

Despite our high profile client base, we're a relatively
small team. This allows us to be flexible and responsive,
turning around jobs faster than larger full service agencies.

Above: iPad app for
participants in luxury
rallies.
Client: The Run To
Year: 2011

Above: identity and related
marketing material for
the Top Drawer and Home
Show 2012, London.
Client: Clarion
Year: 2011

Above: website for the
Reading + Leeds Festival.
Client: BBC1
Year: 2010

# JOSH KING

UK

## Simple, fun observations

**Josh King**
www.josh-king.com
Born UK 1990

**Education**
Graphic design at
Kingston University (UK)

**Philosophy**
Investigating the way we experience something can
lead to new and exciting ideas. For me, design relies
on making simple, fun observations.

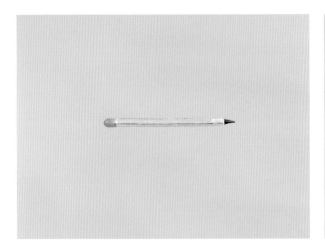

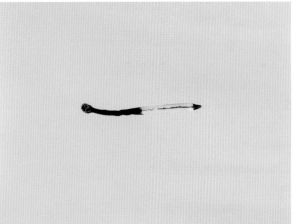

Opposite: Josh says
"Conkers look a lot like ET."
Client: self
Year: 2012

Above: speed-drawing: he
turns matches into pencils
to reduce hesitation and
increase danger.
Client: self
Year: 2012

RING RING RING RING RING

Who's there?  The Olympics.                    *Felix Heyes, Josh King & Ben West*

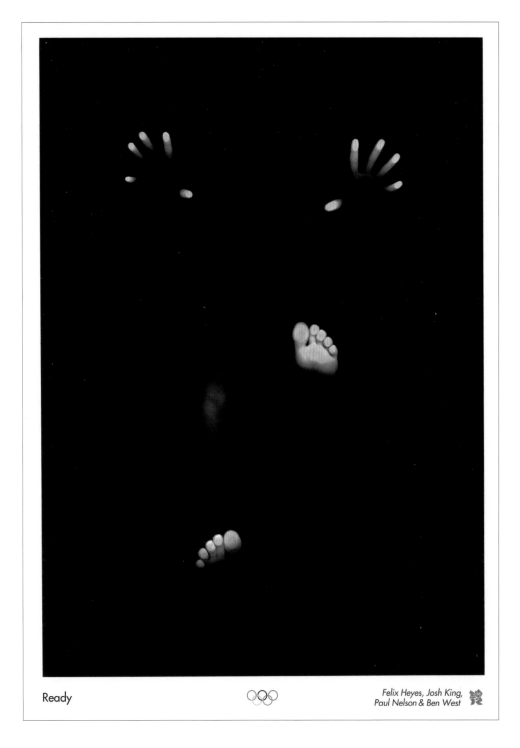

Ready

Felix Heyes, Josh King,
Paul Nelson & Ben West

Opposite and right:
following the unveiling
of 12 posters by leading
artists for the 2012
London Olympic games,
the editor of *Creative
Review* asked Kingston
University students if
they could do better.
Client: *Creative Review*
Year: 2012

Above: Par Fore is an
ongoing project in
collaboration with Felix
Heyes to turn unused and
vandalised rooftops into
a free mini-golf course
for the local community.
Client: self
Year: 2012

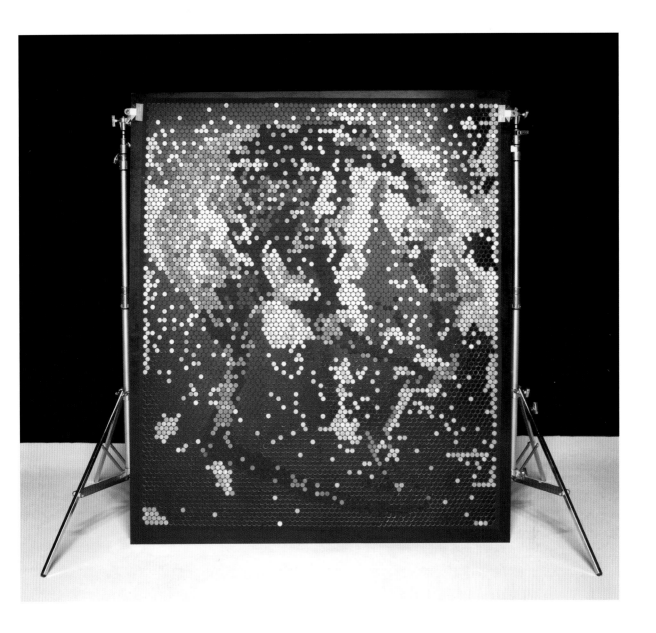

Above: An interactive
installation made in
collaboration with Felix
Heyes, James Ward & Ben
West. It was nominated for
the D&AD student awards
2012.
Client: Coutts Bank
Year: 2012

# LA BOCA

UK

Opposite: poster
advertising Vivid Live, an
annual audiovisual festival.
Client: Sydney Opera
House
Year: 2011

Right: an illustration
designed to be used for
a variety of purposes
including a custom option
on the Aol homepage.
Client: AOL
Year: 2010

## To have played a part

**La Boca**
www.laboca.co.uk
Founded 2002

**Founding member**
Scot Bendall (UK 1975)

**Education**
Graphic design at Central
Saint Martins School of
Art and Design (UK)

**Philosophy**
La Boca is an independent design circus based in
London. We are both image-makers and problem-
solvers, we put the ape into apricot. Our work spans
limited edition record sleeves seen by a few hundred
fans, to film posters and CD covers seen by millions
across the globe. Both are equally important. To
contribute to, and thus be formed by popular culture, is
a responsibility we celebrate and it drives everything we
do. Not for fame or reward (although it helps), but for
the opportunity to exist. To have played a part.

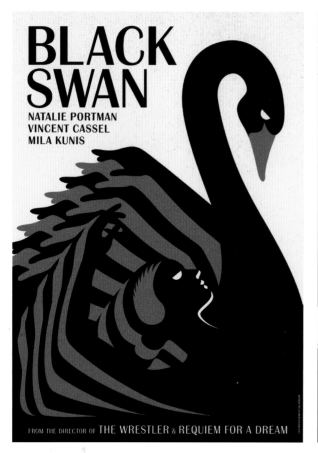

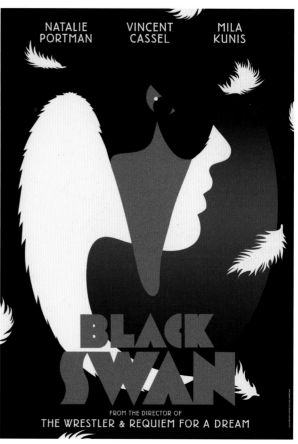

**Above and opposite:**
**set of four official teaser**
**posters for the film**
*Black Swan.*
**Client: 20th Century Fox**
**Year: 2010**

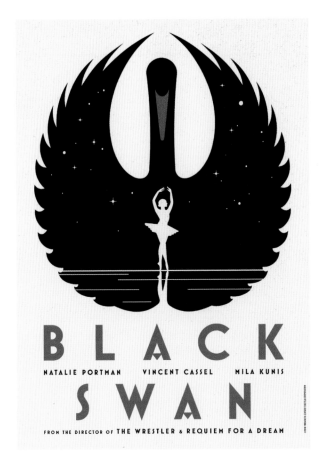

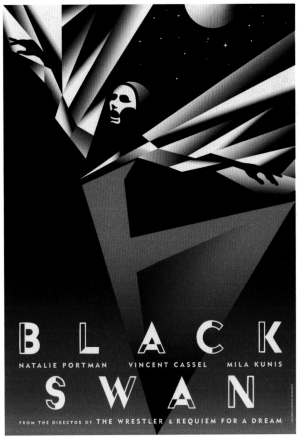

Left: poster from a UK
advertising campaign.
Client: Green Mark Vodka
Year: 2012

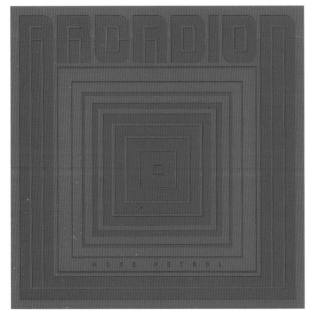

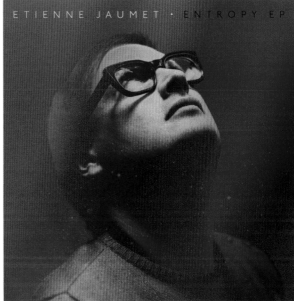

Top left: CD artwork for the debut album *More Petrol* by Arcadion.
Client: DC Recordings
Year: 2011

Above left: CD and gatefold vinyl artwork for Shout Out Out Out's *Spanish Moss and Total Loss.*
Client: Normals Welcome Records
Year: 2012

Top right: 12" vinyl record sleeve for "Respond in Silence" by The Orichaic Phase.
Client: DC Recordings
Year: 2006

Above right: 12" vinyl record sleeve for Etienne Jaumet's "Entropy EP".
Client: Versatile Records
Year: 2009

# LETERME DOWLING

UK

the bar
the restaurant
the pool
the gym
the service
the staff
the rooms

(the white)

Left: identity and
guidelines for The White.
Client: Bubble Hotel
Group
Year: 2009

Opposite: poster design
for a graphic design
exhibition based in
Brussels.
Client: Modern Theory
Year: 2012

## Graphic design that not only communicates but also engages

**Leterme Dowling**
www.letermedowling.com
Founded 2008

**Founding members**
Celine Leterme and Jon
Dowling (Belgium 1981,
UK 1981)

**Education**
Graphic design at
Buckinghamshire
University (UK)

**Philosophy**
Leterme Dowling is a multi-disciplinary design studio
with a global client base. We pride ourselves on our
individual approach to design across a variety of
applications; from logos, websites, promotional
literature and identity systems, to brochures,
packaging and signage. We work on projects of all
scales, place an emphasis on giving each project our
collective commitment and on working closely and
openly with clients from the outset. We believe this
can make the difference in creating appropriate and
distinctive graphic design that not only communicates
but also engages its audience.

Visual Grammar
06.09.2012
to 18.09.2012

Open Daily From
10.00 to 19.00

MAD Brussels
10 Place du Nouveau
Marché aux Grains
1000 Brussels
Belgium

Curated by
Modern Theory

Designed by
Leterme Dowling

Atsuki Kikuchi
Base Design
Claudia Klat
Coast
George Hardie
HORT
Leterme Dowling
Maddison Graphic
Modern Practice
MuirMcNeil
Neubau
Node Berlin Oslo
North
Open Source Publishing
PLMD (pleaseletmedesign)
Project Projects
R2
Studio Astrid Stavro
StudioThomson
Work In Process

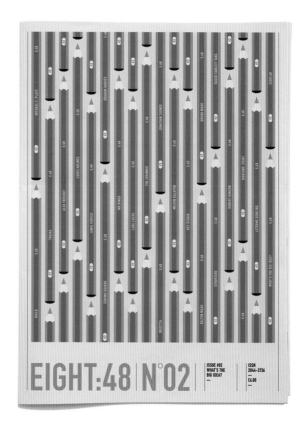

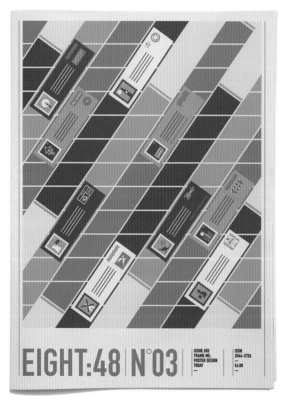

Left and above: cover designs for *Eight:48* and *Counter-Print* magazine.
Client: Counter-Print.co.uk
Year: 2010–Present

Opposite: Urban poster, which formed part of a screen-printed series called Edit. Each designer was asked to represent a musical genre using one shape and one type (stating the genre)
Client: Edit
Year: 2010

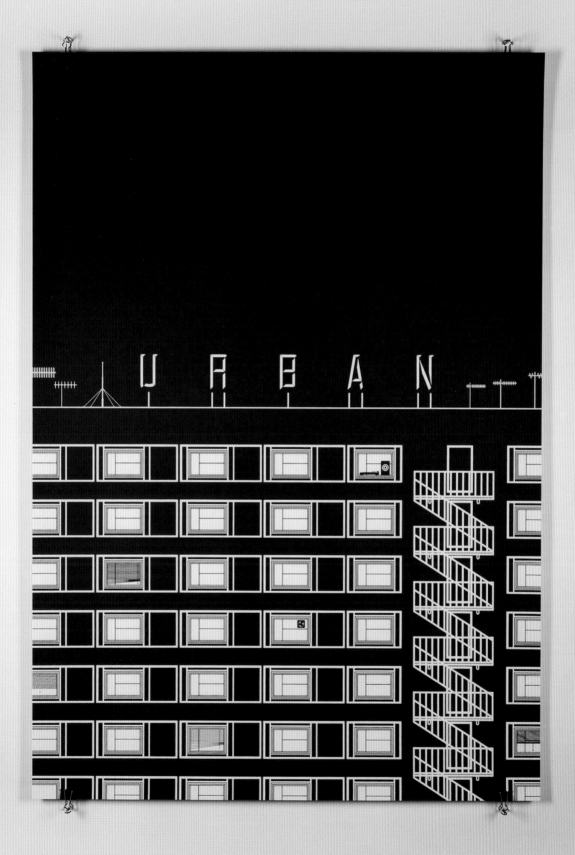

# YANG LIU DESIGN

GERMANY

Below left and right: book
design for *Three Millennia
of Publishing in China.*
Client: China Foreign
Language Press
Year: 2009

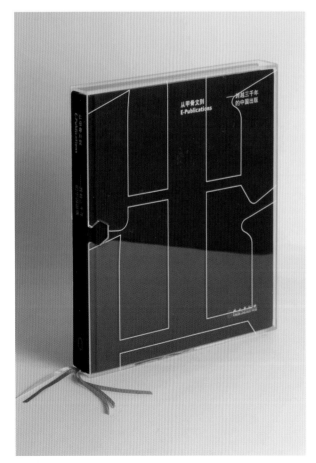

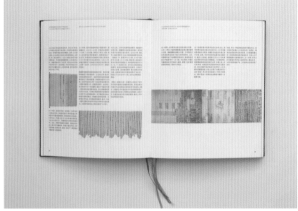

# Highly conceptual and content-led

**Yang Liu Design**
www.yangliudesign.com
Founded 2004

**Founding member**
Yang Liu (China 1976)

**Education**
Design at Berlin
University of the Arts
(Germany)

**Philosophy**
At first I focused my work on poster design, and later moved on to corporate design, books and exhibitions. It is very important for me that my work is highly conceptual and content-led. I'm always trying to use the minimum of elements and still be able to communicate the message of the content. A lot of my new ideas come from my love of travel and discovering new places.

Below: exhibition design for a Chinese photography exhibition called Humanism in China. Client: Staatliche Kunstsammlungen Dresden
Year: 2009

↖ Galerie Neue Meister

↘ Mosaiksaal
Klingersaal

Above and right: a signage
system for the Albertinum
in Dresden, Germany.
Client: Staatliche
Kunstsammlungen
Dresden
Year: 2010

# LUST

NETHERLANDS

Opposite: PolyArc media
installation forming
part of the International
Poster and Graphic Design
Festival of Chaumont,
France.
Client: Poster Festival
Chaumont
Year: 2011

## Media, interactivity and technology

**Lust**
www.lust.nl
Founded 1996

**Founding Members**
Jeroen Barendse
(Netherlands 1973),
Thomas Castro
(Philippines 1967) and
Dimitri Nieuwenhuizen
(Netherlands 1971)

**Education**
Graphic design at Academy of the Arts Utrecht and
Arnhem, Werkplaats Typografie (all Netherlands);
psychology and fine arts at University of California,
graphic design at Academy of the Arts Utrect
(Netherlands); industrial engineering at the Delft
University of Technology, graphic design atthe Design
Academy in Eindhoven (both Netherlands)

**Philosophy**
Our work consists of 40% interactive and time-based
media, 40% traditional & printed media, 15%
self-initiated projects, and 5% fonts and typographic
experimentation. In 2010 we founded a new
research-based media & technology studio laboratory
dubbed LUSTlab, as a platform for researching,
generating hypotheses, and developing new theories
and technologies in the fields of media, interactivity,
and technology.

Left: a typographic poster/invite, made up of scenes from the David Lynch film *Lost Highway*.
Client: Lost & Found Foundation
Year: 2008

Below: a special typeface, based on a super bold version of Letter Gothic, was created for the PolyArc prints and dossiers, and the installation signage and wall text.
Client: Poster Festival Chaumont
Year: 2011

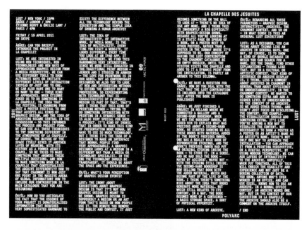

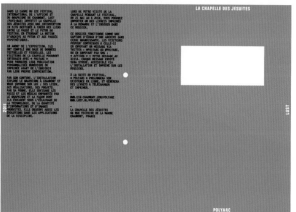

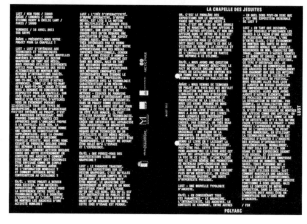

Above: installation of
eight giant pictures in a
city square forming part of
the Experimenta Design
biennale in Lisbon.
Client: Experimenta
Design Festival
Year: 2011

# MARCUS McCABE

IRELAND

Opposite: storyboard
for Carlsberg 360, an
interactive experience
bringing together the
brand and its relationship
with football.
Client: Carlsberg
Year: 2011

Opposite: branding for
the Ceri Hand Gallery
in Liverpool.
Client: Ceri Hand
Year: 2009

## Great ideas, well-crafted above all else

**Marcus McCabe**
www.marcusmccabe.net
Born Ireland 1983

**Education**
Visual communication at
National College of Art &
Design, Dublin (Ireland)

**Philosophy**
I am a freelance designer and art director. After
studying in Dublin at the National College of Art &
Design where I earned a degree in Visual
Communication, I moved to the UK and joined the
award-winning design studio Uniform where I worked
on projects for several notable clients. My work
encompasses most disciplines, from branding, identity,
advertising and communications, online and interactive
to environmental design. My work has been
recognised by the Roses, Design Week and Fresh
Awards (UK) and I have been featured on many major
design sites worldwide. I believe in great ideas,
well-crafted above all else.

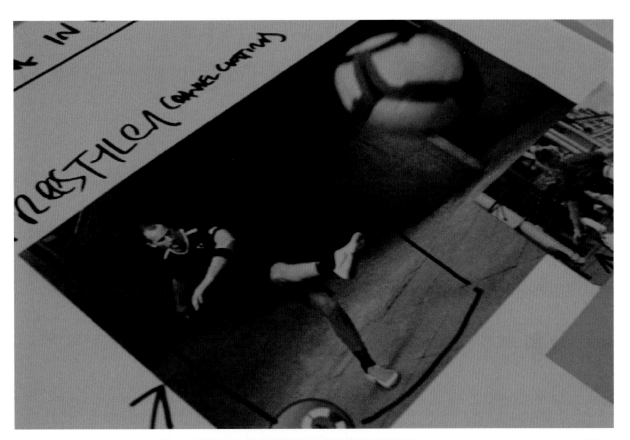

MAKING THINGS HAPPEN
IS OUR EVERYDAY JOB.

Eventful is an experienced and efficient live events and
marketing company, specialising in gloriously memorable
corporate occasions that go smoothly from welcome
to wind-up, bringing you the results you're looking for.
From glittering awards ceremonies and gala dinners
to high quality conferences and exhibitions, for us the
magic is in giving each one its own unique personality.

We know how to translate ideas into action. We have
the skills, we know all the right people, we enjoy doing
it and, above all, we have a proven track record
of solid success.

THE MAGIC IS IN
GIVING EACH ONE
ITS OWN UNIQUE
PERSONALITY.

Above: promotional
brochure for an event
management company.
Client: Eventful
Year: 2011

Opposite: posters for
the AND Film Festival
in Liverpool.
Client: FACT/Corner-
house/Folly
Year: 2009

Opposite top: marketing
and print materials for the
Discovery Film Festival
included characters that
children could download
and print themselves.
Client: DCA (Dundee
Contemporary Arts)
Year: 2010

Above: mailer to be sent
to prospective clients for
Valentine's day.
Client: Uniform
Year: 2009

Above right: an alternative
Christmas card to be sent
to clients – a "Closed" sign
to be hung on the door.
Client: Uniform
Year: 2010

Right: yearbook on
packaging design.
Client: Unilever
Year: 2011

# MICHA WEIDMANN STUDIO

UK

Left: brand identity.
Client: Twinings
Year: 2012

Opposite: newspaper
advertisement for
10 Trinity Square property
development.
Client: KOP Group
Year: 2012

## Helping creators of high-end products to build their brands

**Micha Weidmann Studio**
michaweidmannstudio.
com
Founded 2001

**Founding member**
Micha Weidmann
(Switzerland 1974)

**Education**
SfGB Bern (Switzerland)

**Philosophy**
Micha Weidmann Studio is an art direction and design
studio based in London, helping creators of high-end
products to build their brands. We act as consultants
to publishers and art galleries. The studio's creative
approach is based on Micha Weidmann's background
in Swiss design and art direction defined through
working with brands such as Prada, Tate Modern and
Zaha Hadid.

*Corriere della Sera*

BEYOND RARE

IO

TRINITY SQUARE

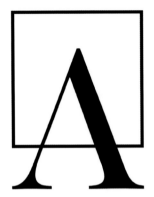

Opposite: book design for
the German photographer
and filmmaker.
Client: Norbert Schoerner
Year: 2012

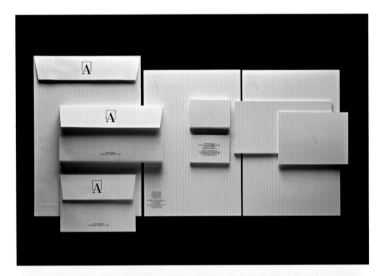

Left top and middle:
identity and stationery
designed as part of
company identity.
Client: Advanced Capital
Year: 2011

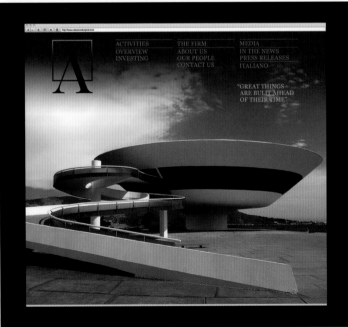

Left: website design.
Client: Advanced Capital
Year: 2011

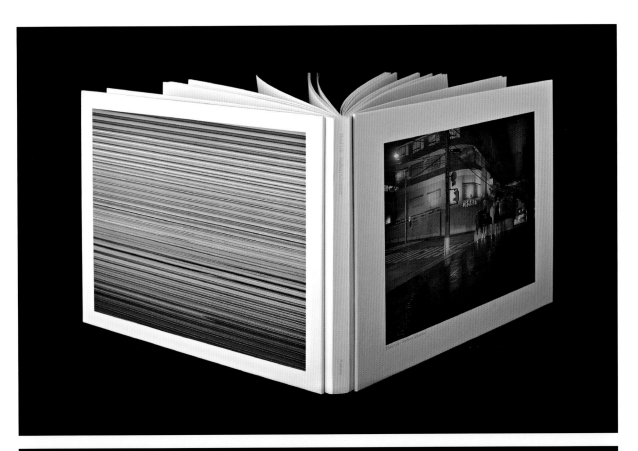

# ADELINE MOLLARD

GERMANY/SWITZERLAND/USA

## My field of interest revolves around creative communities and their networks

**Adeline Mollard**
www.adelinemollard.ch
Born Switzerland 1982

**Education**
Visual communication at
ECAL (University of Art
and Design Lausanne)
(Switzerland)

**Philosophy**
Beyond graphic design, my field of interest revolves
around creative communities and their networks,
which I bring to light through my self-published
publications. By portraying creative individuals in
their personal spaces, it allows me insight into
private moments of artists' lives, their perspectives
and inspirations. I have worked in Berlin as a freelance
editor and designer for Gestalten publishers, an art
director for *OPAK* magazine, a resident artist, and
an independent art director and designer.

AFGHANISTAN / ALBANIA / ALGERIA / ANDORRA / ANGOLA / ARGENTINA / ARMENIA / AUSTRALIA / AUSTRIA AZERBAIJAN / BAHAMAS / BAHRAIN / BANGLADESH / BARBADOS / BELARUS / BELGIUM / BELIZE / BENIN BHUTAN / BOLIVIA / BOSNIA AND HERZEGOVINA / BOTSWANA / BRAZIL / BRUNEI 7 BULGARIA / BURKINA FASO / BURMA / BURUNDI / CAMBODIA / CAMEROON / CANADA /CAPE VERDE / CENTRAL AFRICAN REPUBLIC / CHAD / CHILE / CHINA / COLOMBIA / COMOROS / CONGO (BRAZZAVILLE) / CONGO (KINSHASA) / COSTA RICA / COTE D'IVOIRE / CROATIA / CUBA / CYPRUS / CZECH REPUBLIC / DENMARK DJIBOUTI / DOMINICA / DOMINICAN REPUBLIC / ECUADOR / EGYPT / EL SALVADOR / EQUATORIAL GUINEA / ERITREA / ESTONIA / ETHIOPIA / FIJI / FINLAND / FRANCE / GABON / GAMBIA, THE GEORGIA / GERMANY / GHANA / GREECE / GRENADA / GUATEMALA / GUINEA / GUINEA-BISSAU / GUYANA / HOLY SEE / HONDURAS / HONG KONG / HUNGARY / ICELAND / INDIA / INDONESIA IRAN IRAQ / IRELAND / ISRAEL / ITALY / JAMAICA / JAPAN / JORDAN / KAZAKHSTAN / KENYA KIRIBATI / KOREA, NORTH / KOREA, SOUTH / KOSOVO / KUWAIT / KYRGYZSTAN / LAOS LATVIA / LEBANON / LESOTHO / LIBERIA / LIBYA / LIECHTENSTEIN / LITHUANIA / LUXEMBOURG / MACAU / MACEDONIA / MADAGASCAR / MALAWI / MALAYSIA / MALDIVES MALI / MALTA / MARSHALL ISLANDS / MAURITANIA / MAURITIUS / MEXICO / MICRONESIA / MOLDOVA / MONACO / MONGOLIA / MONTENEGRO / MOROCCO / MOZAMBIQUE / NAMIBIA / NAURU / NEPAL / NETHERLANDS / NETHERLANDS ANTILLES NEW ZEALAND / NICARAGUA / NIGER / NIGERIA / NORTH KOREA / NORWAY OMAN / PAKISTAN / PALAU / PALESTINIAN TERRITORIES / PANAMA / PAPUA NEW GUINEA / PARAGUAY / PERU / PHILIPPINES / POLAND / PORTUGAL / QATAR / ROMANIA / RUSSIA / RWANDA / SAINT KITTS AND NEVIS / SAINT LUCIA / SAINT VINCENT AND THE GRENADINES / SAMOA / SAN MARINO SAO TOME AND PRINCIPE / SAUDI ARABIA / SENEGAL / SERBIA / SEYCHELLES / SIERRA LEONE / SINGAPORE / SLOVAKIA / SLOVENIA / SOLOMON ISLANDS / SOMALIA / SOUTH AFRICA / SOUTH KOREA / SPAIN / SRI LANKA / SUDAN / SURINAME / SWAZILAND / SWEDEN SWITZERLAND / SYRIA / TAIWAN / TAJIKISTAN / TANZANIA THAILAND / TIMOR-LESTE / TOGO / TONGA / TRINIDAD AND TOBAGO / TUNISIA / TURKEY / TURKMENISTAN / TUVALU UGANDA / UKRAINE / UNITED ARAB EMIRATES / UNITED KINGDOM / URUGUAY / UZBEKISTAN / VANUATU / VENEZUELA / VIETNAM / YEMEN / ZAMBIA / ZIMBABWE

The Haiti Poster Project 2010
Adeline Mollard / Switzerland
adelinemollard.ch

3 /30

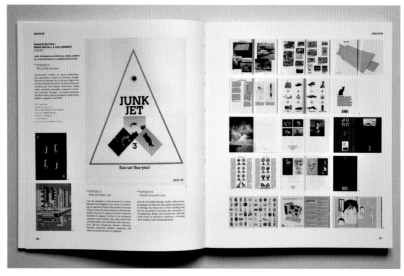

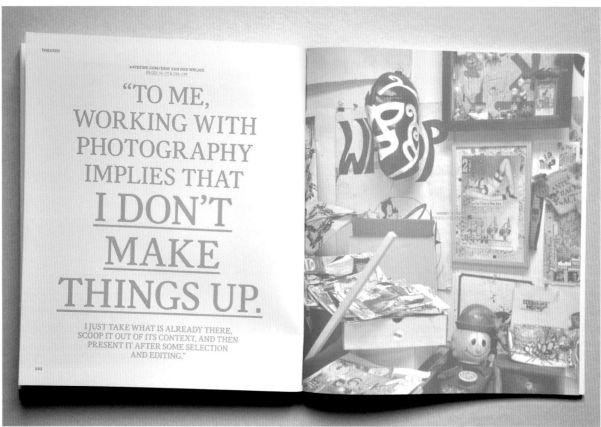

Left and opposite: *Behind the Zines: Self-Publishing Culture* book design.
Client: Gestalten
Year: 2011

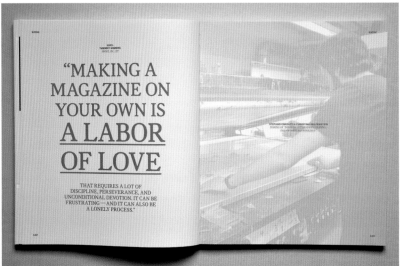

Above and opposite:
*Berlin Subjective Directory*
concept, interviews,
photography and design.
Client: self
Year: 2011

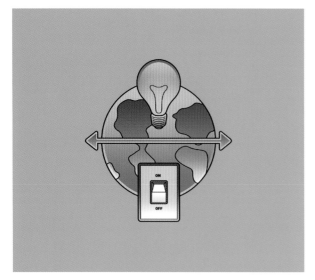

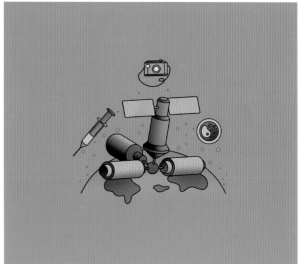

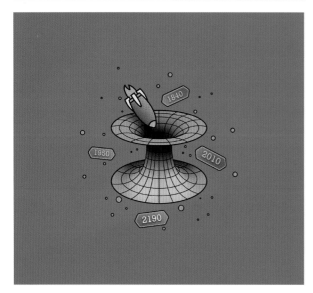

# DIEGO MORALES

BRAZIL

## Sensitive, human and alive design

**Diego Morales**
www.mediainvia.com
Born 1987 Brazil

**Education**
Graphic design at the
Universidade Estadual
Paulista Júlio de
Mesquita Filho
(UNESP) (Brazil)

**Philosophy**
I am a designer and illustrator living and working
in São Paulo, Brazil. I'm truly passionate about
design and all its aspects. I believe that design
is a transdisciplinary communication tool. So we,
designers, should be able to permeate many areas
and create new relationships to be able to do
something really new. We should keep up with the
changes of the world in which we live. Design cannot
be something static, it must reinvent itself in every
situation, every project. And that's what I believe
in: sensitive, human and alive design.

Above: illustration for
article on Super Papo.
Client: Editora Abril/
*Superinteressante*
Year: 2011

# OMG

USA

Opposite: army alphabet.
Client: self
Year: 2009

## I believe in thinking more and designing less

**OMG**
www.olivermunday.com
Founded 2008

**Founding member**
Oliver Munday
(USA 1984)

**Education**
Maryland Institute
College of Art

**Philosophy**
It's hard to subscribe to one philosophy, but when possible I believe in thinking more and designing less. I think the aesthetic should be conceptually informed and not be driven by the desire to use trends and styles of the moment. It's tough to completely separate yourself from tropes of the day, but the more I try and align my thinking with the content of the project, the less likely I am to impose my own preferential treatment to the aesthetic. Beyond that, I find that thinking more about the idea behind a piece makes for a quick turnaround on the visual deliverable. But of course, there are always exceptions to this rule.

# MUSEUM OF UNNATURAL HISTORY

OOOOOOOOOOOOO!

CATCH IT *LIVE!* IN THE *202*

# 8·2·6·DC

# CAVE!

Marvel AND Gape

FULL of INTRIGUE and MYSTERY

??????????????

UNSETTLING

WWW.826DC.ORG

SQUID

BATS

WEIRD

QUAACK!

SPLENDID

MUSEUM OF UNNATURAL HISTORY

WASHINGTON, DC

THE UNNATURALIST SOCIETY was founded on August 26, 1826 in Quito, Ecuador, when eight extensively unknown scientists sat down around a large octagonal table and declared they would "no longer cling like helpless little babies to the so-called scientific method."

Oh — Leave — My ASTONISHED...

EST. *The* 1826 UNNATURALIST SOCIETY

They spoke up for an emerging class of sciencticians, explorographers, and experimentationists fed up with the rigid formalities of "if-then" statements and posterboard science fairs. Over the next two centuries, the Society's members compiled knowledge of plants, animals, and not-so-precious stones using a combination of haphazard observation, creative inquiry, and rampant, unnchecked speculation.

At their headquarters in Washington, DC, Unnaturalists from all over the world gather to swap stories from the field and share their discoveries with the public. At the Museum of Unnatural History, all of the exhibits, events, and educational programs therein are dedicated to a simple truth: The world is as strange as you imagine it to be.

·FIN

3255 14TH STREET, NORTHWEST WASHINGTON D.C. 20009

# SPLENDIFEROUS! & UNVERIFIED!

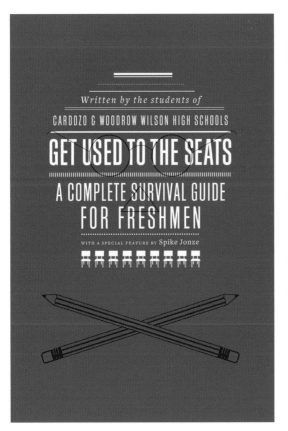

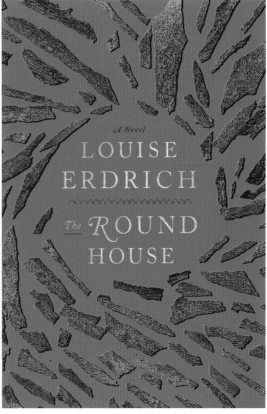

Above: *Get Used to the Seats,* book jacket design.
Client: 826DC
Year: 2010

Above right: *The Round House,* book jacket design.
Client: HarperCollins
Year: 2012

Right: *The Mansion of Happiness,* book jacket design.
Client: Knopf
Year: 2012

Opposite: 826DC Museum of Unnatural History poster.
Client: 826 National
Year: 2010

WHO THE HELL IS ANGELA DAVIS?

Angela Davis will be coming to speak at MICA for "The State of Women's Rights" conference along with Helen Molesworth, curator of the Harvard Fogg museum, on Sept. 12th 2009.

MICA

Below: business card.
Client: Robson DeSouza
Year: 2011

Right: *The New York Times
Book Review* cover design.
Client: *The New York
Times*
Year: 2011

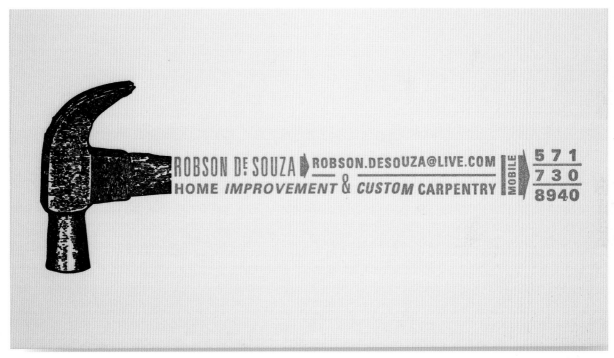

Opposite: Angela Davis
poster design.
Client: MICA
Year: 2010

# NAM

JAPAN

Below: Artwork for NAM's
solo exhibition "A Fantasy
in Life".
Client: self
Year: 2011

# We create work with hints of fantasy

**NAM**
n-a-m.org
Founded 2006

**Founding members**
Takayuki Nakazawa
(graphic designer) and
Hiroshi Manaka
(photographer)
(Japan 1968, Japan 1974)

**Education**
Kuwasaka Design School
Tokyo (Japan)

**Philosophy**
NAM is a Tokyo-based graphic/art collective, formed
in May 2006 by graphic designer Takayuki Nakazawa
and photographer Hiroshi Manaka. We create work
with hints of fantasy, fusing a graphic designer's
aesthetic into photographic expression.

Above and left: artwork
and book design for a
postersize book, *NAM:
A Fantasy in Life*, to
accompany the exhibition.
Client: self
Year: 2011

Right: campaign
advertising for Harbour
City Chocolate Trail 2012.
Client: Harbour City
Year: 2012

Below: advertising
and a music video
for cotto x capsule.
Client: Bascule Inc.
Year: 2012

Below: installation for
NUMABOOKFACE
exhibition.
Client: self
Year: 2011

# NICK BELL DESIGN

UK

Right: exhibition design:
Museum of the Post
Office in the Community.
Client: British Postal
Museum & Archive
Year: 2009

## Our design approach is curatorial

**Nick Bell Design**
nickbelldesign.co.uk
Founded 1988

**Founding member**
Nick Bell (UK 1965)

**Education**
Graphic Design at
London College of
Communication (UK)

### Philosophy

We are visual communicators designing for three-dimensional interactive environments. We have spent the last ten years collaborating with architects, museum directors and curators on exhibition interpretation design, digital interactive/audio-visual media design and wayfinding. During that time we have developed a visitor-centred editorial concern for the voices and visual language of interpretation and interactivity within physical information-rich environments. We try to make museums absorbing and inspirational places to be. We always aim to make it easier and more appealing for people to strengthen the connections they have with an organization. We strive to deepen this affinity by developing ways of communicating that spark interest, encourage participation and provoke action. We fuel action by making visitor engagement tangible and intelligible through building distinctive graphic identities specific to the content and experience that each attraction offers. Our design approach is curatorial. Our interpretive understanding is steered by objects and issues in context, how people find meaning in them and how they might be further engaged. This curatorial approach grew out of our extensive editorial design experience, in print (most notably on influential critical writing magazine, *eye*). It is an approach that is winning plaudits not merely for design, but for effectiveness too.

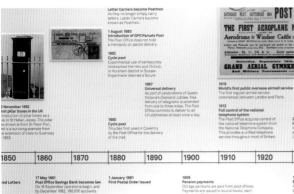

Letter Carriers become Postmen
As they no longer simply carry
letters, Letter Carriers become
known as Postmen.

1 August 1883
Introduction of GPO Parcels Post
The Post Office does not hold
a monopoly on parcel delivery.

1882
Cycle post
Experimental use of pentacycles
(nicknamed the Hen and Chicks),
in Horsham district in Sussex.
Experiment deemed a failure.

1897
Universal delivery
As part of celebrations of Queen
Victoria's Diamond Jubilee, free
delivery of telegrams is extended
from one to three miles. The Post
Office commits to deliver to all
UK addresses at least once a day.

1880
Cycle post
Tricycles first used in Coventry
by the Post Office for the delivery
of the mail.

1919
World's first public overseas airmail service
The first regular airmail service
commences between London and Paris.

1912
Full control of the national
telephone system
The Post Office acquires control of
the national telephone system from
the National Telephone Company.
This provides a unified telephone
service throughout most of Britain.

THE FIRST AEROPLANE M
Aerodrome in Windsor Castle a

GRAND AERIAL GYMKH
And Military Tournament o

| 1850 | 1860 | 1870 | 1880 | 1890 | 1900 | 1910 | 1920 |
|------|------|------|------|------|------|------|------|

3 November 1852
First pillar boxes in the UK
Introduction of pillar boxes as a
trial in St Helier, Jersey. The pillar
box shown is from St Peter Port,
and is a surviving example from
the extension of trials to Guernsey
in 1853.

red Letters

17 May 1861
Post Office Savings Bank becomes law
On 16 September operations begin, and
by December 1862, 180,000 accounts
have been opened. Becomes National
Savings from 1 October 1969.

1 January 1881
First Postal Order issued

1909
Pension payments
Old age pensions are paid from post offices.
Payments are issued in bound books, each
containing 25 pension orders.

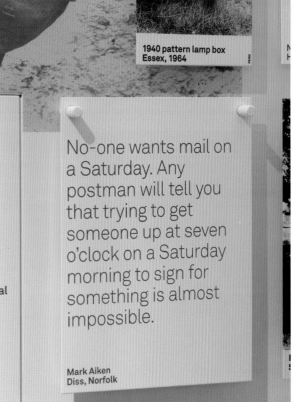

1940 pattern lamp box
Essex, 1964

No-one wants mail on
a Saturday. Any
postman will tell you
that trying to get
someone up at seven
o'clock on a Saturday
morning to sign for
something is almost
impossible.

Mark Aiken
Diss, Norfolk

Left and below:
permanent exhibition
design for the Great
North Museum.
Client: Tyne & Wear
Museums and Newcastle
University
Year: 2009

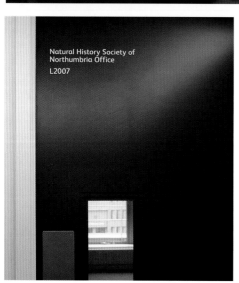

Natural History Society of
Northumbria Office
L.2007

Above and left: design
for permanent exhibition
called "Atmosphere:
exploring climate science".
Client: Science Museum.
Year: 2010

# OHYES-COOLGREAT

NETHERLANDS

Opposite: poster design
for a lecture series.
Client: Sandberg Instituut
Amsterdam
Year: 2011

## Signal, observe, discuss, react, make, strategize and publicize

**Ohyescoolgreat**
www.ohyescoolgreat.com
Founded 2007

**Founding Members**
Jeroen Sikma and
Janneke de Rooij
(Both Netherlands 1985)

**Education**
Graphic design identity
at the Willem de Kooning
Academie (Netherlands )

**Philosophy**
Ohyescoolgreat focuses on the communication of identities through graphic design. We develop strong visual languages for corporate identities, books, magazines, websites etc. We art direct, design and give advice. We signal, observe, discuss, react, make, strategize and publicize. Ohyescoolgreat is based in Rotterdam, Netherlands, and we have worked together with other creative professionals in Amsterdam, Enschede, Arnhem, Brussels and Berlin.

Above and right: research,
art direction, identity,
design and launch for
*24,95*, a book by a
collective of four freelance
photographers.
Client: TOT
Year: 2012

Above: WickedChairTobac-
coPlant: Lookbook poster
for fashion label.
Client: Daisy Kroon
Year: 2010

Above: flyers and poster
design for an Amsterdam
art gallery.
Client: Dek22
Year: 2010

Below: poster and flyer for
the exhibition "On The Wall."
Client: Kunstvlaai
Year: 2010

## KEEP AN EYE /

## ON THE WALL

**Voor** 'On the Wall' nodigt de Keep an Eye Foundation jonge kunste-
naars uit om een eigentijdse wandschildering te maken. Daarmee
wordt een nieuw hoofdstuk toegevoegd aan de lange geschiedenis
van de muurschilderkunst, van de graffiti van Keith Haring, kerkelijke
fresco's tot de allereerste rotstekeningen in Lascaux.

Een meer dan zes meter hoge houten toren fungeert als drager.
De toren is verdeeld in zes horizontale stroken van één meter hoog
en zestien meter lang, die zich om het rechthoekige volume slin-
geren. Ze werken als 'regels' die je kunt 'lezen' en zo verandert de
toren in een bundeling van beeldverhalen.

De Keep an Eye Foundation is initiatiefnemer en opdrachtgever
van 'On the Wall'. Het concept werd ontwikkeld met het Sandberg
Institute en curator Gijs Frieling. Deze kunstenaar hecht grote waarde
aan de communicatieve kracht van kunst, zoals ook bleek uit zijn
recente muurschilder project Dr. Faustus in W139.

De toren is een blikvanger tijdens de 'Kunstvlaai' in mei 2010. Deze
alternatieve kunstbeurs werd in 1997 voor het eerst georganiseerd
als reactie op de KunstRai, (nu bekend als Art Amsterdam).
De Kunstvlaai is een uniek podium voor aanstormend talent en expe-
rimentele, niet commerciële kunst in Amsterdam.

## COLOFON

**Conceptontwikkeling:**
Jos Houweling, Sandberg Institute
& Vera Poelmann–Wolfs, Keep an Eye Foundation
**Curator:** Gijs Frieling
**Tekst:** Anne Berk

**Productie:** Riet Wijnen
**Grafisch ontwerp:**
Anja Groten, Janneke de Rooij
& Maartje Smits
**Drukkerij:** SSP

Opposite above left:
poster for an art gallery in
Amsterdam.
Client: Dek22
Year: 2010

Opposite above right:
poster for the exhibition
"Tangible Traces".
Ciient: OPA, Arnhem
Year: 2009

Opposite below left:
poster and identity design
for a collective of
photographers from
Amsterdam.
Client: TOT
Year: 2009

Opposite below right:
poster for "Face Value",
an exhibition to re-evaluate
the question of autonomy
in the design process.
Client: TENT
Year: 2011

# PETER ØRNTOFT

DENMARK

Opposite: Framing Copenhagen poster design research
and implementation.
Client: self
Year: 2009

Right: Rating the City
interactive postcard
(conceptual project).
Client: Posterheroes.org
Year: 2011

RATING:

**COPENHAGEN**
DENMARK

## Tell more stories

---

**Peter Ørntoft**
www.peterorntoft.com
Born Denmark 1983

**Education**
Graphic and media
design at London
College of
Communication (UK),
visual communication
at the Danish Design
School (Denmark)

**Philosophy**
I am a designer in the field of visual communication.
I usually work with a context and research-based
approach to traditional fields of visual communication,
and by using this approach my projects are able to
contain multiple layers and tell more stories about
the subject or the client I'm working with.

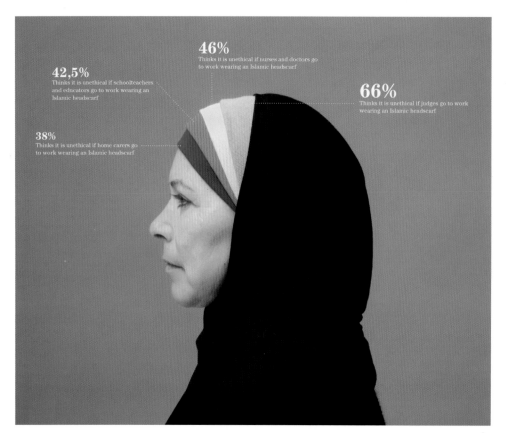

46%
Thinks it is unethical if nurses and doctors go to work wearing an Islamic headscarf

42,5%
Thinks it is unethical if schoolteachers and educators go to work wearing an Islamic headscarf

66%
Thinks it is unethical if judges go to work wearing an Islamic headscarf

38%
Thinks it is unethical if home carers go to work wearing an Islamic headscarf

Left and below: design research into information graphics and conceptual implementation.
Client: self
Year: 2011

18%
Have changed their behaviour a lot because of gang related crime

26%
Have changed their behaviour because of gang related crime

55%
Have not changed behaviour because of the gang related crime

Opposite: data visualization showing the results of a paint brand's survey on the use of colour and space.
Client: Jotun Coatings Turkey
Year: 2012

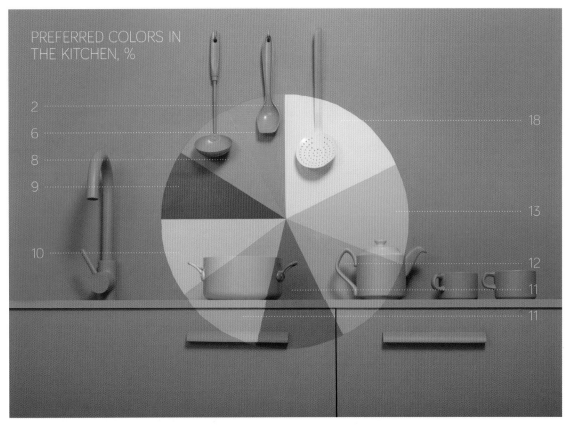

PREFERRED COLORS IN
THE KITCHEN, %

2        18
6        13
8
9
10       12
          11
          11

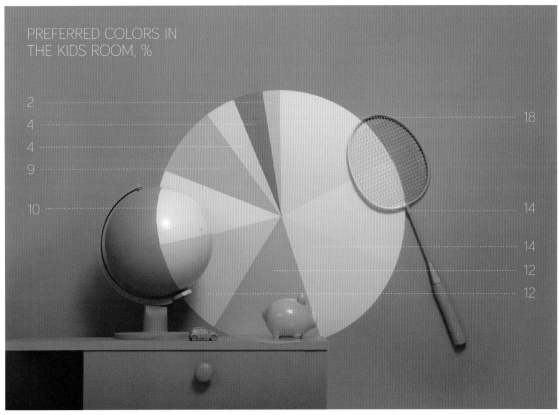

PREFERRED COLORS IN
THE KIDS ROOM, %

2        18
4        14
4        14
9        12
10       12

# KOSMA
# OSTROWSKI

POLAND

Below and opposite:
features in an online
culture and contemporary
art magazine.
Client: ZIN
Year: 2012

# Art is like masturbation, design is like sex

**Kosma Ostrowski**
www.wix.com/
kosmaostrowski/portfolio
Born Poland 1983

**Education**
Graphic design and
digital media art at Maria
Curie-Skłodowska
University (Poland)

**Philosophy**
I teach graphic design at the School of Art and Design
in Lublin, Poland, and am a co-founder of
the Kamienica Cudów Gallery. My favourite quote is
from designer Colin Wright: "Art is like masturbation. It
is selfish and introverted and done for you and you
alone. Design is like sex. There is someone else
involved, their needs are just as important as your
own, and if everything goes right, both parties are
happy in the end."

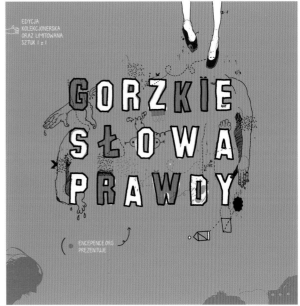

Above: CD and vinyl cover
design for the radioplay
*Bitter Words of Truth*, part
of Radio Lublin's
celebrations for five years
of broadcasting "Studnia
Akademicka".
Client: Encepence.org
Year: 2011

Opposite: poster for
the third International
Theatre Festival, held
in Lublin, Poland.
Client: International
Theatre Festival
Date: 2012

Right: "Visual Noise"
photographs and print
designs.
Client: self
Year: 2012

# DANIEL PETER

SWITZERLAND

Below: silkscreen poster design.
Client: Kulturwerk
Year: 2008

Below: poster design.
Client: Detectiv Bureau
Year: 2010

# Work as pleasure!

**Daniel Peter**
www.herrpeter.ch
Born Switzerland 1983

**Education**
Graphic Design at
Hochschule Luzern
(Switzerland)

**Philosophy**
Work as pleasure!

Below: concert poster design.
Client: Südpol
Year: 2010

Below: poster design.
Client: Südpol
Year: 2009

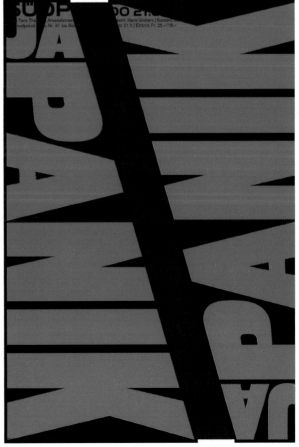

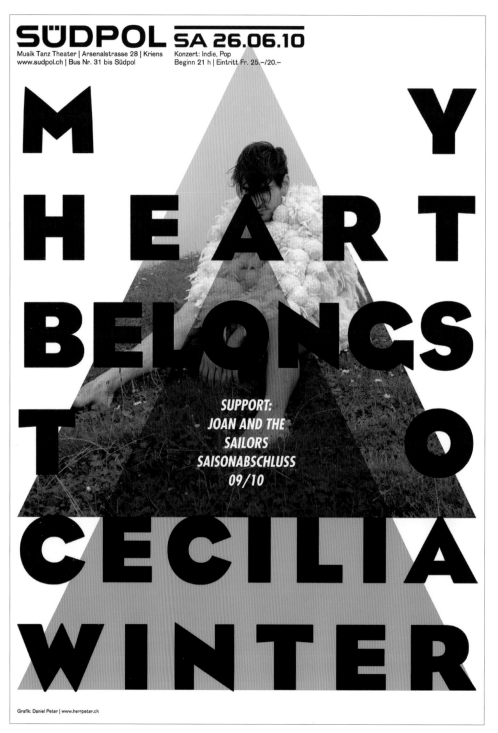

Left: poster advertising
a concert by the Swiss
indie/pop band My Heart
Belongs to Cecilia Winter.
Client: Südpol
Year: 2010

Opposite: poster design
for Play Again.
Client: Detectiv Bureau
Year: 2010

# PRALINE

UK

Opposite: "From the
House to the City"
exhibition identity, signage,
handout and all graphics.
Client: Rogers Stirk
Harbour + Partners.
Interior Design: Ab Rogers
Design
Year: Singapore 2011,
Hong Kong and Beijing
2012

## Energy, thoughtfulness and visual impact

**Praline**
www.designbypraline.
com
Founded 2000

**Founding Member**
David Tanguy
(France 1973)

**Education**
Graphic design/
typography at Central
Saint Martins, London
(UK)

**Philosophy**
At Praline we love working on different kinds of
projects, from graphic design to branding, exhibitions
and art direction. We love challenges and new ideas.
We are based in London and Paris and, over the years,
have developed a dedicated team of highly talented
colleagues, collaborators and consultants.
Since our inception in 2000, we have grown into a
highly respected design agency, having worked with
clients such as Richard Rogers + Partners, TATE
Modern, Royal Academy, Heston Blumenthal, Nick
Knight, Little Chef, Central Saint Martins, the Barbican
Centre and many others. Our graphical thinking is
characterised by an instinct for typography, colour and
materials, expressed in a bold yet understated visual
language. Our work is recognized for its unmistakable
energy, thoughtfulness and visual impact.

Below: *POLPO: a Venetian
Cookbook (of sorts)* book
design.
Client: Bloomsbury
Year: 2012

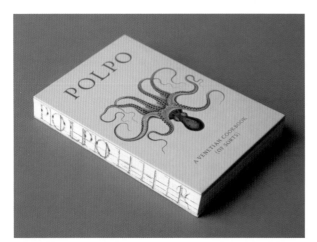

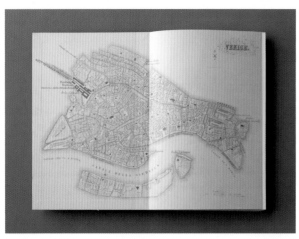

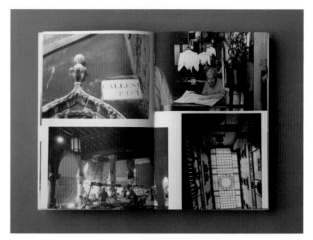

Right: Scape branding, wayfinding and environmental graphics
Client: Gravis Capital Partners.
Architect: Jefferson Sheard Architects.
Interior Design: Ab Rogers Design
Year: 2012

All: "Designing 007:
50 Years of Bond Style"
exhibition identity,
graphics and catalogue.
Client: Barbican Centre,
London.
Exhibition Design:
Ab Rogers Design
Year: 2012

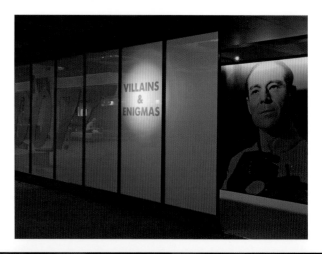

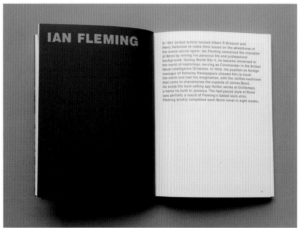

# QUINTA-FEIRA

BRAZIL

06/01NEPALDIOG
69 RUA FARME DE AMOEDO 50          WWW.FESTACOMBO.COM
OREIS(MOO)

Left: flyer design.
Client: Combo
Year: 2009

# Before anything else, design should be a pleasure for everyone

**Quinta-Feira**
www.quinta-feira.org
Founded 2000

**Founding Member**
Odete de Aruanda
(Brazil 1977)

**Philosophy**
Before anything else, design should be a pleasure for everyone.

Below: two flyer designs.
Client: Combo
Year: 2009

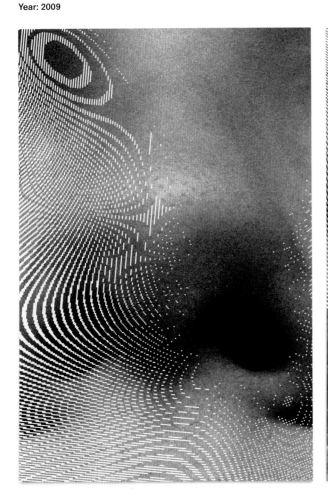

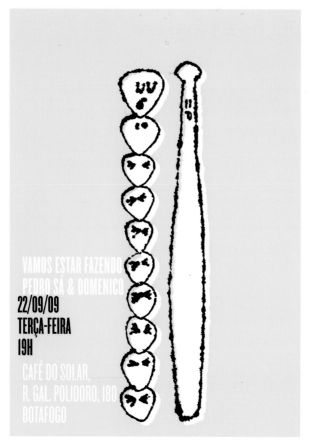

VAMOS ESTAR FAZENDO
PEDRO SÁ & DOMENICO
22/09/09
TERÇA-FEIRA
19H
CAFÉ DO SOLAR,
R. GAL. POLIDORO, 180
BOTAFOGO

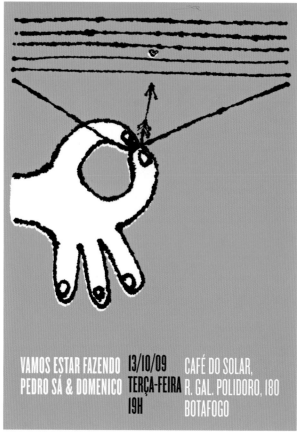

VAMOS ESTAR FAZENDO    13/10/09      CAFÉ DO SOLAR,
PEDRO SÁ & DOMENICO    TERÇA-FEIRA   R. GAL. POLIDORO, 180
                       19H           BOTAFOGO

12/12
MORGANGEIST
(METROAREANY)
BADENOV

Above: flyers and posters
designs for music events.
Client: Café do Solar
Year: 2009

Left: flyer design.
Client: Combo
Year: 2009

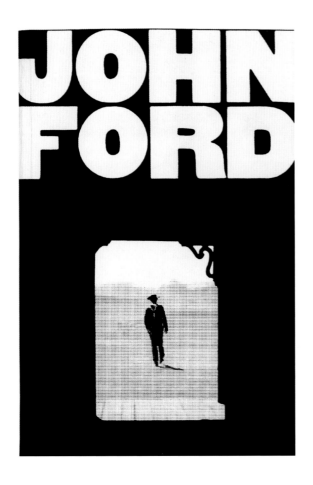

Above: John Ford
exhibition identity,
catalogue and poster
design.
Client: Centro Cultural
Banco do Brasil.
Designed with Miguel
Nóbrega
Year: 2012

Left: magazine
illustrations.
Client: *S/Nº – Envy*
Year: 2012

# RUDD
# STUDIO

UK

Opposite: On-air
programme menus
with television
channel branding.
Client: Channel 4
Year: 2010

## New ways of seeing

---

**Rudd Studio**
www.ruddstudio.com
Founded 2002

**Founding member**
Matthew Rudd
(UK 1972)

**Education**
Graphic design at Central
Saint Martins,
communication art and
design at the RCA (UK)

**Philosophy**
Rudd Studio is a small, London-based studio of specialists who work in moving image, music and design. Inspired by art and music, we are also bound together by our belief in the creative power of integrating the disciplines of moving image, music and design. We have learned that by developing the visual and the musical in tandem and by working closely with our clients, we are able to create surprising and beautiful design solutions through a subtle alchemy of ideas, function and form. This quite artistic process allows us to develop big ideas that are then realised and crafted in exquisite detail. And while we work like artists to create impact, we do not follow our own individual artistic agendas. Instead, we listen to our clients' and their customers' agendas and create relevant and enduring solutions which evoke an instinctive response inspiring recognition and loyalty in consumers. Every project has its own complexion, and requires new thinking. We look for inspiration in unexpected places and avoid following trends. We are continually searching for innovation and new ways of seeing, thereby avoiding complacency and tiredness.

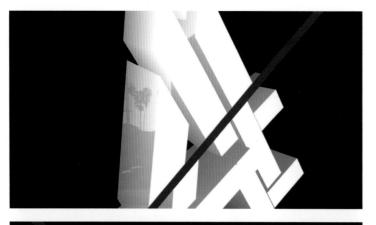

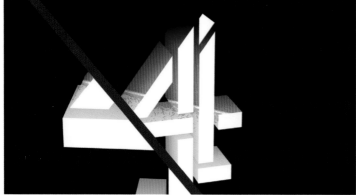

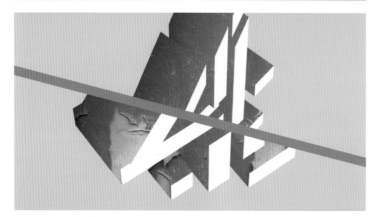

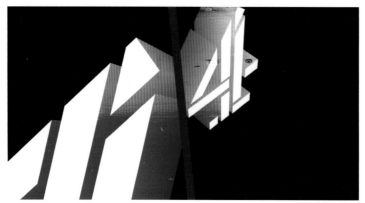

Left: updated television channel brand idents used in the one-second stings that precede ad breaks.
Client: Channel 4
Year: 2010

Opposite: various logo designs for television channel sub-brands. These static logos were the starting point for developing the print and on-air branding.
Client: Channel 4
Year: various dates between 2001 and 2010

# SAGMEISTER & WALSH

USA

## Try out as many things as possible

**Sagmeister & Walsh**
www.sagmeisterwalsh.
com
Sagmeister Inc. founded
in 1993, Sagmeister &
Walsh in 2012.

**Founding Members**
Stefan Sagmeister
(Austria 1962), Jessica
Walsh (USA 1986)

**Education**
Graphic design at the
University of Applied
Arts, Vienna (Austria);
graphic design at Rhode
Island School of Design
(USA)

**Philosophy**
As a studio, we embrace technology, sometimes
hesitantly, when we redesign sites because of higher
screen resolutions and sometimes passionately, when
we work with programmers to create custom
generative tools created to design logos or
installations. Jessica concentrates on our more
commercial work while I take care of the more self
generated projects. We support each other in each of
these endeavours. The biggest changes in our
industry continue to be technology driven. Everything
that can be animated, will be animated. I would not
want to miss working in either analogue or digital.
When I started my career it was with the aim of being
honest. I wanted to see if it was possible to touch the
heart of the viewer. If I were advising myself as a
recent graduate, I would say: work hard. Only take on
jobs that have the potential to be worthwhile. Try out
as many things as possible. Embrace technology.

Left: a wall featuring 10,000 bananas, created for an exhibition in New York. Text created with green bananas gradually disappeared then reappeared as the bananas ripened.
Client: Deitch Projects
Year: 2008

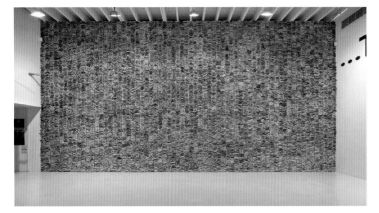

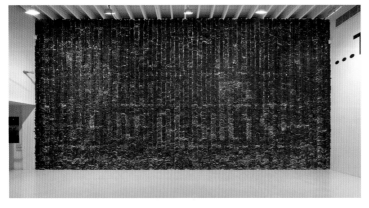

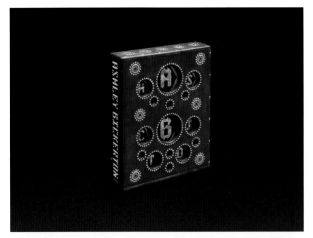
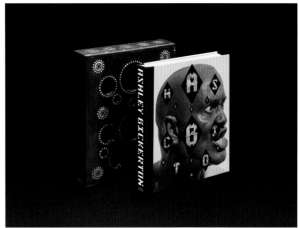

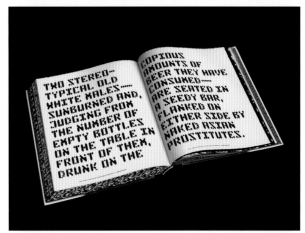

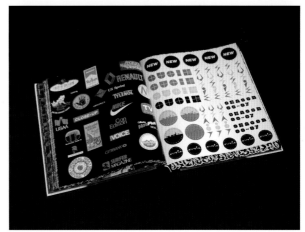

Above: design of visual
artist Ashley Bickerton's
monograph.
Client: Other Criteria
Year: 2011

**Above:** a 60 second
advertisement with a
global, typographic
approach.
**Client:** Standard Chartered
**Year:** 2010

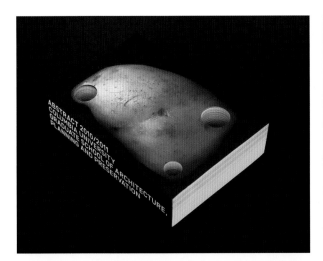

Above: publication design for the Graduate School of Architecture, Planning and Preservation's yearbook.
Client: Columbia University
Year: 2011

# SAWDUST

UK

## Do what you love

Below: "This is Now"
poster created for
exhibition.
Client: Oh Yeah Studio
Year: 2012

Below: poster designed to
commemorate the fiftieth
anniversary of the founding
of the city of Brasilia.
Client: Brasilia Prima
Year: 2010

## Sawdust
www.madebysawdust.
co.uk
Founded 2006

### Founding Members
Rob Gonzalez and
Jonathan Quainton
(UK 1980, UK 1982)

### Education
Graphic design at Bath
Spa University College,
graphic design at
Banbury College (both
UK)

## Philosophy
Milton Glaser was once asked what advice he would give to young designers. He told a story about how he chose art school over other academic subjects as a career path, after which one of his teachers (who he thought might disapprove) pulled him to one side, gave him a set of pencils (if we recall correctly) and said "do good work". This sums it up really, we always wanted to create beautiful work, it really isn't any more complicated. In terms of advances in technology, we continue our work as usual while embracing new technologies as and when appropriate. For instance if we create a typeface, it could then be used in print, in a digital capacity, it could be used in motion/animation and so forth. The same goes for image-making… We were recently commissioned by *Wired* magazine to create some typographic artwork for an article; when they saw our idea they asked if it could be animated as it lent itself nicely to moving image. For us it's just a natural progression, embracing what's around us but

not feeling the need to reinvent ourselves or the need to gear ourselves toward something specifically based around emerging technology. To answer the "analogue vs. digital" debate, we would say: can't we all just get along? We are both passionate about visual culture and producing work that is beautiful, effective and thoughtful. Our approach is often typographically driven because it's a passion of ours, which subsequently attracts clients who require work with a typographic edge or focus. Perhaps a good way to explain who specializes more in each area is: Jonathan: 60% type obsessed, 40% image-making and other visual culture, and Rob: 60% image-making (often typographic but not specifically), 40% type. It's a difficult thing to "box" – it's probably better not to try as interests evolve as you do. Our advice to graduates would be to do what you love. It took us longer than we'd hoped to discover that. Unfortunately finding what you love the most is often half the battle and there's no shortcut.

Below: Interactive
"Granimator" wallpaper
app for the iPad
Client: ustwo
Year: 2011

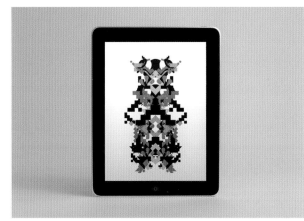

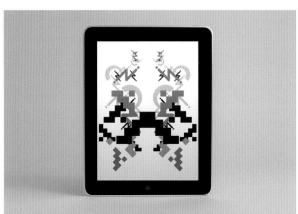

Below: Typographic
illustration and editorial
design.
Client: *Who's Jack*
Year: 2012

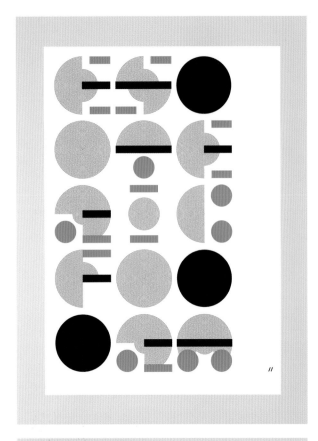

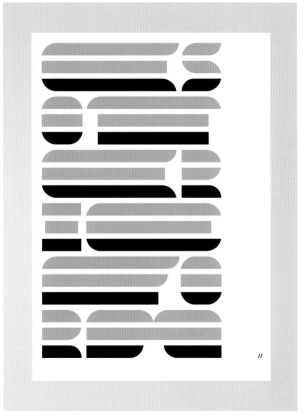

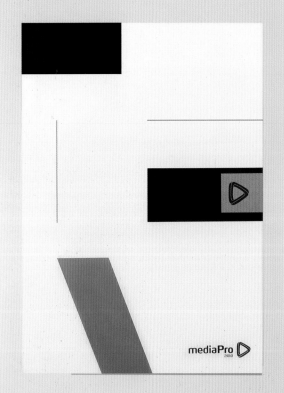

Above left: "Esoteric
Form – Edition One"
limited edition poster.
Client: Art Mosh
Year: 2011

Above right: "Esoteric
Form – Edition Two"
limited edition poster.
Client: Art Mosh
Year: 2011

Left: brochure for an event
focusing on the future of
integrated marketing and
communication.
Client: yumyumcreative/
CloserStill/mediaPro
Year: 2010

Opposite above: Editorial
spread design for launch
publication on bikes and
cycling culture.
Client: Fixed & What
Year: 2011

Opposite below: custom
designed typeface,
available to buy online.
Client: HypeForType
Year: 2011

# SECOND STORY INTERACTIVE STUDIOS

USA

## Pique curiosity, engage and entertain

Opposite above: Live
Positively Portrait Wall
interactive installation.
Client: The Coca-Cola
Company
Year: 2011

Opposite below and
overleaf left: design and
development for
the Vault of the Secret
Formula, a series of
12 interactive media
experiences.
Client: The Coca-Cola
Company
Year: 2011

**Second Story
Interactive Studios**
www.secondstory.com
Founded 1994

**Founding members**
Brad Johnson and
Julie Beeler (both USA)

**Education**
Philosophy at
Washington and Lee
University; graphic
design and art history
from the University of
the Pacific (both USA)

### Philosophy
Since 1994, Second Story has been forging powerful,
personal, and memorable connections between
individuals and ideas by focusing on how people learn
and how they experience environments. How we think
leads to what we make. We approach our interactive
concepts and creations from the standpoint of audiences
– what will pique curiosity, engage, and entertain in
the most direct and beautiful way? As strategists,
planners, and concept developers, we rethink
interactive media experiences at the highest levels.
Our knowledgeable team blends new technologies,
compelling design, and proven storytelling techniques
to bring information intuitively to people's fingertips
within elegant interfaces. We implement information
design strategies that empower people with
ready-at-hand tools to explore sound, visuals, and the
written word. Our deep understanding of technology
allows us to take innovative risks and push the
boundaries of interactive design. Working across
industry disciplines, we bring clarity and efficiency
to complex projects.

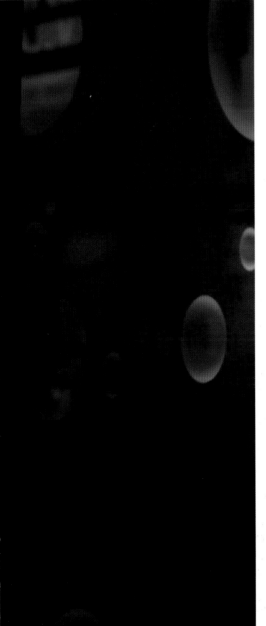

Below: design and
development for an
interactive gallery.
Client: Adler Planetarium
Year: 2011

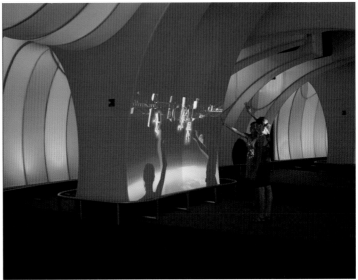

# SIGNAL | NOISE

UK

Below: Parkhouse
interactive blueprints
Client: AllofUs / Land
Securities
Year: 2010

Below: Peugeot Peep
showroom
Client: pd3/Peugeot
Year: 2010

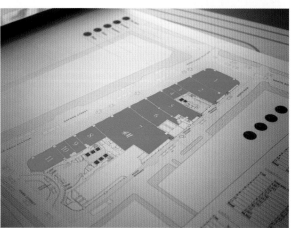

# Touch, swipe, gesture

**Signal | Noise**
www.matthewfalla.com
Founded 2010

**Founding members**
Matthew Falla, Hem Patel, and Christian Thümer (UK 1980, UK 1976, Germany 1980)

**Philosophy**
The World Wide Web is over 20 years old and has completely redefined the way we live and work. The next 20 years are going to see another shift to a truly connected world shaped by an Internet of things and ubiquitous, often invisible technology. This is the world of always-on-mobile, RFID, flexible screens... touch, swipe, gesture. We are a full-service interactive design company and our mission is to educate our clients – from big financial institutions to fashion brands – about this new world and to work with them to develop the products, services and experiences that will come to define it. We provide interaction and information design services and develop our own products and intellectual property.

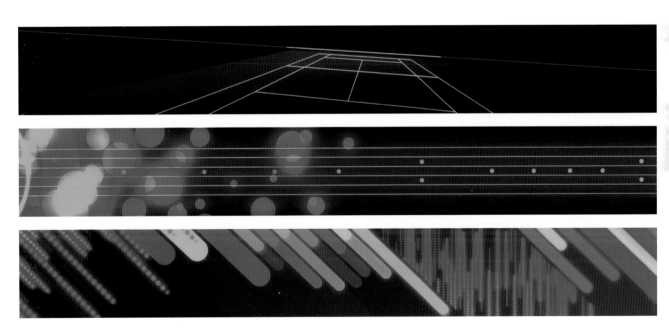

Above: the O2 Bluebar
animated wallpaper
Client: pd3/O2 Arena
Year: 2011

Left: custom bike
generator
Client: 14 Bike Co.
Year: 2011

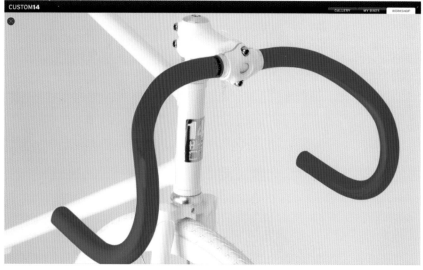

Opposite: snowboard
data digital poster
Client: Hyper/Nokia/
Burton
Year: 2011

# FRODE SKAREN

NORWAY

## Work harder and do better

**Frode Skaren**
www.uglylogo.no
Born Norway 1982

**Education**
Illustration at NKF
Oslo, visual
communication at
Oslo National Academy
of the Arts (both Norway)

**Philosophy**
I try not to follow trends, and usually I start with
defining the client's problem and trying to figure
out the best solution for them. This working method
means my work isn't in a specific style, and the final
product might not always be what I want it to be, but
I try to keep in mind that the client's needs come first.
I use my illustration work to be more personally
creative, and I can work for days with detail that only
I will see in the end. But for me, it's important. It's the
same with graphic design – the detail that I see and
admire in others' work is what inspires me to work
harder and do better.

Above and right: poster
and identity design for
Norway's largest club
music festival.
Client: By:Larm
Year: 2011

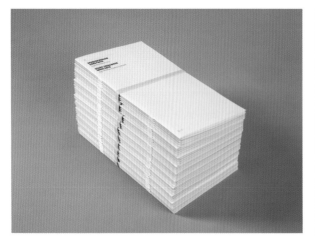

Above: design for a
study catalogue.
Client: Oslo National
Academy of the Arts
Year: 2009

374

Above: *Feite Forestillinger*,
design of a book on
arranging music concerts.
Client: Norsk Rockforbund
Made with Rune
Mortensen
Year: 2010

Right: magazine cover
illustration for Norway's
newest music magazine.
Client: ENO magazine
Year: 2011

# MICHAEL SPITZ

CROATIA

Opposite: Drink me Now
and Forget me Later
poster.
Client: self
Year: 2012

## I love what I do, and my hope is that it translates

**Name**
michaelspitz.com
Born USA 1984

**Education**
Communication design
at Parsons the New
School for Design,
New York (USA)

**Philosophy**
Effective communication, distilled and driven by
carefully considerd conceptual foundations. A great
love and respect for typography, and an affinity for
making people think. In determining my role, I like to
consider myself a thinker and a problem-solver first
and foremost. The bulk of my commercial work
focuses on conceiving and crafting the faces of others
and their endeavours. The general goals for my clients
are providing them with a means to create memorable
lasting impressions, and a solid platform for future
growth and development. The goal for myself is to
keep things interesting. I love what I do, and my hope
is that it translates.

Left: personal branding.
Client: self
Year: 2010

Right: logotype script.
Client: Drupalr
Year: 2011

Far right: Bumpy Road
Films logotype.
Client: Heather
Year: 2011

Right: identity and
branding for multi-purpose
entertainment venue.
Client: Debut London
Year: 2011

# STUDIO AAD

IRELAND

Below: compliment cards
with branding for Studio Aad.
Client: self
Year: 2010

Bottom: poster and flyer
design for a visual arts
season.
Client: The Ark, A Cultural
Centre for Children
Year: 2010

Below: cultural festival
identity and programme.
Client: Cork Midsummer
Festival
Year: 2012

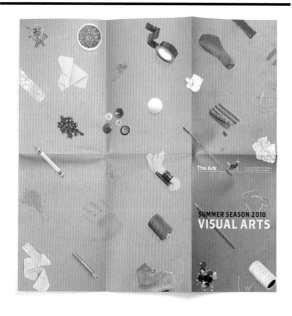

# Finding the truth in the subject matter

**Studio aad**
www.studioaad.com
Founded 2003

**Founding members**
Scott Burnett and
Johnny Kelly (Scotland
1973, Ireland 1974)

**Education**
Visual communication
at Grays School of Art
(Scotland)
Print management
at Dublin Institute of
Technology (Ireland)

**Philosophy**
Aad stands for art and design. This in turn stands
for the craft and thought that goes into making
something well. We apply this not just to the logos,
identities, books, brochures, websites and environments
we design but also to the design process itself. We
design to connect people and do so with the studio
philosophy of honest invention – finding the truth in
the subject matter and being inventive in how we
communicate it.

Below: publication design
for a festival programme.
Client: Absolut Fringe
Year: 2012

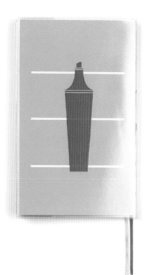

This page: book design.
Client: Self
Year: 2011

This page: print and digital
festival identity design
and branding.
Client: Dublin Writers
Festival
Year: 2011

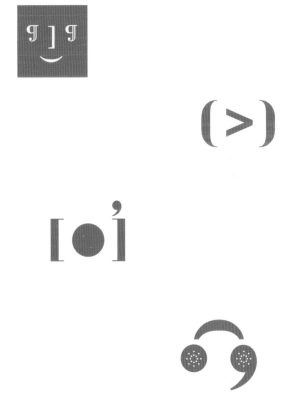

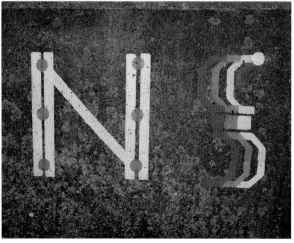

# STUDIO FRITH

UK

Opposite: Belvedere River
Wall, typographic mural
and typeface system.
Client: London Borough
of Bexley & Design for
London
Year: 2011

## We experiment with the relevant

**Studio Frith**
www.studiofrith.com
Founded 2008

**Founding Member**
Frith Kerr (UK 1973)

**Education**
Graphic design at
Camberwell College
of Arts and the Royal
College of Art (both UK)

**Philosophy**
Studio Frith's work is collaborative and conceptual.
We experiment with the relevant.

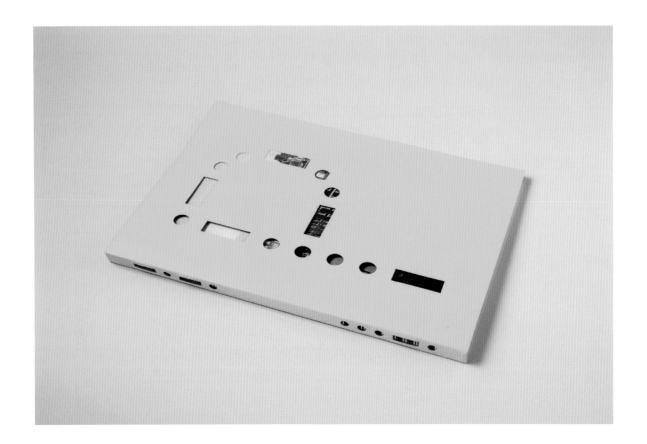

Opposite: presentation
folders and branding.
Client: Publica
Year: 2010

Above: seasonal tote bag
designs.
Client: Melrose and
Morgan
Year: 2009 – present

Right: Hussein Chalayan
exhibition poster.
Client: Les Arts Decoratifs
Year: 2011

A NEW PERFORMANCE BY PABLO BRONSTEIN
ONE NIGHT ONLY
THURSDAY 14 JANUARY 2010, 7–9PM

WWW.CHISENHALE.ORG.UK
64 Chisenhale Road, London, E3 5QZ
+44 (0)20 8981 4518
Registered Charity no.1026175

ADMISSION FREE. NO BOOKING REQUIRED.

Left: website homepage
design.
Client: Chisenhale Gallery
Year: 2009

Opposite and below:
exhibition posters.
Client: Chisenhale Gallery
Year: 2009 – present

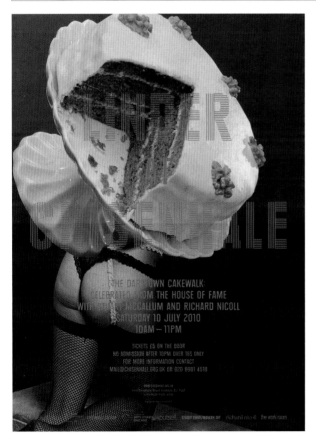

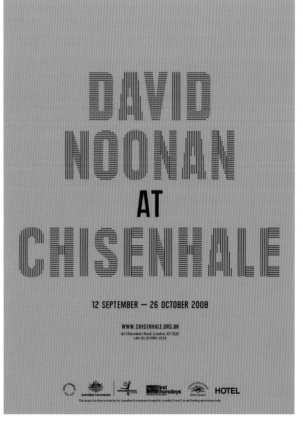

# STUDIOKXX

POLAND

## We seek the most creative solution

**StudioKxx**
www.studiokxx.com
Founded 2006

**Founding member**
Krzysztof Domaradzki
(Poland 1979)

**Education**
Drawing and metal
techniques at Academy
of Fine Arts Poznan
(Poland)

**Philosophy**
We are a multidisciplinary design studio that focuses on
providing high quality work for a diverse group of clients
in a wide range of professions. Since establishing the
studio in 2006, we have developed into an enterprise that
practises in a broad range of disciplines, including art
direction, graphic design, illustration, visual identity, brand
design, web-design and app design. Whether the client
is a multinational corporation or a small struggling
start-up, we always strive to deliver a unique message
that captures the client's vision. Regardless of the
scale and budget, we seek the most creative solution
and enjoy every kind of creative challenge.

BRANDO

**Above and opposite: design
for a poster and CD cover.
Client: self
Year: 2009**

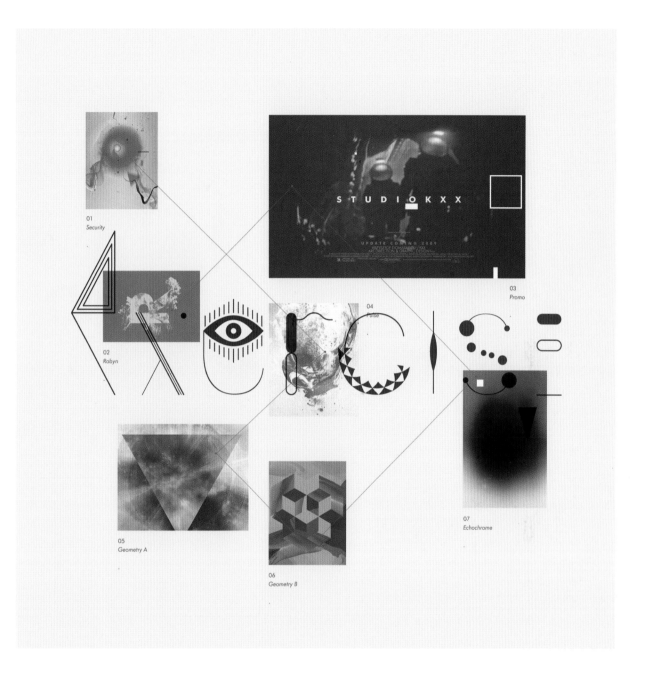

01
Security

02
Robyn

03
Promo

04
Pulse

05
Geometry A

06
Geometry B

07
Echochrome

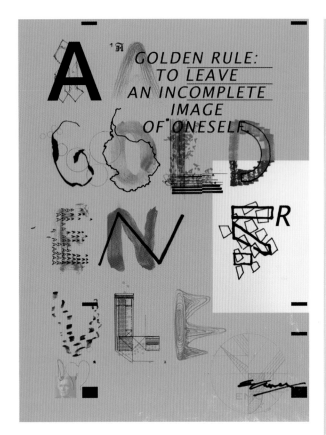

Above: poster design.
Client: self
Year: 2011

Above: CD sleeve and
packaging design made
for the album *Of Sand
and Stone*.
Client: Drawing North
Year: 2012

Above: design for a poster.
Client: self
Year: 2009

Above: t-shirt design proposal.
Client: Diesel
Year: 2010

# STUDIO
# NEWWORK

USA

Below: branding for a
concept store for a
Japanese fashion label.
Client: Markaware
Year: 2011

# We design with passion, care, and love.

**STUDIO NEWWORK**
www.studionewwork.com
www.newworkmag.com
Founded 2007

**Founding members**
Ryotatsu Tanaka, Ryo
Kumazaki, Hitomi Ishigaki
(Japan1976, Japan1979,
Japan 1981)

**Education**
Graphic design at
Fashion Institute of
Technology New York
(USA) (all)

**Philosophy**
Studio Newwork is a graphic design studio
based in New York. Together we are a team of
passionate typographic designers committed to
searching for excellence in design. We design
with passion, care, and love.

**Below: typography design
published in an
international design
magazine from Denmark.
Client: *FAT*
Year: 2012**

BESPOKE ISSUE No.3

D

Derek Kettela

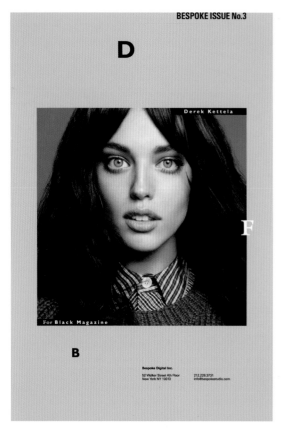

For Black Magazine

F

B

Bespoke Digital Inc.
52 Walker Street 4th Floor
New York NY 10013
212.226.3731
info@bespokestudio.com

BESPOKE ISSUE No.1

ENRIQUE BADULESCU for ELLE UK

AGENCY: ART PARTNER

Bespoke Digital Inc.
52 Walker Street 4th Floor
New York NY 10013
212.226.3731
info@bespokestudio.com

BESPOKE ISSUE No.2

SANTIAGO & MAURICIO
FOR 25 MAGAZINE

AGENCY: CADENCE

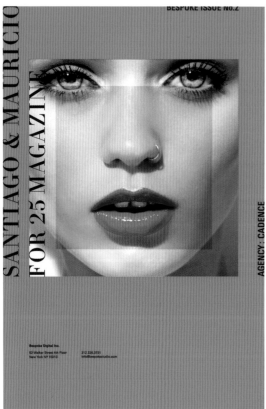

Bespoke Digital Inc.
52 Walker Street 4th Floor
New York NY 10013
212.226.3731
info@bespokestudio.com

Above and left: a
bi-monthly email
newsletter to clients.
Client: Bespoke Studio
Year: 2012

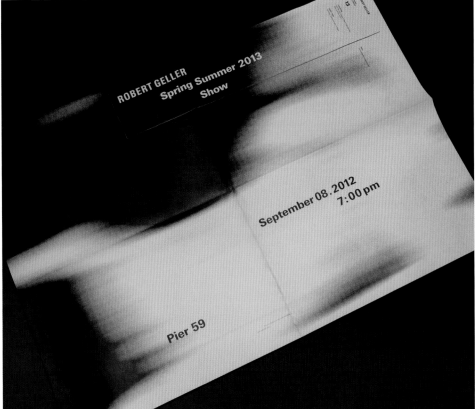

Right: branding, including
these show invitiations,
for a men's fashion label.
Client: Robert Geller
Year: 2011

# STUDIO-THOMSON

UK

Below and right:
advertising campaign for
the UK Music Video
Awards.
Client: Ballistic
Year: 2011

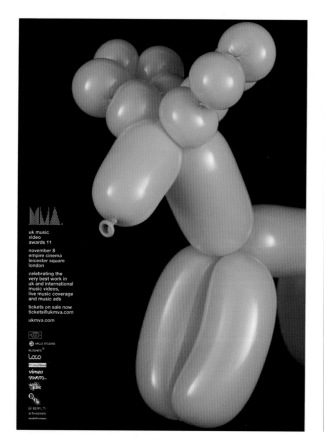

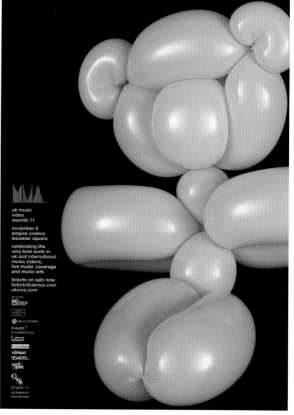

# Contemporary with a very British twist

**StudioThomson**
www.studiothomson.com
Founded 2004

**Founding members**
Christopher and Mark
Thomson (UK 1969,
UK 1975)

**Education**
University of Salford;
University of Brighton
(both UK)

**Philosophy**
StudioThomson is a multi-disciplinary creative agency specializing in design and art direction. Our approach to every project is from a unique perspective. We collaborate with the best creative talent available and our love of research, craft, and innovative creative concepts produces work that is classic and contemporary with a very British twist, earning us a global reputation. We like to do great work and have fun doing it, forging long term client relationships while providing consistent, clear, intelligent solutions that communicate with impact.

Below: CD cover design
for electronica duo
Norken & Deer's *Micro
Don Juan*.
Client: Hydrogen Dukebox
Records
Year: 2012

Below: brand identity
design for a fashion
designer.
Client: Richard James
Savile Row
Year: 2011

PREEN
BY
THORNTON BREGAZZI

A / W 2011-12

Above and opposite:
design for the brochure
and show invitation for
a fashion label's new
collection.
Client: Preen
Year: 2011

# made in italy

A series of talks on the influence of Italian design
in partnership with Peroni Nastro Azzurro

PERONI ITALY | DESIGN MUSEUM

Opposite: branding and
poster design for the
exhibition "Made in Italy".
Client: Design Museum
Year: 2010

Right: brochure design
for a clothing company.
Client: Wrangler
Year: 2011

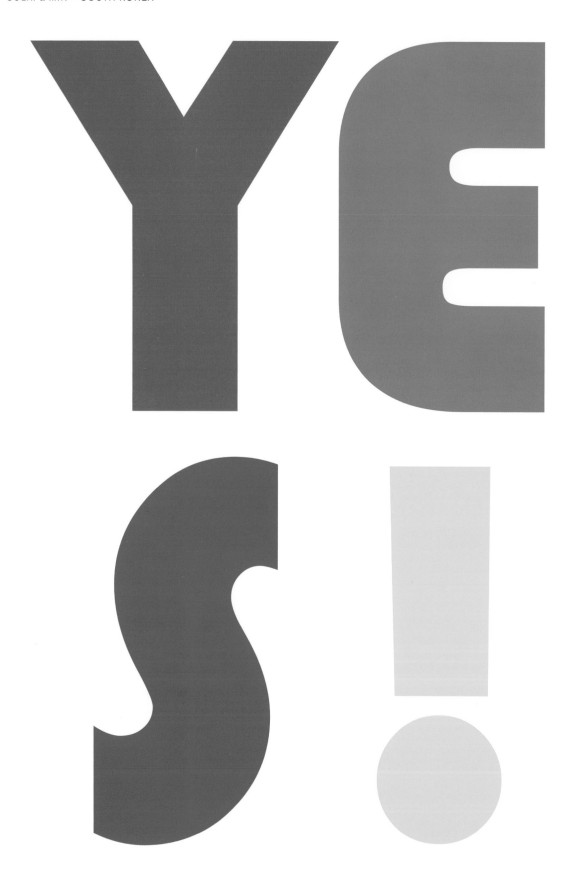

# SULKI & MIN

SOUTH KOREA

## We value precision.

---

### Sulki & Min

www.sulki-min.com
Founded c.2003
somewhere between
Newhaven, Maastricht
and Seoul

### Founding members

Sulki Choi and Min Choi
(South Korea 1977, South
Korea 1971)

### Education

Graphic design at Yale
University (USA), research
in design at Jan Van Eyck
Academie Maastricht
(Netherlands) (both)

### Philosophy

We design graphic identities, marketing materials,
publications and websites for museums, galleries,
publishers, artists and writers. We take constraints
seriously, and do not challenge briefs or budget limits.
We work with them. We compromise, and we often
find ourselves surprised by the results. Alongside
commissioned projects, we make self-initiated works,
often to show in museums and galleries. We publish
books through our own Specter Press, producing
unique artist publications that become works on their
own right. We edit – often silently – and write. We
also translate: sometimes we think this is all about
translation, from one language to another. We always
start with ideas, and try to find a way to translate them
in a less obvious way, which will include the most
obvious possible way. We work very hard on a very
limited set of projects. We work with other people,
but we don't usually have other people work for us.
We keep things close to ourselves, and spend a lot
of time on unnecessary details that no one else cares
about – not that they should. We prefer words to
imagery, and numbers to words. We value precision. For
example, this paragraph is composed of exactly 200
words.

Left: poster for a
performing arts
festival held in Seoul.
Client: Festival Bo:m
Year: 2010

Right: poster designed
for the exhibition "Life:
A User's Manual".
Client: Culture Station
Seoul 284
Year: 2012

Opposite: poster
designed for the
exhibition "Works
in the Open Air."
Client: Gyeonggi
Museum of Modern
Art, Ansan
Year: 2010

Right: magazine cover
design.
Client: Print, New York
Year: 2012

Below: corporate typeface,
based on the typeface
Kraliçe.
Client: SALT, Istanbul
Year: 2012

IF POSSIBLE, THEN,
WE WOULD HAVE CALLED
THE FONT 'KRALIÇE
STICKY GRAY SMOGGY
SESAME SALT FRECKLED
SPONGE'.

# KENICHI TANAKA

JAPAN

## Make people happier through simple design.

**Kenichi Tanaka**
www.kenichi-design.com
Born Japan 1985

**Education**
California College of
the Arts (USA), Aichi
Prefectural University
of Fine Arts and Music
(Japan)

**Philosophy**
Recently I've been dedicated to creating simple vector graphics. Simplified graphic design can be stronger and potentially reach more people. Infographic movies are very powerful tools for teaching something new, and they can show viewers a different perspective about certain issues. Through exploring motion graphics, I believe that design can contribute to addressing and solving social issues. I also work with typography, and use both traditional and new media to create my work. My objective is to make people happier through simple design, and maybe even help change the world.

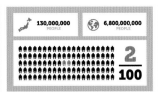
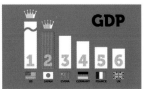

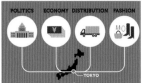
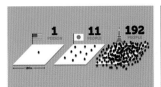
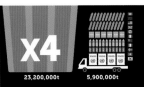

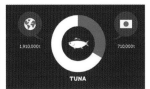

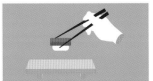

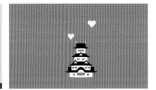

Above: infographic movie
*Japan – The Strange
Country*, produced as a
final thesis project.
Client: self
Year: 2010

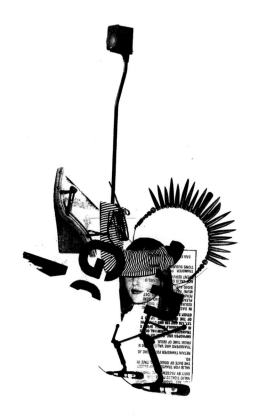

Opposite: collages made for *Delightmare Zine*.
Client: self
Year: 2009

Right: motion graphics produced for a dummy movie festival commercial.
Client: self
Year: 2009

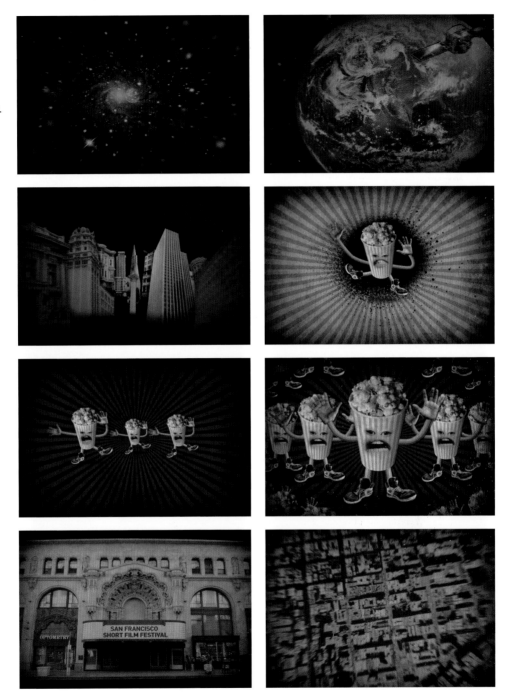

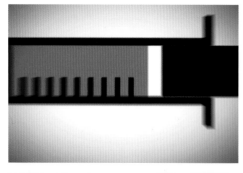

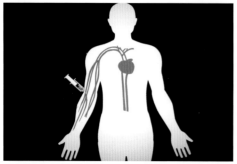

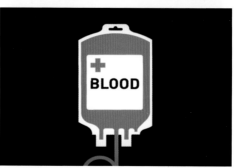

Left: screenshots from the infographic movie *Performance Enhancement.*
Client: self
Year: 2009

Left: illustration created for self-promotion, branding and design identity.
Client: self
Year: 2011

Right: poster design.
Client: self
Year: 2010

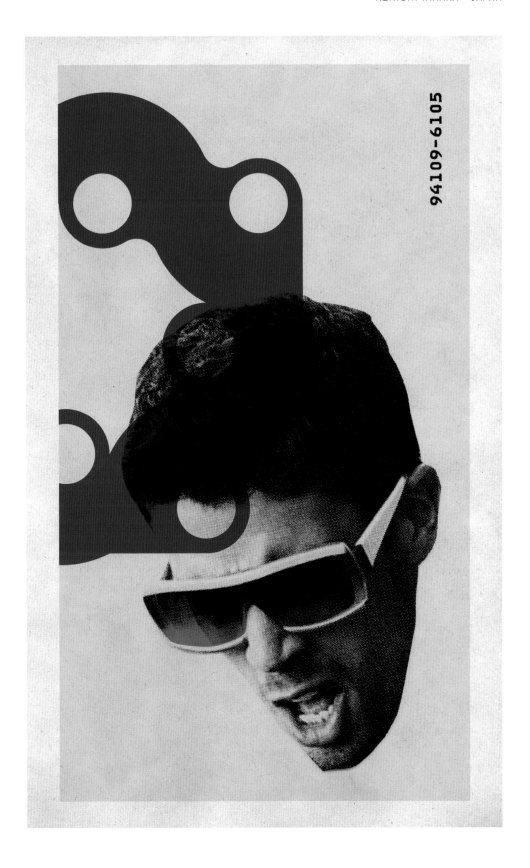

# TANKBOYS

ITALY

Below: installation
Client: Triennale
Design Museum
Year: 2009

Below: publication
design for the second
edition of *Manifesto*.
Client: self
Year: 2010

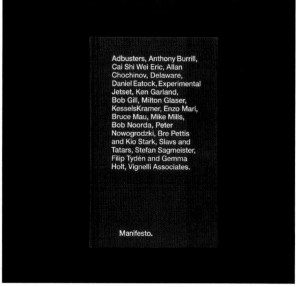

# We'll describe our working method only when we feel sure we have achieved an unfailing one. We will probably be quite old.

**Tankboys**
www.tankboys.biz
Founded 2005

**Founding members**
Lorenzo Mason and
Marco Campardo
(Italy 1983, Italy 1982)

**Education**
Arts and design at
Venice IUAV university
(Italy)

**Philosophy**
We will describe our working method only when we
feel sure we have achieved an unfailing one. We will
probably be quite old.

Overleaf: magazine cover
designed for the Venice
International Short Film
Festival.
Client: Circuito Off
Year: 2009

Below: catalogue design
for an architecture
exhibition.
Client: Venice Biennale
Year: 2010

Below: publication design
for an Italian lighting
company's brochure.
Client: Pallucco
Year: 2011

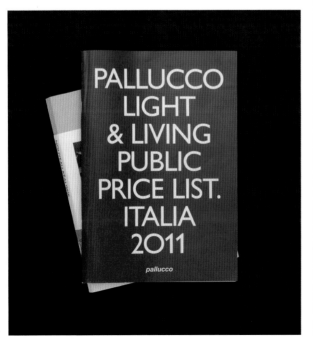

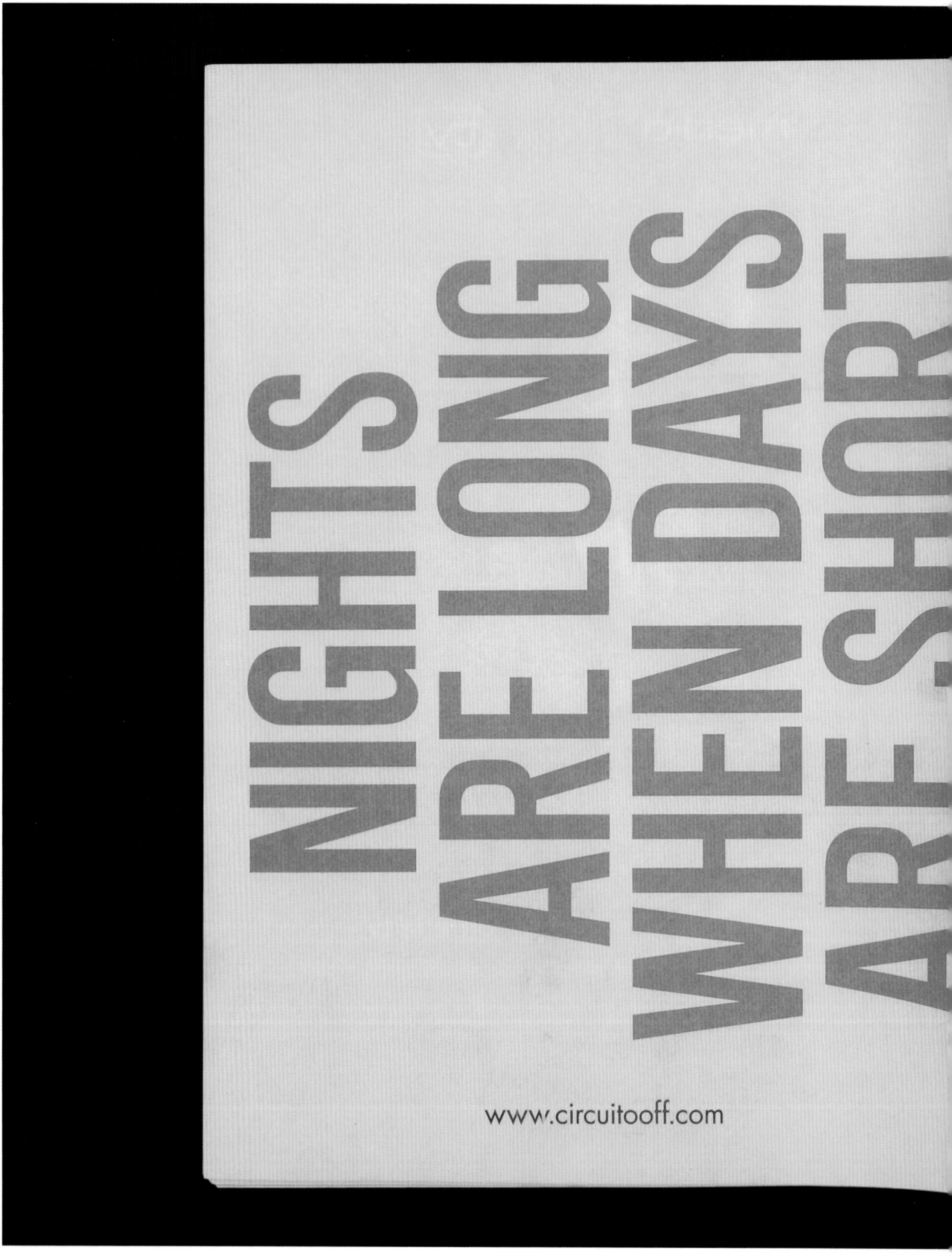

NIGHTS
ARE LONG
WHEN DAYS
ARE SHORT

www.circuitooff.com

11 Circuito Off
Venice International Short
Film Festival

DAYS ARE SHORT WHEN NIGHTS ARE LONG

August 31—September 4 2010
Ca' Foscari University—Venice
Blue Moon Beach—Lido

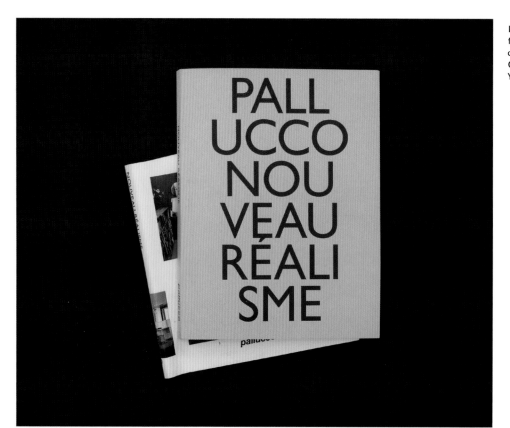

Left: publication design for a lighting company's catalogue.
Client: Pallucco
Year: 2010

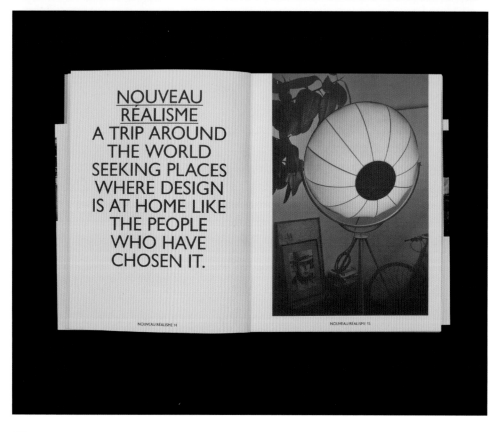

Right: "Love Mail" book
and exhibition based
on spam email messages.
Client: self
Year: 2009

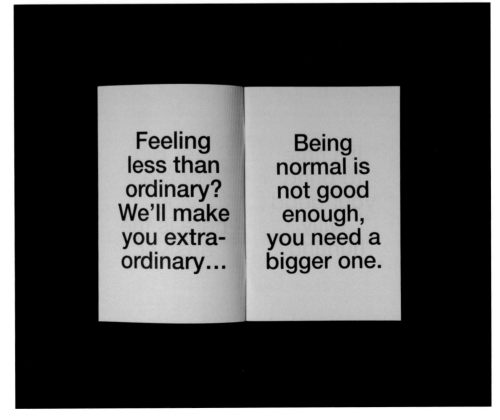

# THE LUXURY OF PROTEST

UK

Opposite: silk-screen poster representing "Love Will Tear Us Apart" by Joy Division, mapped with information design techniques in relation to original recordings of the track.
Client: self
Year: 2007–09

Overleaf left: Real Magick, a silk-screen poster with 23 carat gold gilding representing the 4_21 polytope, an algebraic form known as the centre of the "universal theory of everything".
Client: self
Year: 2010

Overleaf right: Everyone Ever in the World, laser engraved cotton paper poster, a visual representation of the number of people to have lived versus been killed in wars, massacres and genocide during the recorded history of humankind.
Client: self
Year: 2010–12

## The integration of science and art

**The Luxury of Protest**
theluxuryofprotest.com
Founded 2009

**Founding member**
Peter Crnokrak
(Croatia 1970)

**Education**
Biology at University of Western Ontario, evolutionary genetics at McGill University, computational art at Concordia University (all Canada)

### Philosophy

The Luxury of Protest is the *nom de guerre* of London-based designer and artist Peter Crnokrak. Established in 2009, the practice is an experimental design platform that develops critical design projects that are socially relevant and conceptually provocative. Projects use design language to communicate meaning in complex and nuanced social systems. A primary goal is to challenge the perception that our lives are based on a collective, agreed-upon understanding of the nature of existence. The practice is a continual crossover between art, design and new technologies with work that addresses culturally relevant themes including geopolitics, generative aesthetics and the integration of science and art. Projects take the form of data visualisation pieces which explore overarching themes such as the transient nature of empire, the geometric structure of the universe and the degree to which conflict has shaped human history. The Luxury of Protest is a question as much as it is a statement. It is a design that presents a new way of seeing – that which is futuristic and not yet experienced, but most powerfully questioning that which is so familiar as to be accepted as inherent truth.

# love will tear us apart again.

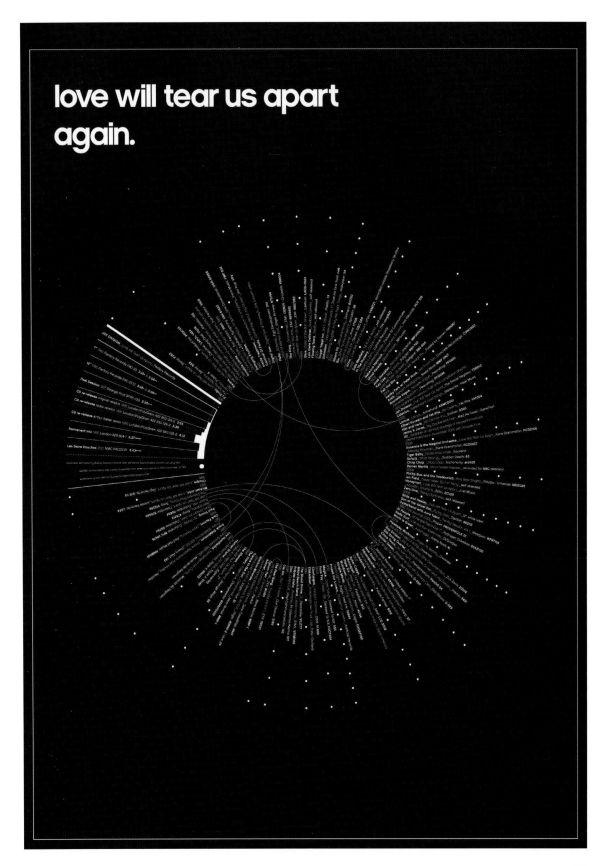

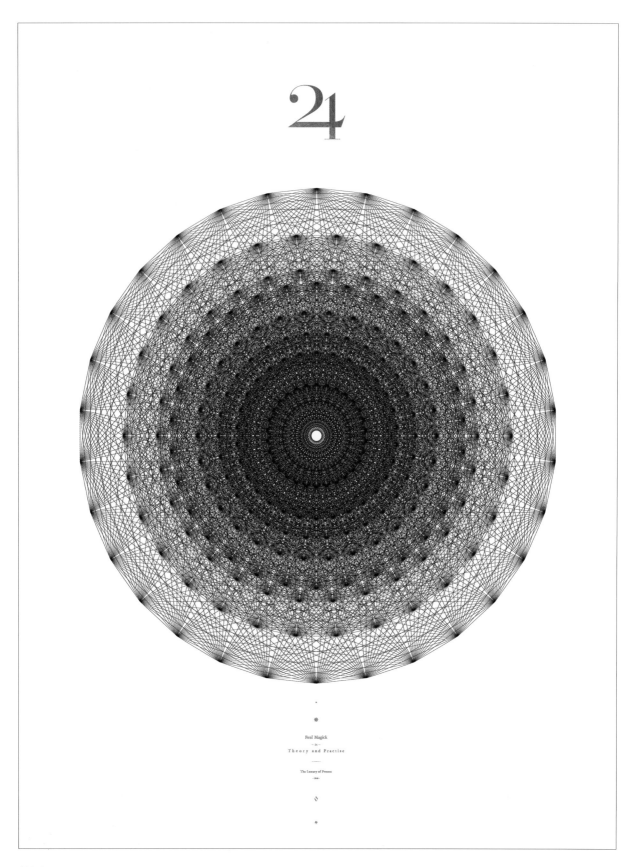

Real Magick
— in —
Theory and Practise

The Luxury of Protest

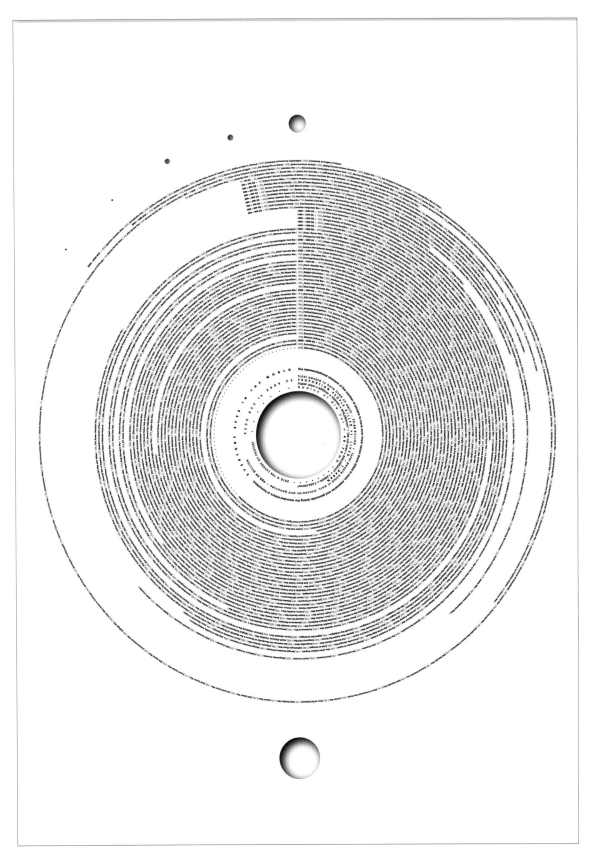

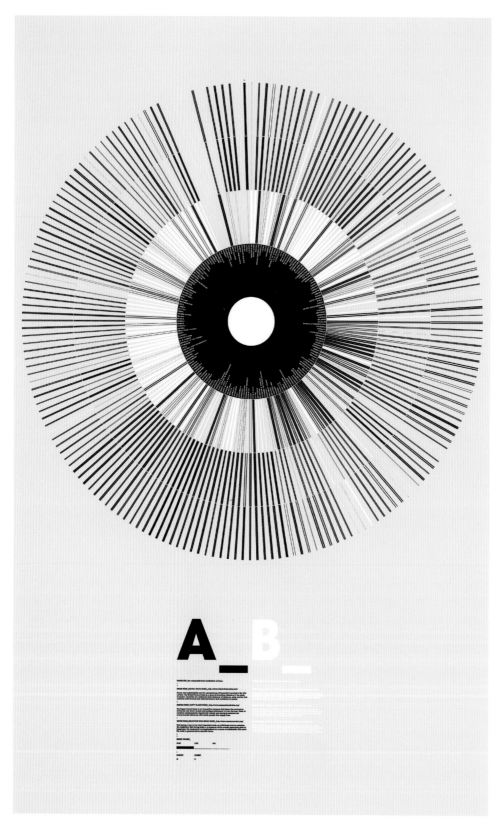

Left: A_B_ Peace and Terror, dual-sided silk-screen printed poster, a geopolitical survey of the 192 member states of the United Nations with regard to the quantitative degree to which each contributes to peace and terror in the world.
Client: self
Year: 2008–10

Opposite: digital Giclée poster created to raise money for the Japan earthquake relief campaign.
Client: self
Year: 2011

11/03/2011.
A LIGHT IN THE DARKNESS FOR THE PEOPLE OF JAPAN IN THEIR TIME OF NEED.

# RICHARD THE

USA/GERMANY

## Design for new social interactions

**Richard The**
www.rt80.net
Born Germany 1980

**Education**
Visual communication
at University of the Arts
Berlin (Germany) and
media arts and sciences
at the MIT Media Lab
(USA)

**Philosophy**
I am a graphic and interaction designer. After having
studied at University of the Arts Berlin and the MIT
Media Lab, I worked at Sagmeister Inc. I now work
independently in Brooklyn, New York, and am part of
design studio The Green Eyl in Berlin. I focus on new
forms of visual expression using computation, and on
design for new social interactions and situations.

Right: *Appeel,* an
interactive installation.
Client: self
Year: 2007 – present

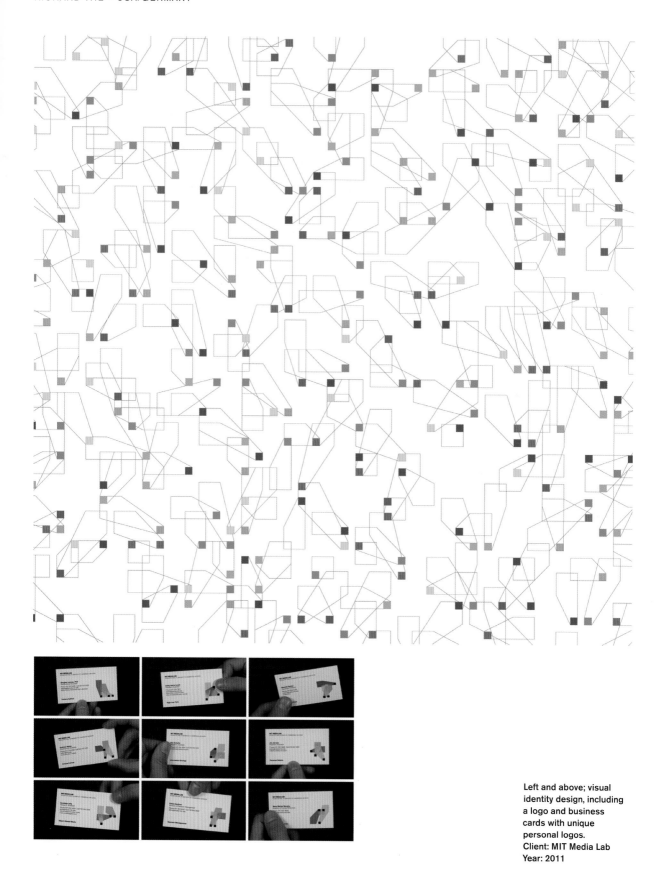

Left and above; visual
identity design, including
a logo and business
cards with unique
personal logos.
Client: MIT Media Lab
Year: 2011

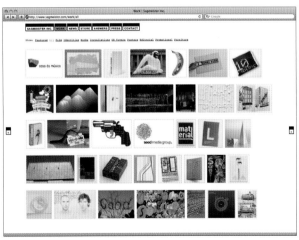

Above: website design for
a New York-based design
studio, including a live
webcam feed.
Client: Sagmeister Inc.
(now Sagmeister & Walsh)
Year: 2010

# THOMAS. MATTHEWS

## UK

Left: permanent exhibition
design, The Jodrell Bank
Discovery Centre.
Client: The University
of Manchester
Year: 2011

## Good design: appropriate, sustainable and beautiful

**thomas.matthews**
thomasmatthews.com
Founded 1998

**Founding members**
Sophie Thomas (and
Kristine Matthews, who
has since left the studio)
UK 1973

**Education**
Graphic design at Central
Saint Martins School of
Art and Design,
communication design
at the Royal College of
Art (both UK)

**Philosophy**
thomas.matthews is an award-winning communication design practice that creates high quality, innovative design at a time when simplicity of solution and clarity of message matters. Or to put it another way, we believe in Good Design: appropriate, sustainable, and beautiful. When we say appropriate, we mean communicating the message through the most effective medium to the best audience. Sustainable, we define as design that has embedded systemic sustainable thinking throughout the process. And beautiful, through the creation of an outcome that is eye-catching and uplifting. The result is clever design that reduces negative impact and enhances the positive. Our team has built up a vast network of interesting and knowledgeable people who work on the cutting edge of sustainable practice and creative experimentation. We call them in for specific knowledge on materials, structures, waste streams, policy, carbon certification and auditing – to name but a few areas. Our studio teams up with global corporations, architects and planners, museums, governments and world-changing NGOs to create a whole range of projects. Whether it's branding, consultation, campaigns, print, web design, signage strategies, or exhibitions – each has been designed with consideration for the purpose and with true sustainable principles at its core.

Above: branding and
design identity.
Client: self
Year: 2009

This page above:
sketchbooks with
velodrome design.
Client: Expedition
Year: 2012

This page below: design
and installation of
an exhibition at the
Big Bang Fair.
Client: ISE/Think Up
Year: 2011

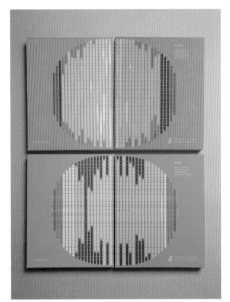

# RÉGIS TOSETTI

UK

Below and opposite:
design for the catalogue
accompanying an
exhibition on the
collective Jikken Kobo.
Client: Bétonsalon
Year: 2011

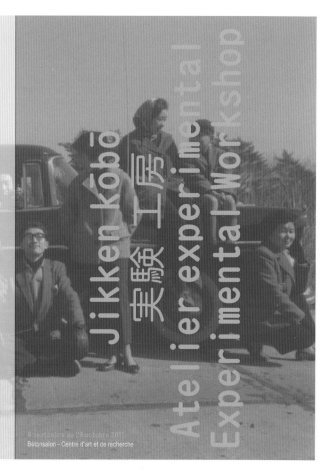

**Jeudi 8 septembre 2011**
Bétonsalon – Vernissage & Performance
➤ 18h: Vernissage de l'exposition
≪ Jikken kōbō 実験工房 ≫.
➤ 20h: Performance ≪ Be a Speaker.
So be it... ≫.
El Arakawa, Sergel Tcherepnin,
Gela Patashuri.

**Jeudi 22 septembre 2011**
CAC Brétigny – Vernissage
➤ 18h: Navette au départ de Paris
Bibliothèque, 104 avenue de France,
75013 Paris (sur inscription).
➤ 19h: Vernissage de l'exposition
≪ Be a Speaker. So be it... ≫
El Arakawa, Sergel Tcherepnin,
Gela Patashuri.

**Samedi 24 septembre 2011**
CAC Brétigny/Bétonsalon – Conférence & Visite
➤ 14h: Navette au départ de Paris
Bibliothèque, 104 avenue de France,
75013 Paris (sur inscription).
➤ 17h30: Conférence ≪ Broken Mirror. Propos
sur la musique japonaise dans ses marges
de 1945 à aujourd'hui ≫ de Michel Henritzi au
CAC Brétigny.
➤ 18h30: Visite de l'exposition
Jikken kōbō à Bétonsalon.

**Samedi 8 octobre 2011**
CAC Brétigny/Bétonsalon en RER C
– Performance & Concert
➤ 17h: The Ensemble Performance avec
Sergel Tcherepnin au CAC Brétigny.
➤ 20h: Concert de Aki Takahashi,
avec la participation d'El Arakawa et
Sergel Tcherepnin, à Bétonsalon.

**Samedi 15 octobre 2011**
CAC Brétigny/Bétonsalon/Maison de la culture
du Japon à Paris.
Évenement Taxi Tram édition ≪ Hospitalités ≫
– Performance, Visite, Cinéma.
➤ 12h: Rendez-vous au métro Bibliothèque
Francois Mitterrand (L14) 104 Av de France.
➤ 13h00: The Ensemble Performance avec
El Arakawa au CAC Brétigny.
➤ 15h00: Visite de l'exposition Jikken kōbō
à Bétonsalon.
➤ 17h30: ≪ Autour de Ginrin ≫, séance de
films expérimentaux à la Maison de la culture
du Japon à Paris.
Réservation pour le parcours en bus:
taxitram@tram-idf.fr

**Mercredi 19 octobre 2011**
Bétonsalon – Conférence
➤ 19h–21h: Conférence de Reiko Tomii (historienne
de l'art, NYC) et Joji Yuasa (Compositeur,
membre de Jikken kōbō, Tokyo).

**Vendredi 28 octobre 2011**
Maison de la culture du Japon à Paris – Cinéma
➤ 19h: ≪ Autour de Kiné calligraph ≫, séance de
films expérimentaux.

www.betonsalon.net

Jikken kōbō
実験工房
Atelier experimental
Experimental Workshop

8 septembre au 29 octobre 2011
Bétonsalon - Centre d'art et de recherche

# Terroirism

**Régis Tosetti**

www.registosetti.ch
Born Switzerland 1982

**Education**

Visual communication at University of Art and Design Lausanne (ECAL) (Switzerland)

## Philosophy

My work develops a form for a given content, but also seeks to be involved in the process, and even the creation of the work itself. In my self-initiated projects I regularly explore what I define as "Terroirism", the design work of amateurs, the creative potential of common operations and everyday tasks. As co-director and founder of Helvetic Centre London, I initiate and curate art and design exhibitions, bringing together designers across disciplines. I've collaborated with Swiss photographer Yann Gross as well as other London-based designers including artist Scott King and fashion designer Christopher Ræburn.

---

**Lumière
Lights
照明**

**14–15**

**Noaji Imai**

Born in 1928, Noaji Imai is still living in Tokyo today. While writing his PHD in Philosophy at the University of Hosei on the artistic use of light in history, Noaji Imai got involved in stage lighting. He is twenty-three years old when he joins the Jikken Kobo for their first event *The Joy of Life* and at that time he has been already working on stage lighting for two years. Recalling that time, Imai remembers he had to deal with somewhat dangerous lights system and that only few members of the group agreed to help him, fearing electricity accidents. He developed several new lighting displays, sometimes using rudimentary techniques, as plugging off and on the general power supply of the theatre to create the first stroboscopic effects on stage. All along his career he participated in more than 500 projects, among which Kabuki, Nô, exotic dance revue and the light conception of three pavillions at the Expo'70 in Osaka.

The following excerpts are taken from an article published in 1961 in the well-known Japanese art magazine *Bijutsu techo*. This is quite particular for any art magazine to devote an article on lighting stage. The article is split in three sections, an interview of Noaji Imai, a presentation of his work by his friend and stage director Hisamitu Noguchi, and documents on the play he had just finished at that time, *The Red Cocoon*, directed by Makoto Moroi and presented at the legendary Sogatsu Art Center.

神は「光あれ」と言われ
た。すると光があった。

**Noaji Imai**

Né en 1928, Noaji Imai vit aujourd'hui toujours dans les environs de Tokyo. Alors qu'il rédige son doctorat en philosophie à l'Université de Hosei sur l'utilisation artistique de la lumière dans l'histoire, Noaji Imai commence à travailler sur des projets d'éclairage au théâtre. Il a vingt-trois ans et travaille déjà depuis deux ans sur différents projets de théâtre lorsqu'il participe au premier événement du Jikken kôbô, le ballet *La Joie de vivre*. À l'époque, à cause de la dangerosité des systèmes d'éclairage, peu de membres du groupe acceptaient de l'aider, craignant des accidents. Tout en utilisant des techniques rudimentaires, il a développé des dispositifs d'éclairage innovants pour l'époque, à l'exemple des premiers effets stroboscopiques sur scène en branchant et débranchant l'alimentation électrique générale du théâtre. Tout au long de sa carrière, il a pris part à plus de 500 projets, que ce soit dans le théâtre classique (Kabuki ou Nô), pour des concerts de musique, des revues de danse exotique, ou encore trois pavillons de l'Expo'70 à Osaka.

Les extraits suivants sont tirés d'un article publié en 1961 dans le magazine d'art japonais *Bijutsu techo*. Il semble assez singulier de trouver un article entièrement consacré à la conception de la lumière dans un magazine d'art. L'article est divisé en trois parties : un témoignage de Noaji Imai, une présentation de son travail par son ami et metteur en scène Hisamitu Noguchi, et des documents sur la pièce de théâtre *Le Cocon Rouge*, mis en scène par Makoto Moroi et présenté au fameux Sogatsu Art Center, pour lequel Imai venait de terminer la conception lumière.

**LE COCON ROUGE (EXTRAITS) [2]**
NOAJI IMAI.

Dieu dit : ≪ Que la lumière soit ≫ Et la lumière fut.
— Ancien Testament

Composition : Makoto Moroi
Scénario : Kôbo Abe
Mise en scène : Hiroshi Shibzle
Scénographie : Hiroshi Manabe
Éclairages : Naoji Imai
Chorégraphie : Mamako Yoneyama
Acteurs : Hiroshi Akutagawa, Kazuo Kumakura, Hisano Yamaoka
Théâtre : Sôgetsu Art Center / contemporary series

≪ Le moment présent est quelque chose arrêté, quelqu'un crie, quelqu'un se déplace, mais il n'y a pas de lumière, ou... l'on ne voit rien.≫

Pour la composition, le scénario, la mise en scène, la scénographie, l'éclairage, nous sommes entrés en conflit. Cela a finalement permis, à restaurer chacun de nos axes de travail, et nous avons avancé dans un même but. J'ai beaucoup appris et c'est cela est née une nouvelle énergie.
Voilà le vrai processus de création théâtrale. ● [1]

— Naoji Imai, ≪ Le Cocon Rouge ≫, in *Bijutsu Techo*, n°193, septembre 1961, p. 95.

**EXPLICATION DU SCHÉMA DU COCON ROUGE**
NOAJI IMAI.

≪ Voilà que quelque chose arrive, quelqu'un crie, quelqu'un se déplace, mais il n'y a pas de lumière... ou l'on ne voit rien.≫

Dans le graphique pour ≪ Le Cocon rouge ≫ représenté ci-dessous, une partie ne se conçoit de l'éclairage qu'est substantielle afin de montrer le fonctionnement et les mouvements tridimensionnels des lumières.

≪ L'éclairage de demain (le futur aura à dépasser les longueurs d'onde de la lumière visible pour explorer une nouvelle dimension ≫ ● [1]

— Naoji Imai, ≪ Le Cocon Rouge ≫, in *Bijutsu Techo*, n°193, septembre 1961, p. 95.

**THE RED COCOON (EXCERPTS). [2]**
NOAJI IMAI.

Composition : Makoto Moroi
Script : Kôbo Abe
Stage direction : Hiroshi Shibwa
Scenography : Hiroshi Manabe
Lighting : Naoji Imai
Choregraphy : Mamako Yoneyama
Actors : Hiroshi Akutagawa, Kazuo Kumakura,
Theatre : Sôgetsu Art Center / contemporary series

God said : ≪ Let there be light ≫. And there was light.
— Old Testament

≪ The moment (play The Red Cocoon of Makoto Moroi demanded a lot of work, but it is a project that I liked a lot. For the composition, scenario, scenography, lighting, we all entered into conflict. In the end this reinforced our works and we progressed towards the same goal. I learnt a lot and a new energy was born from this experience. That's the true process of theatrical creation ≫.

— Naoji Imai, ≪ The Red Cocoon ≫, in *Bijutsu Techo*, n°193, September 1961, p. 95.

**THE SCHEMA OF THE RED COCOON**
NOAJI IMAI.

≪ Here is something happening, someone is shouting, someone is in love, someone is dancing, but if there is no light, we cannot see anything.≫

In the work of lighting the stage takes place in space and time, it is therefore difficult to describe it on paper, it is nonetheless possible to represent the work that took place with the help of a diagram. In the diagram of ≪ The Red Cocoon ≫ below, part of the lighting concept has been drawn in order to show the functioning and the three-dimensional movements of the lights.

≪ Theatre lighting of the future will have to move beyond the wavelengths of visible light in order to explore a new dimension.≫ ● [1]

— Naoji Imai, ≪ The Red Cocoon ≫, in *Bijutsu Techo*, n°193, September 1961, p. 95.

[1] Schéma de Noaji Imai, ≪ The Red Cocoon ≫, in *Bijutsu Techo*, n°193, September 1961, p. 97-100.
[2] Article de Hisamitu Noguchi, ≪ Interview Naoji Imai ≫, in *Bijutsu Techo*, n°193, Septembre 1961, p. 94-101.

## APN
あぷん

**APN**

From January 1952 to the Spring of 1954, the photographer Ohtsuji is collaborating with many artists such as two members of the Jikken Kobo (Yamaguchi and Kitadai) for a project of ≪ assemblies photographed ≫ entitled APN. This project proposes to design every week a new image title for the topic ≪ Asahi picture News ≫ in the Japanese magazine, *Asahi Girafu*, equivalent of *Life* in the United-States. These photographs were not photomontages, but photographs of objects, shapes, or structures which, when staged, designed the letters A, P or N (acronym of title of the topic). The caption accompanying the photo showed the precise materials of the assemblage of objects.

**APN**

De janvier 1953 au printemps 1954, le photographe Kiyoji Ohtsuji collabore avec de nombreux artistes dont deux membres du Jikken kôbô (Yamaguchi et Kitadai) sur un projet d'≪ assemblages photographiques≫ intitulé APN. Il s'agit de produire chaque semaine une nouvelle image-titre pour la rubrique ≪ Asahi Picture News ≫ du magazine japonais *Asahi Girafu*, équivalent du *Life américain*. Il ne s'agit pas exactement de photomontages, mais de photographies d'objets, de formes, ou de structures qui, une fois mis en scène, forment les lettres A,P ou N (acronyme du titre de la rubrique). La légende qui accompagne la photo indiquait précisément les matériaux du montage d'objets.

[3] ≪ APN ≫, *Asahi Gurafu*, 4th of February 1953, p. 22.
Production : Kitadai Shozo
Photography : Ohtsuji Kiyoji
On the left : Assemblage of three elements in flexible katsura wood planed and polished.
Two celluloid bowls fixed together with piano strings.
On the right : One structure in Japanese cypress.
≪ APN ≫ was made in laminated bristol board.
Around these objects, some green and red celluloid plates.

[3] ≪ APN ≫, *Asahi Gurafu*, 4 février 1953, p. 22.
Fabrication : Kitadai Shozo
Photographie : Ohtsuji Kiyoji
À gauche : assemblage de trois éléments en bois souple d'essence de katsura raboté et poli. Deux boules en celluloïd liées avec des cordes de piano.
À droite : une structure en cyprès du Japon, le titre ≪ APN ≫ a été dessiné sur du bristol contre-collé. À côté de ces objets, des plaques vertes et rouges en celluloïd.

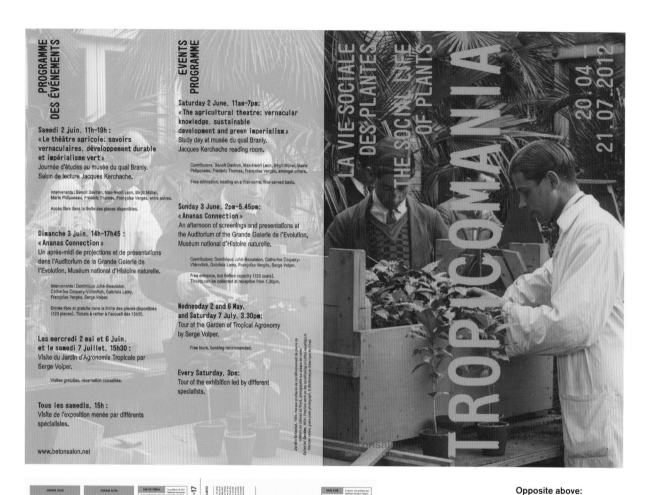

Above: catalogue design
for the exhibition
"Tropicomania: The Social
Life of Plants".
Client: Bétonsalon
Year: 2012

Opposite above:
art direction and
poster design for
a fashion designer.
Client: Christopher
Ræburn
Year: 2012

Opposite below:
catalogue design to
accompany an Antonio
Saura retrospective.
Client: Antonio Saura
Foundation/
Kunstmuseum Bern/
Museum Wiesbaden
Year: 2012

# DIMO TRIFONOV

UK

## I am inspired by really simple things

**Dimo Trifonov**
www.di-t.com
Born Bulgaria 1990

**Education**
No further education

**Philosophy**
I am often inspired by really simple things – objects, materials, light. These things are the basic elements of my work. The other essential element is 3D software, with which I can experiment a lot and combine different materials and shapes in a way that doesn't exist in the real world. My dream is to one day have a workshop where I can make all those abstract shapes a reality.

POISON CANDY

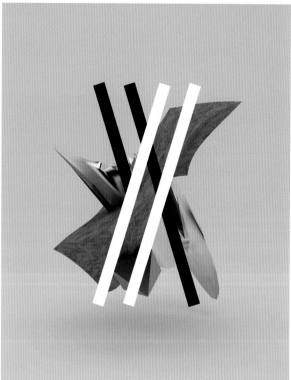

**Above left:** artwork
entitled *I am curious about
you.*
**Client:** self
**Year:** 2011

**Above right:** artwork
entitled *My riches consist
not in the extent of my
possessions but in the
fewness of my wants.*
**Client:** self
**Year:** 2010

**Left:** artwork entitled
*You Are We.*
**Client:** KDU
**Year:** 2010

**Opposite:** photograph
entitled *UUTheory.*
**Client:** self
**Year:** 2010

# TSK DESIGN

INDIA

Opposite: poster created
for exhibition "Zeebelt –
Views on the West."
Client: Zeebelt Theater
Year: 2010

## Global and local

---

**Tsk Design**
www.tsk-design.com
Founded 1996

**Founding member**
Tania Singh Khosla
(India 1970)

**Education**
Graphic design at Yale
University School of
Art (USA)

**Philosophy**
We're a design consultancy creating print, web and space graphics for clients across industries and the arts. Located in India, a rapidly evolving urban landscape and a culture that is undeniably rooted in its unique sense of self – and creates an exciting set of possibilities for communication and design. Responding to this challenge, we aim to create designs that are smart, effective and culturally relevant. Our process is research-based, rigorous and fun. Every project, big or small, is handled with utmost attention. We believe in a cross-disciplinary approach to design and if required, we draw upon our wide network of resources, bringing together the best heads for a project. This holistic approach delivers design solutions that are well thought out, carefully crafted and the highest quality. Parallel to, and enriching our commercial practice, we engage in design projects that are self-initiated, for cultural institutions and the arts. Across our work, we negotiate a fine balance between an internationalist and a modern Indian design aesthetic. We are inspired and informed by technology and craft, the modern and traditional, the global and local.

Inspired

Committed

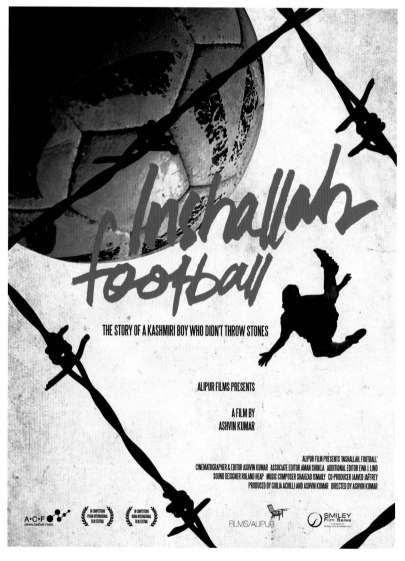

Above: identity
and rebrand.
Client: Apeejay
Surrendra Group
Year: 2010

Left: publicity design for
the film *Inshallah Football*.
Client: Alipur Films
Year: 2010

Above and right:
typeface and type
specimen book design,
created for Experimenta
Design Lisbon.
Client: self
Year: 1996–2009

# TSTO

FINLAND

Opposite: illustrations for
magazine publication.
Client: Suomen Kuvalehti,
Yhtyneet Kuvalehdet
Year: 2010

## Breaking the subject apart

**Tsto**
www.tsto.org
Founded 2010

**Founding members**
Antti Uotila, Inka
Järvinen, Jaakko
Pietiläinen, Johannes
Ekholm, Jonatan
Eriksson and Matti
Kunttu (1979, 1981,
1986, 1984, 1984, 1982,
all Finland)

**Education**
Graphic design at
University of Art and
Design Helsinki (Finland)

**Philosophy**
Tsto is a Helsinki-based studio working in the field
of communication design and creative direction.
The name Tsto is an abbreviation of the Finnish word
"toimisto" which means "office". The name reflects our
serious attitude towards business, as a contrast to the
fact that we still enjoy the experience of collaborating
together as friends. Our approach has a lot to do with
breaking the subject apart and building the final
solution from scratch regardless of the level we are
working on. This might result in a crafted typeface or
a playful concept. Nevertheless we want to leave our
mark deep in the roots of the project.

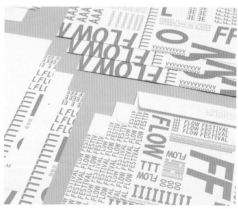

Above: visual identity, type
and print design for an
arts and science festival.
Client: Flow Festival
Year: 2011

Right: branding,
typography and
website design.
Client: Husky Rescue
Year: 2011

ABCDEFGHIJKLM
NOPQRSTUVWXYZ
abcdefghijklm
nopqrstuvwxyz
123456789

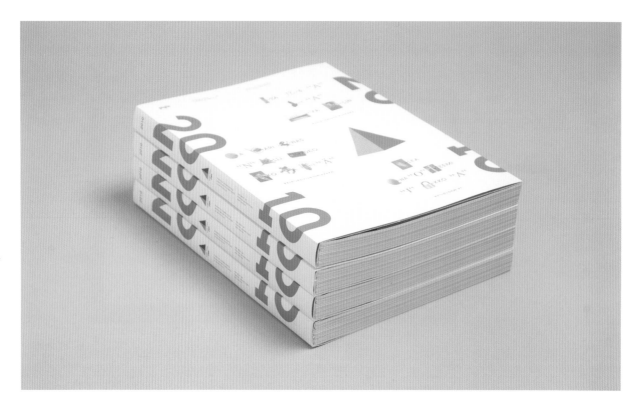

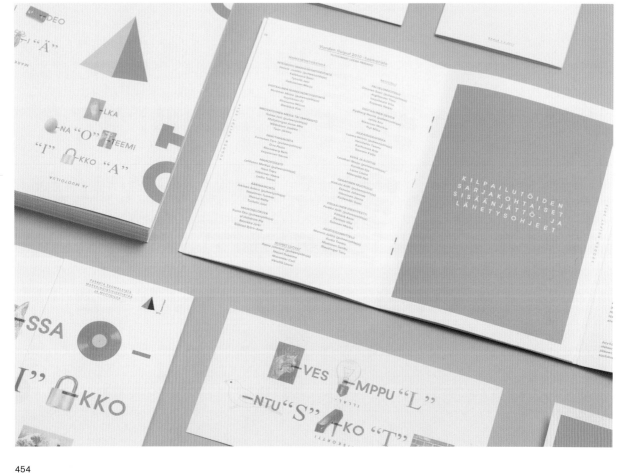

Opposite: branding,
visual identity and
book design.
Client: Grafia
Year: 2011

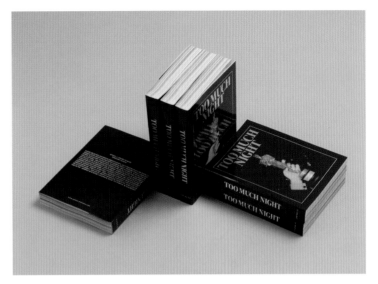

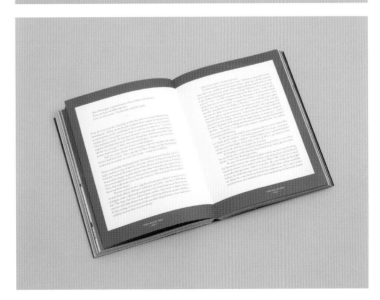

Right: *Too Much Night*,
book design.
Client: Syntax Editions
Year: 2010

# UMBRELLA DESIGN

INDIA

Opposite: advertising
campaign for a Mumbai
arts festival.
Client: *The Times of India*
and Kala Ghoda Festival.
Year: 2012

Right: logotype.
Client: Indian Cancer
Society
Year: 2009

## Listen more and talk less

**Umbrella Design**
www.umbrelladesign.in
Founded 2004

**Founding member**
Bhupal Ramnathkar
(India 1957)

**Education**
Applied Arts at the J. J.
School of Arts (India)

**Philosophy**
Umbrella Design specialize in branding and corporate
identity, design for retail, corporate and industrial spaces,
packaging, visual merchandising, signage, brochures,
magazines, books, annual reports, websites, and the
occasional advertising campaign. Our philosophy:
we try to listen more and talk less; we create all work
in the context of emotional relevance; integrity –
intellectual, creative and financial – is important to us;
we try to build respectful, long-term relationships with
all our clients.

Left: advertising campaign
with eco-friendly theme.
Client: *The Times of India*
Year: 2012

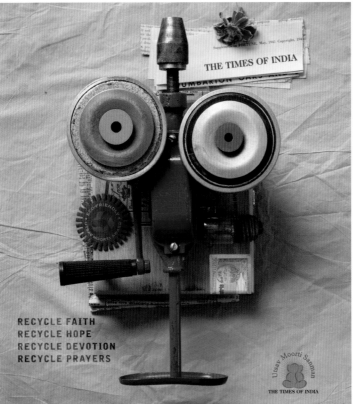

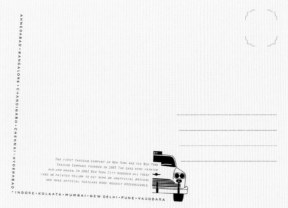

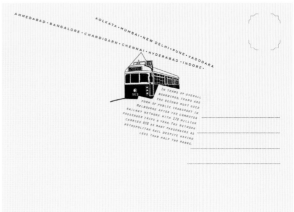

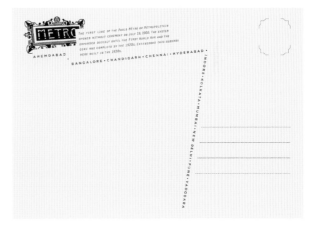

**Above: postcards
designed as part of
an advertising campaign
for a fashion label.
Client: Chemistry
Year: 2010**

# JONTY VALENTINE

NEW ZEALAND

Opposite: wood-cut
printed poster.
Client: Split/Fountain
Year: 2009

Overleaf left: screen
printed poster.
Client: AUT University
Year: 2009

Overleaf right: poster
shown in the exhibition
"Quotidian."
Client: Objectspace
Gallery
Year: 2010

## Observe, gather, parody, order, and align

**Jonty Valentine**
index.org.nz
Born New Zealand 1970

**Education**
University of Canterbury,
Christchurch (New
Zealand), Yale University
(USA)

**Philosophy**

I like to see my work as that of a journeyman graphic designer: I take what I can get, I hand the important work over to other people – writers and printers. If I have a discernable pattern of working, in hindsight, it could be characterized as a documentary method. I don't mean that in a neutral or scientific way at all: I observe, gather, parody, order, and align other people's stuff into my own. Partly because of this, and maybe to contradict the above, I also find this works well when I self-initiate projects – "Of all the ways of acquiring books, writing them oneself is regarded as the most praiseworthy method" (Walter Benjamin, *Unpacking my Library*). Another thing that influences my work is a project to uncover and publish histories of graphic design in New Zealand. Part of this endeavour involves trying to make connections between these mostly hidden stories and other local/ international discourses. But I should confess that conversely, by making these connections, I hope to differentiate graphic design from other disciplines and cultural spheres.

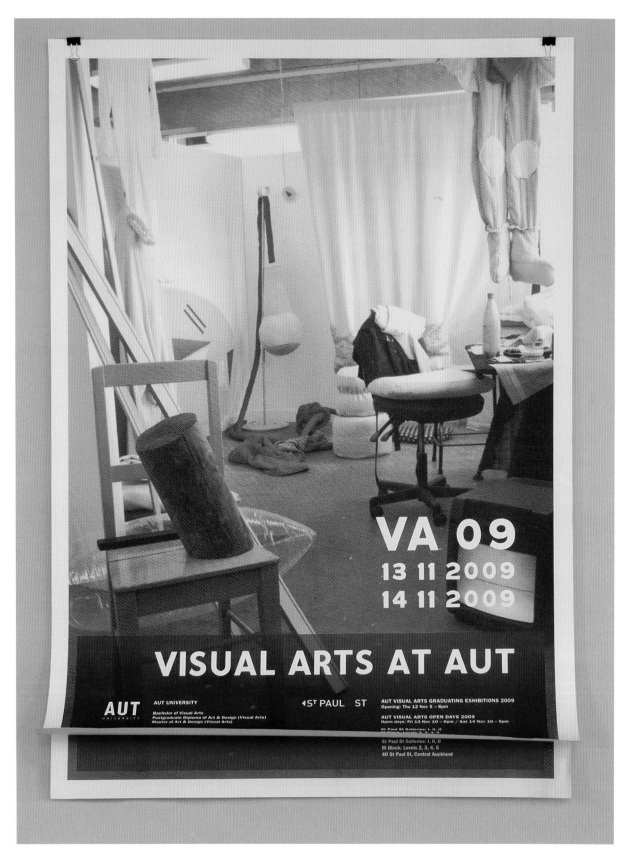

Yonkers
Jonty Valentine, 2006

Yonkers Line
Yonkers

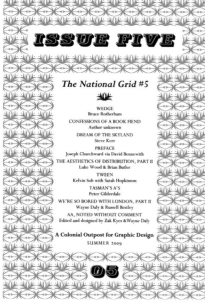

Above and left: cover design for a graphic design publication.
Client: *The National Grid*
Year: 2006-2012

The Book Borders
Robert Coupland Harding, 1877

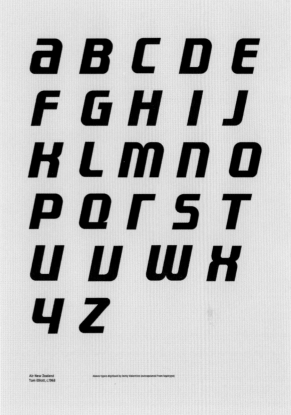

Air New Zealand
Tom Elliott, c.1968

Above types digitised by Jonty Valentine (extrapolated from logotype)

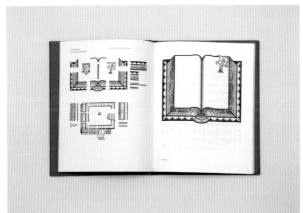

Above: posters and book
to accompany the
exhibition "Printing Types:
New Zealand Type Design
since 1870" (curated by
Jonty Valentine).
Client: Objectspace Gallery
Year: 2009

# JULIEN VALLÉE

CANADA

Below: *Supernova*, an
installation created for an
exhibition in Seoul at the
Samwon Paper Gallery.
Client: self
Year: 2009

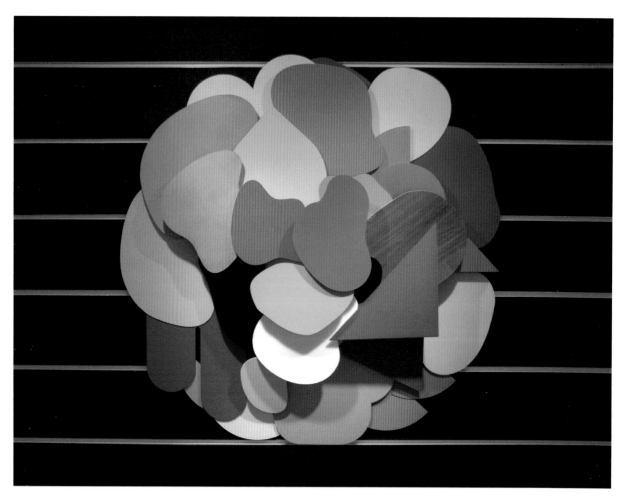

# I like it when an image, first and foremost, communicates a message

**Julien Vallée**
www.jvallee.com
Born Canada 1983

**Education**
Graphic design at UQAM,
Montreal (Canada), ESAG
Pennighen, Paris (France)

**Philosophy**
I like it when an image, first and foremost,
communicates a message, but for it to have enough
detail that it can be broken down into parts, and
through this process the steps by which the image
was made can be revealed.

Left: magazine
cover visual.
Client: *Computer
Art Projects*
Year: 2010

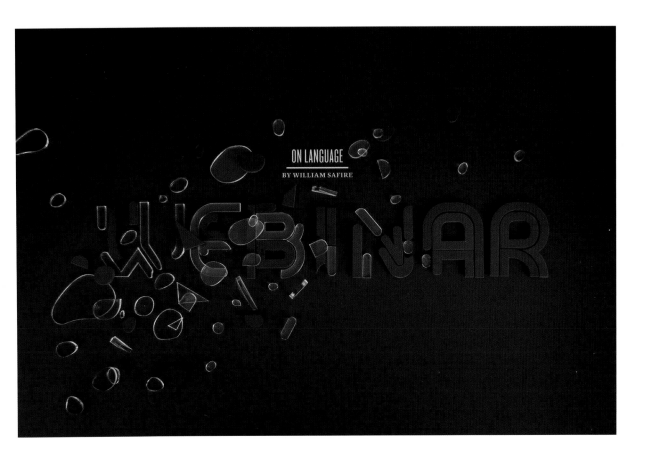

Opposite: re-interpretation
of the artwork Icon, for
inclusion in the book
*ExtraBold*.
Client: Serial Cut
Year: 2012

Above: illustration
to accompany a
magazine article.
Client: *The New York
Times Magazine*
Year: 2010

Left: stills from a video
created to present the
major partners in an
arts festival.
Client: OFFF festival
Year: 2010

Opposite: poster designed
for a music festival.
Client: We Love Fantasy
Year: 2009

we love art
PRÉSENTE

— WE LOVE —
FANTASY

SAMEDI 11 JUILLET '09 / 23Hrs.

PRÉVENTES 25 € (hors frais de loc.)
DISPONIBLES SUR DIGITICK

LA CHESNAIE DU ROY – BOIS DE VINCENNES
PLUS D'INFOS : WELOVEART.NET

SIMIAN MOBILE DISCO LIVE
WHO MADE WHO LIVE
SUPERMAYER
GUI BORATTO LIVE
WARM UP : SISTERS SOUND SYSTEM

# JÓNAS VALTÝSSON

ICELAND

Opposite: album cover
and booklet design for
the rock band The Boxer
Rebellion.
Client: Absentee Records
Year: 2011

## Music is the main reason I got into graphic design

**Jónas Valtýsson**
www.jonasval.com
Born Iceland 1982

**Education**
Graphic design at IAA
(Iceland)

**Philosophy**
A graphic designer and image-maker from a cold
island in the north, I was born in Reykjavík, but my
heart lies in a place called Mosfellsbær where the
mountains see everything and the trees keep secrets.
I've lived there for the bigger part of my life and in
a strange way that place has shaped me more than
I can imagine. I dream of the day when I can go back
to this magical place and spend the rest of my life
there, eating good food, getting grey hair and growing
an enormous beard. I love music and I can't really get
through the day without it. Music is the main reason
why I got into graphic design and photography. The
most exciting thing for me about getting a new CD
was going through the album artwork and seeing the
band's photos, so it's not surprising that I got into
creating music-related work. It's something I love to
do and would like to keep on doing.

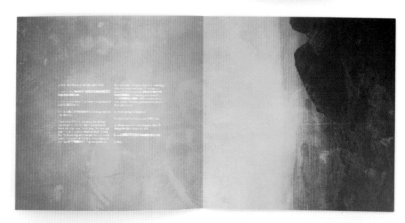

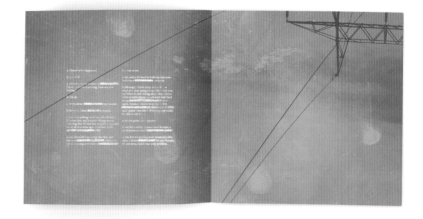

Top: cover and fold-out
booklet design for an
Olafur Arnalds album.
Client: Erased Tapes
Records
Year: 2010

Above: photography and
album cover design for the
band Codes in the Clouds.
Client: Erased Tapes
Records
Year: 2011

Above: album cover
design for an Icelandic
heavy metal band.
Client: Myra
Year: 2009

# CRAIG WARD/ THE WORDS ARE PICTURES STUDIO

USA

## With a thousand words, who needs to paint a picture?

**Words are Pictures**
wordsarepictures.co.uk
Founded 2011

**Founding Member**
Craig Ward (UK 1981)

**Education**
Fine Art and Design
at the University of
Lincolnshire and
Humberside, graphic
design at Bucks New
University

**Philosophy**
The Words Are Pictures Studio exists to bring words
to life in all manner of media and mediums. Sharing
David Carson's belief that legibility should not be
confused with communication, I constantly explore
the notion of word as image. With a thousand words,
who needs to paint a picture?

Above: book design and
authorship of *Popular Lies
About Graphic Design*.
Client: Actar
Year: 2012

Opposite: photography
project: Collapsed in Love.
Client: self
Year: 2011

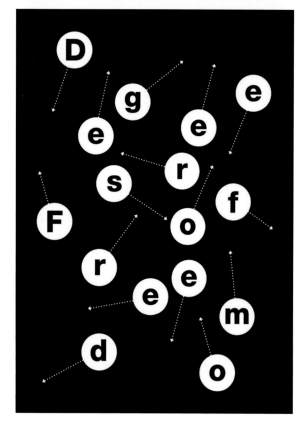

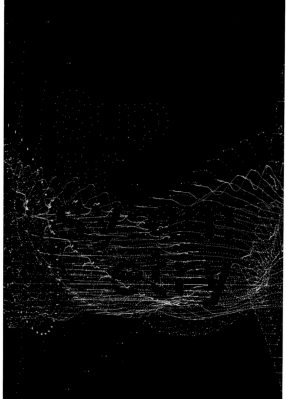

Right: custom type
treatment for an
advertising campaign.
Client: Mulberry
Year: 2011

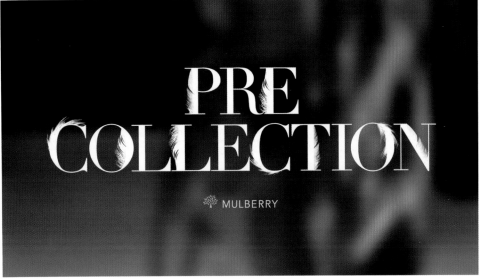

Opposite: typographic
project: The Bulk of
Reality.
Client: self
Year: 2010–ongoing

# CARDON
# WEBB

USA

Below: *Circumstance*
book jacket design.
Client: The Office
of Letters and Light
Year: 2010

Below: Oliver Sacks book
jacket series design.
Client: Vintage Books
Year: 2010

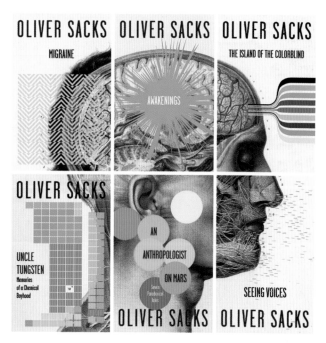

# A hobby, a vice, an outlet, a source of income, a source of frustration, and a source of elation.

**Cardon Webb**
cardondesign.com;
cardoncopy.com;
cardonuncovers.com
Born USA 1982

**Education**
Art at Utah State
University, graphic design
at the School of Visual
Arts NY (both USA)

**Philosophy**
I design because I have to, it is ingrained in almost every aspect of my life. It's my good and bad habit. A hobby, a vice, an outlet, a source of income, a source of frustration, and a source of elation. I sometimes design for discovery, and sometimes for failure. I design because I love variety, to be as creative, ambiguous, literal, sloppy or Swiss as I want. I design for the endless possibilities and surprises. Creativity for me often begins with a stepping stone. I rarely, if ever, sit down at the computer to design without some reference, research or sketch. I try to plan a direction that I feel is appropriate for the subject matter, keeping in mind my own personal style and aesthetic. I want the process and design to retain a good energy, keeping me engaged and interested. Though I most often start with a loose plan, the design process usually takes on its own momentum and begins to deviate (this is a good sign). The original idea often differs from the end result – becoming something new and fresh, standing on its own, something original.

Below: Missing Cat poster.
Client: self
Year: 2009

Below: Zeno poster.
Client: self
Year: 2009

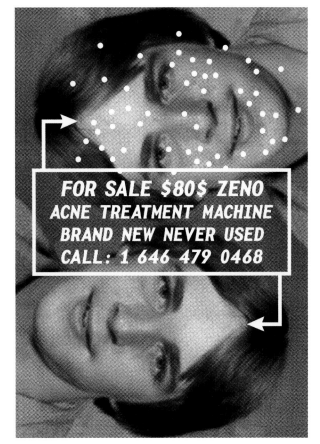

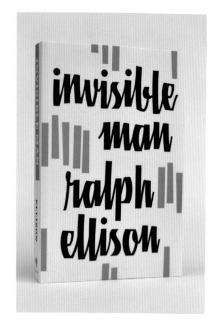

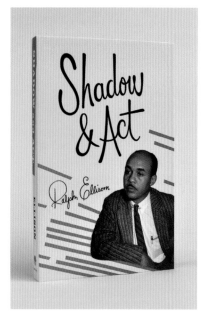

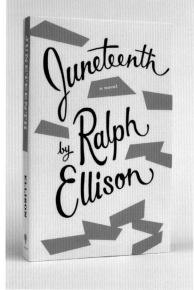

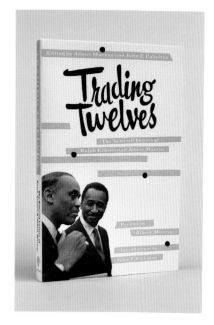

Above: jacket designs for
a series of Ralph Ellison
books.
Client: Vintage Books
Year: 2012

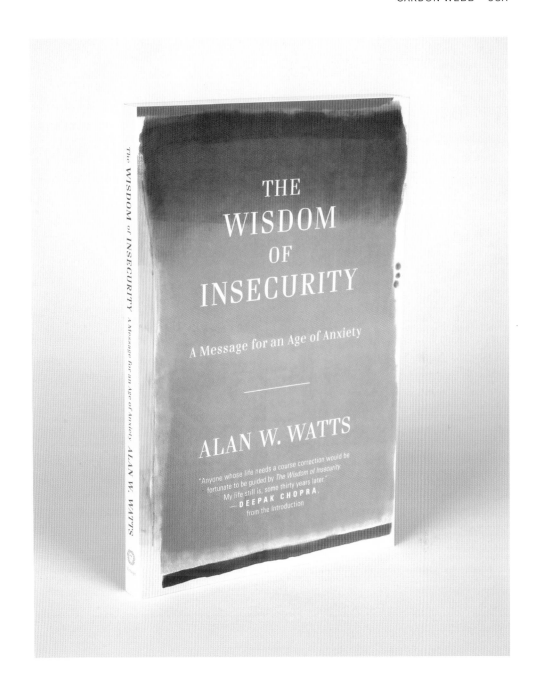

**Above:** *The Wisdom of Insecurity*, book jacket design.
**Client:** Vintage Books
**Year:** 2010

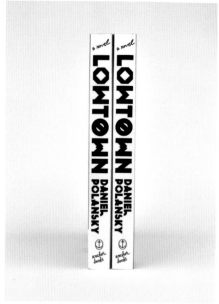

**Above: book cover design
for *Low Town*.
Client: Anchor Books
Year 2012**

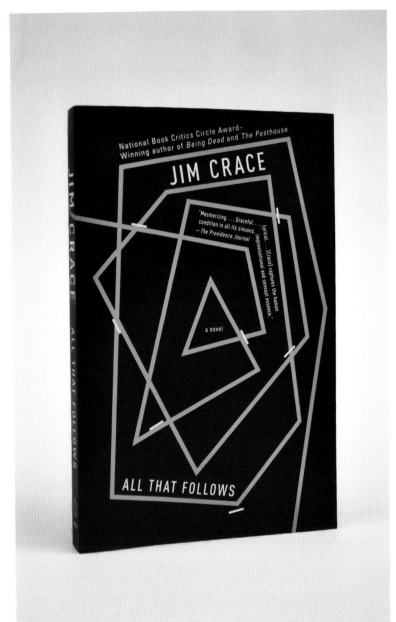

**Above:** *All That Follows*
book cover design,
Client: Vintage Books
Year: 2011

# YVETTE YANG

FRANCE

Left and opposite: custom
typography.
Client: self
Year: 2010

**Yvette Yang**
www.nmyv.com
Born South Korea 1979

**Education**
SCECGS Redlands
Sydney (Australia),
communication design
at SADI (South Korea),
graphic design at AKV |
St.Joost (Netherlands)

## Philosophy

A font makes up a word which can then become part of a sentence or a paragraph, delivering a story and a message. But a font itself has no way of delivering messages. I believe that image is message – so I tried to design a font that is made up of images, and is more visually meaningful – a font that could communicate messages without forming words. I have been creating a "Fashion Font" for each fashion season (biannually) since 2007. This example of the Fashion Font (overleaf left) shows trends from the 2010 spring/summer collections. The Surrealist technique of collage engages viewers' imaginations and enriches their senses, while the clothes themselves are visually appealing, and viewers dream of owning them. As I used only 2010 collection images, this font is truly showing the transience of the collections. It will be old news next year, and in 10 to 20 years time it will be history – the font will still say "I am 2010 spring/summer". That's the message. The archive of this font series will contain fashion history.

YVETTE YANG – FRANCE

Left: typography
designed using
fashion photography.
Client: self
Year: 2010

Opposite: custom
typography for use
in a fashion magazine.
Client: *Vogue Korea*
Year: 2009

BURBERRY 150

Calvin Klein 40

DOLCE & GABBANA 20

HERMÈS 170

Jean Paul GAULTIER 80

Maison Martin Margiela 20

MISSONI 50

RALPH LAUREN 50

SONIA RYKIEL 40

# NOD YOUNG

CHINA

Opposite: poster for an
environmental campaign.
Client: Greenpeace
Year: 2009

## Break down the boundaries.

**Nod Young**
www.nodyoung.com
Born China 1979

**Education**
Tsinghua University
(China)

**Philosophy**
I am a visual artist specializing in digital design and
visual arts. My work mixes Chinese culture with
various elements, avant-garde and traditional, always
trying to break down the boundaries. As an artist, my
work has been widely exhibited around the globe,
from the UK to Spain, Finland to Singapore, the US to
South Africa. I hope to bring changes to life, through
art and creativity that are able to influence the world
and enrich people's sensations.

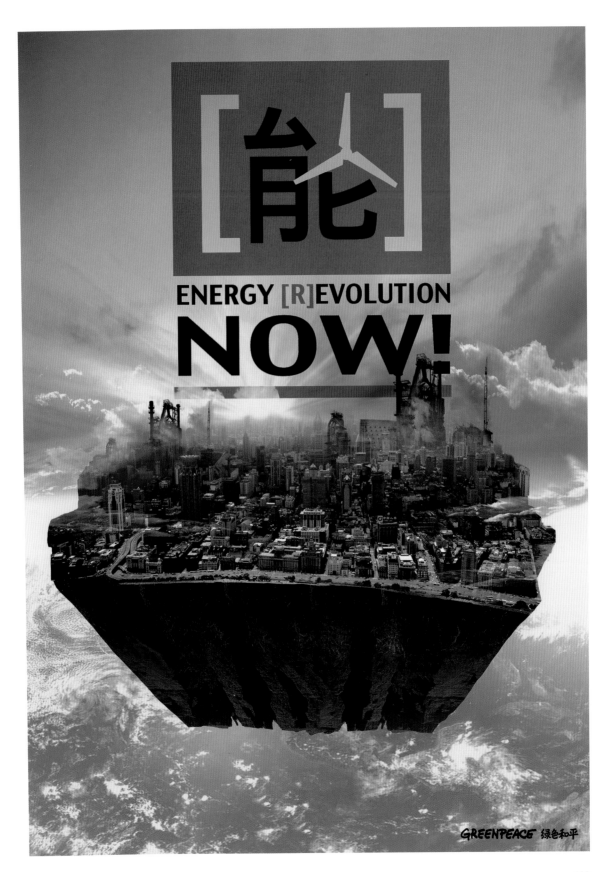

Above left and right:
posters.
Client: 2XS
Year: 2010

Opposite: poster
to advertise limited
edition sportswear.
Client: Nike
Year: 2010

# ZIM&ZOU

## FRANCE

**Opposite: paper
installation for a
leaflet cover design.
Client: ENI
Agency: Pocko
Year: 2010**

# A polyvalent duo

**Zim&Zou**
www.zimandzou.fr
Founded 2009

**Founding members**
Thibault Zimmermann
and Lucie Thomas
(France 1986,
France 1987)

**Education**
Graphic design BTS
(France)

**Philosophy**
We propose a contemporary approach to design that
is a mixture of different fields such as paperart,
installation, graphic design, illustration and web
design. Rather than composing images on a computer,
we prefer creating real objects with paper and taking
photos of them. Our choice of paper is down to the
versatility and quality of the material, especially when
it is sculpted and photographed. Our strength is to
be a complementary and polyvalent duo.

Top: leaflet design.
Client: Microsoft/*Wired*
Year: 2010

Bottom: 3D paper object
designs.
Client: self
Year: 2010

Right: poster design.
Client: Réglisse et
Coconut
Year: 2010

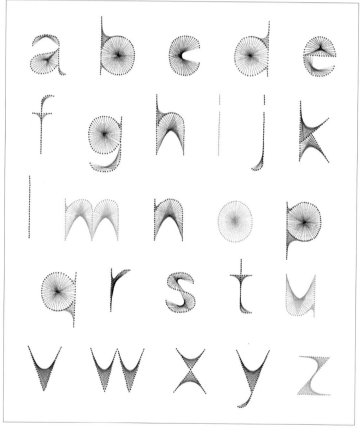

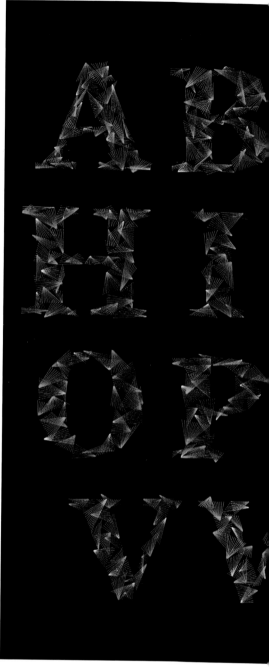

Above: custom woven
typography.
Client: self
Year: 2010

Above and opposite:
custom woven typography.
Client: self
Year: 2011

# ZOVECK ESTUDIO

MEXICO

## A travelling two-ring circus

**Zoveck Estudio**
www.zoveck.com
Founded 2004

**Founding members**
Sonia Romero and Julio
Carrasco (both Mexico)

**Education**
Graphic Design at
Universidad Autónoma
Metropolitana (Mexico)

**Philosophy**
We are a travelling two-ring circus, and we play all
sorts of roles: Sonia is the bearded lady, tightrope
walker, mistress of ceremonies and much more.
El Valiente is the fire-eater, clown, contortionist, and,
last but not least, the magician – bowler hat and rabbit
included. The juggling act began in 2004, after
wandering about with other circuses, from town
to town, from fair to fair, until one day, drunk with
applause, we decided it was time to have our own
circus where we could perform tricks in our very own
way. At this circus, we juggle editorial design, web
design, corporate image, multimedia and illustration…

on a tightrope, riding a monocycle, without a safety
net, while the band plays on. Finally, our circus talents
have been recognised in various publications in
Mexico, abroad, and beyond.

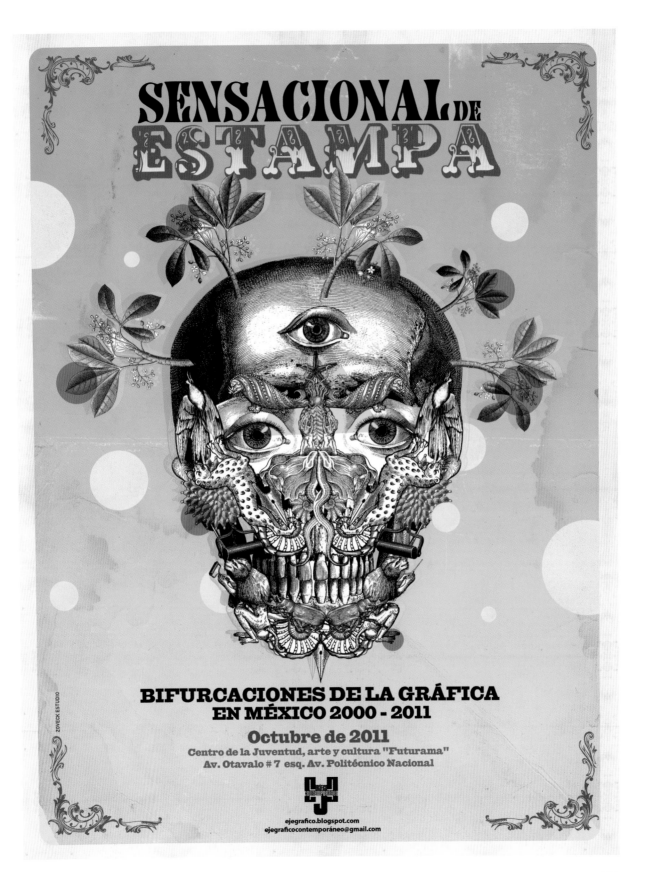

Above left: poster
designed for an
exhibition on Darfur.
Client: Amnistia
Internacional y
Vertigo Galeria
Year: 2010

Above right: poster
advertising the film
festival Hola Mexico.
Client: Samuel Doueck
Year: 2009

Left: design for a
magazine publication.
Client: *Picnic Magazine*
Year: 2010

Opposite: magazine
cover design.
Client: *Let's Motiv*
Year: 2011

# GRADE

## UK
## (DESIGNERS OF *NEW GRAPHIC DESIGN*)

Specialists in illustrated book design, below and opposite is a selection of the many titles designed by Grade for a range of their international publishing clients. Titles designed include subject matters as diverse as architecture, art, design, fashion, food, history, music and travel.

Old to New_

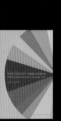

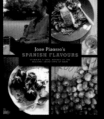

# "Passion, Commitment, Creativity, Coffee = Solutions"

**Grade Design
Consultants**
www.gradedesign.com
Founded 2000

**Founding members**
Peter Dawson and Paul
Palmer-Edwards (UK
1969, UK 1962)

**Philosophy**
London-based and an award-winning graphic design consultancy, we design a wide range of print and online media for the commercial, charitable and publishing sectors. Specializing in typography, editorial and book design, corporate identity and art direction. Since our founding we have earned a reputation for bright ideas – creative, relevant and successful solutions which regularly exceed our client's expectations (even winning a number of awards from our peers and industry along the way). We are passionate about our work; we take pride in our attention to detail and the enthusiasm we bring to everything we do, regardless of the nature of the project. Our process is to tackle every project by first understanding the clients' needs and then the challenge of the brief. From there, with research, thought and development, we go on to consistently produce exciting and relevant design solutions. In our work, we believe in the "big idea", whether conceptual or strategic, reinforced by a strong aesthetic and a high level of attention to detail in composition and typography.

# PICTURE CREDITS

The publishers would like to thank the following sources for their kind permission to reproduce the pictures in this book.

A is a Name: 18, 20–23 (all). A Practice For Everyday Life: 24–29 (all). Reza Abedini: 31–33 (all). Alva: 34–39 (all). BachGärde Design and Communication: 40–44 (all); photography by Marcus Gärde: 45 (both). Marian Bantjes: 47–49 (all); photograph by Benedict Redgrove: 50, 51. Barnbrook: 13, 52–57. Coralie Bickford-Smith: 58–63 (all). Big Fish: 64–67 (all). Irma Boom: 7, 68–73 (all). Brighten the Corners: 75–79 (all). Jonathan Budenz: 80–85. Build: 87, 88, concept, design and direction by Build, original character design by Edik Katykhin, typeface alterations & enhancements by Si Billam, teasers/idents: animation production and direction Animade, sound design by Sonica Studio: 89; 90, 91. Büro Achter April: performer: Bora T., concept: Büro Achter April, director: Moritz Reichartz, art direction: Michael Fragstein, DoP: Julia Schlingmann, lighting technician: Anna Göhrig, Benjamin Wieg, stylist: Ulé Barcelos, editor/animation/compositing: Moritz Reichartz, sound design: Marc Fragstein, producer: Turan Tehrani, production company: Büro Achter April: 93; concept, animation and production by Büro Achter April: 94; director: Michael Fragstein, animation: Moritz Reichartz, Michael Fragstein, illustration: Vania Oliveira, music: Vania and the Master, production company: Büro Achter April: 95 (all). Buro-GDS: 96–99 (all). Carnovsky: 100–103 (all). Catherine Casalino: 104, design and photography by Catherine Casalino: 106l; design and illustration by Catherine Casalino: 106r; 107 (both). Alvin Chan: 108–113 (all). Conor & David: 114–119 (all). Coy! Communications: 120–125 (all). Lottie Crumbleholme: 126–129 (all). Isotta Dardilli: picture by Gonçalo Campos: 130; 132, 133; picture by Piero Martinello: 134; curated and design directed by Carrè Rotonde: 135. Oder Ezer: 136, 137; edited by Jonathan Safran Foer and translated by Nathan Englander: 138, 139; photograph courtesy of Dror Ben Naftalli: 140; 141. Kiko Farkas: 142; design

assistance by Mateus Valadares: 143, 144, 145. Farrow: 146–151 (all). Louise Fili: 152–157 (all) Forsman & Bodenfors: 158–163 (all). Michael Freimuth: 164–169 (all). Hilary Greenbaum: photography by Jens Mortensen, illustrations by Hilary Greenbaum: 170 (both), 171 (both); illustrations by Hilary Greenbaum: 172, 173; photograph by Dan Winters: 174tl; monograms by Mother New York, Photographs by Susan Tibbels and The Robert Mapplethorpe Foundation/Art + Commerce: 174tr; photograph by Jens Mortensen: 174bl; 174br; photo illustration by Reinhard Hunger, set design by Sarah Illenberger: 175tl; icons designed by Celeste Prevost: 175tr; Killer Earth illustration by Andrew Blauvelt, The Kitchen That Puts Out Fires illustration by Nick Kaloterakis: 175bl; Music for Monkeys illustration by Himi Kozue, The Myth of the Deficient Older Employee chart by Lamosca: 175br. Catherine Griffiths: 177; David Reid: 178tl; 178tr; Paul McCredie: 178bl; 179 (all). H55: 181–183 (all). Charlotte Heal: 184–189 (all). Lisa Hedge: 190–193. © Helmo: photography of "Gunter Baby Sommer" by Christophe Urbain for Helmo: 195; 196, 198; in collaboration with Alice Guillier: 199 (all). Alberto Hernandez: 200–203 (all). Hey: 204–207 (all). Heydays: 208–211 (all). Hyatt Associates: 213–215 (all). Pedro Inoue: 217–221 (all). Irving & Co: design by Julian Roberts and Ana Rachel: 222 (all); 223, 224, 225; design by Julian Roberts and Ian Robertshaw, photography by David Parfitt: 225bl, 225br. Ishan Khosla Design: 227–229 (all). Áron Jancsó: 230–233 (all). Lucas Jatoba: 235–237 (all). Ben Jeffery: 238–241 (all). John Morgan Studio: 242–245 (all). Karlsson Wilker: 247–249 (all). © Kellenberger-White: photography © 2011–12 Kellenberger-White: 250–253 (all); illustration © 2012 Jesse Kanda: 251. Neil Kellerhouse: art direction by Neil Kellerhouse and David Fincher, design by Neil Kellerhouse, copy by Neil Kellerhouse and John Blas, photography by Frank Ockenfels: 254bl; art direction, design and copy by Neil Kellerhouse: 254br; art direction and design by Neil Kellerhouse, photography by Michael

Muller: 255bl; art direction and design by Neil Kellerhouse, photography by Jean-Baptiste Mondino: 255br; art direction by Neil Kellerhouse and Sarah Habibi, design by Neil Kellerhouse, photography by Lars Von Trier: 256 (both); art direction by Neil Kellerhouse and Sarah Habibi, design by Neil Kellerhouse, photography by Matteo Garrone: 257. Kent Lyons: 258–261 (all). Josh King: 262–267 (all). La Boca: 268–273 (all). Leterme Dowling: 274–278 (all). Yang Liu Design: 278–281 (all) . Lust: 282–285 (all). Marcus McCabe: designed at Uniform.net: 287–291 (all). Micha Weidmann Studio: 292–295 (all). Adeline Mollard: 297; edited by Robert Klanten, Adeline Mollard and Matthias Hübner: 298–299 (all); typefaces Euclid BP and Simplon BP mono by Emmanuel Rey/b+p swiss typefaces, illustrations by Anna Hilti, preface by Oliver Koch, translation by Kitty Bolhöfer: 300–301 (all). Diego Morales: 302–305 (all). OMG: 307–311 (all). NAM: art direction by Takayuki Nakazawa, photography by Hiroshi Manaka: 8–9, 312–317 (all). Nick Bell Design: © James Morris, exhibition design and graphic design by Nick Bell Design with Nick Coombe Architecture: 319 (all); © Casson Mann, exhibition design by Casson Mann, exhibition graphics and AV art direction by Nick Bell Design: 320 (all); exhibition design by Casson Mann, Exhibition graphics and AV art direction by Nick Bell Design: 321 (all). Ohyescoolgreat: 323–327 (all). Peter Ørntoft: 328–331 (all). Kosma Ostrowski: 332; © 2012 Kosma Ostrowski: 333–335 (all). Daniel Peter: 336l; with Roland Lämmli: 336r; with Mathis Pfäffli and Nadine Gerber: 337l; 337r, 338; with Nadine Gerber: 339. Praline: 341 (all); author Russell Norman, photographs Jenny Zarins: 342 (all); 342 (all), 344 (both), 345 (all). Quinta-Feira: 346–349 (all). Rudd Studio: 351–353 (all). Sagmeister & Walsh: 10 (all); creative director Stefan Sagmeister, design Joe Shouldice and Richard The, photography by Tom Schierlitz Photography: 354; creative director Stefan Sagmeister, design Joe Shouldice and Richard The: 356 (all); art direction Stefan Sagmeister, design and typeface Philipp Hubert, graphic artist Ignacio Noé,

editor Kara Vander Weg: 357 (all); director Stefan Sagmeister, design  Joe Shouldice, Stephan Walter and Andrew Byrom, design studio Sagmeister Inc., New York, agency TBWA Asia Pacific, agency CD John Merrifield, agency producer Shareen Thumbo, production company Passion Pictures: 358 (all); art direction Stefan Sagmeister, design Philipp Hubert, editor Scott Marble: 359 (all). Sawdust: 360–363 (all). Second Story Interactive Studios: 365–367 (all). Signal | Noise: 368–371 (all). Frode Skaren: 373–375 (all). Michael Spitz: 377–379 (all). Studio AAD: 380–383 (all). Studio Frith: 384–389 (all). StudioKXX: 17, 390–395 (all). Studio Newwork: 396–399 (all). StudioThomson: ph: Luke Stephenson: 400 (both); 401l; ph: Peter Guenzel: 401r; 402, 403 (both), 404; art: David Buckingham: 405 (all). Sulki & Min: 406–411 (all). Kenichi Tanaka: 413–417 (all). Tankboys: 418–423 (all). The Luxury of Protest: 425–429 (all). Richard The: authors Frédéric Eyl, Gunnar Green, Willy Sengewald, Richard The: studio: TheGreenEyl: 431 (all); creative direction and design Richard The, E Roon Kang: programming and design Willy Sengewald: 432 (both); authors Stefan Sagmeister, Willy Sengewald, Richard The: 433 (all). Thomas.Matthews: 434–437 (all). Régis Tosetti: 438–441 (all). Dimo Trifonov: 443–445 (all). Tsk Design: 446–449 (all). Tsto: 451–455 (all). Umbrella Design: 456–459 (all). Jonty Valentine: designed with Luke Wood and Max Lozach: 461; 462, 463; designed and edited with Luke Wood: 464 (all); 465. Julien Vallée: 466–471 (all). Jónas Valtýsson: 473–475 (all). Craig Ward/The Words Are Pictures Studio: 476–481 (all). Cardon Webb: 482–487 (all). Yvette Yang: 488–491 (all). Nod Young: 493–495 (all). Zim & Zou: 496–501 (all). Zoveck Estudio: 503–505 (all).

Every effort has been made to acknowledge correctly and contact the source and/or copyright holder of each picture and Carlton Books Limited apologises for any unintentional errors or omissions, which will be corrected in future editions of this book.

# ACKNOWLEDGEMENTS

Immense thanks must go to Isabel Wilkinson for her project management of this book, from its beginning to its final beautiful completion, and for her many insightful inputs along the way, and to Steven Heller for his delightful, lively foreword. We are also grateful to our former interns Julie Hrischeva and Kristina Kiselyte for their additional research and to Sam Morley for giving us his insight into life as a graphic design student. Lastly but by no means least we would like to thank all the graphic designers and studios who kindly took the time to share their thoughts and allowed us to use their imagery. There wouldn't be a book without you.

# SELECTED BIBLIOGRAPHY

Curtis, A., *The Century of the Self*, television
documentary BBC Four, 2002.

Fiell, C. & Fiell, P., *Graphic Design for the 21st
Century*, Taschen GmbH, Cologne, 2003

Fiell, C. & Fiell, P., *Contemporary Graphic Design*,
Taschen GmbH, Cologne, 2007

Heller, S. & Vienne, V., *100 Ideas that Changed
Graphic Design*, Laurence King, 2012

Heller, S. & Talarico, L., *Graphic: Inside the
Sketchbooks of the World's Great Graphic
Designers*, Thames & Hudson, 2010

Küsters, C. & King, E., *Restart: New Systems in
Graphic Design*, Thames & Hudson, 2001

Lehni, J., *Teaching in the spaces between code and
design. Eye*, issue 81, 2011

Shaugnessy, A., *How to be a Graphic Designer
Without Losing Your Soul*, Laurence King, 2010

http://eyemagazine.co.uk/opinion.
php?id=160&oid=453

http://www.eyemagazine.com/blog/post/letter-to-jane

http://www.theatlantic.com/entertainment/
archive/2011/08/retromania-why-is-pop-culture-
addicted-to-its-own-past/242868/

A is a Name

Pedro Inoue

A Practice for Everyday Life

Barnbrook

Alva

Reza Abedini

Big Fish

Lucas Jatoba

BachGärde Design and Communication

Ben Jeffery

Brighten the Corners

Marian Bantjes

John Morgan Studio

Irma Boom

Build

Jonathan Budenz

Coralie Bickford-Smith

Büro Achter April

Karlssonwilker

Buro-GDS

Kent Lyons

Leterme Dowling

Carnovsky

Catherine Casalino

Lottie Crumbleholme

Isotta Dardilli

Coy! Communications

Alvin Chan

Kiko Farkas/Máquina Estúdio

Diego Morales

Conor & David

NAM

Oded Ezer

Farrow

Lust

Kosma Ostrowski

Forsman & Bodenfors

Michael Freimuth

Hilary Greenbaum

Louise Fili

H55

Charlotte Heal

Catherine Griffiths

Lisa Hedge

Helmo

Alberto Hernandez

Hyatt Associates

Hey

Heydays